PRELUDE TO THE MAHDIYYA

AFRICAN STUDIES SERIES 62

GENERAL EDITOR

J. M. Lonsdale, *Lecturer in History and Fellow of Trinity College, Cambridge*

ADVISORY EDITORS

J. D. Y. Peel, *Charles Booth Professor of Sociology, University of Liverpool*

John Sender, *Faculty of Economics and Fellow of Wolfson College, Cambridge*

Published in collaboration with

THE AFRICAN STUDIES CENTRE, CAMBRIDGE

For a list of other books in this series see page 193

PRELUDE TO THE MAHDIYYA

Peasants and Traders in the Shendi Region, 1821–1885

ANDERS BJØRKELO

The right of the
University of Cambridge
to print and sell
all manner of books
was granted by
Henry VIII in 1534.
The University has printed
and published continuously
since 1584.

CAMBRIDGE UNIVERSITY PRESS

CAMBRIDGE

NEW YORK NEW ROCHELLE MELBOURNE SYDNEY

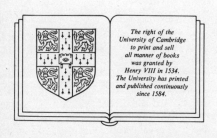

Published by the Press Syndicate of the University of Cambridge
The Pitt Building, Trumpington Street, Cambridge CB2 1RP
32 East 57th Street, New York, NY 10022, USA
10 Stamford Road, Oakleigh, Melbourne 3166, Australia

First published 1989

Printed in Great Britain at the University Press, Cambridge

British Library cataloguing in publication data

Bjørkelo, Anders.
Prelude to the Mahdiyya: peasants and
traders in the Shendi Region, 1821–1885.
(African studies series).
1. Sudan. Shendi region. Agricultural
industries. Development, 1821–1885
I. Title. II. Series.
338.1′09625

Library of Congress cataloguing in publication data

Bjørkelo, Anders J.
Prelude to the Mahdiyya: peasants and traders in the Shendi
region, 1821–1885 / Anders Bjørkelo.
p. cm. – (African studies series: 62)
Revision of thesis (doctoral – University of Bergen, 1983)
presented under the title: From king to Kashif: Shendi in the
nineteenth century.
Bibliography.
Includes index.
ISBN 0 521 35336 X
1. Shendi Region (Sudan) – Economic conditions. 2. Agriculture –
Economic aspects – Sudan – Shendi Region – History – 19th century.
3. Shendi Region (Sudan) – Commerce – History – 19th century.
4. Sudan – History – 1820–. 5. Ja'aliyyīn (Arab tribe).
I. Title. II. Series.
HC835.Z7S543 1988
330.9625′03 – dc 19 88-10234 CIP

ISBN 0 521 35336 X

CE

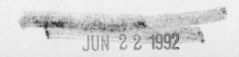

To my family, in gratitude

Contents

Figure

Maps

Tables

Preface

This is a history of a region and its people during a period of profound change. It seeks to describe and analyse the impact of Turco-Egyptian colonial rule (1821–85) on the Northern Sudan with particular reference to the peasants and traders among the Jaʿaliyyīn people of the Shendi region. It will also to some extent be concerned with other groups such as the Shāyqiyya and the Danāgla, who were both neighbours of and settlers among the Jaʿaliyyīn, and with whom the latter both cooperated and competed at home or in the diaspora.

According to the 1956 census, this region (roughly between 16½° and 18° latitude in the Nile Valley, i.e. between the Sixth Cataract and the Atbara River) contained about 300,000 people, including the population of Shendi town (11,031). By the early 1980s the population of the town had grown to around 20,000. Emigration from the rural areas is widespread and tends to keep the population growth in these areas down. The region's population figures from the early nineteenth century can only be guessed at, but it seems reasonable to assume a population figure of 40,000 to 50,000.

This book is a revised and concentrated version of my doctoral dissertation 'From King to Kāshif. Shendi in the Nineteenth Century', at the Faculty of Arts, University of Bergen, 1983. I have profited from the critical comments offered by the evaluation committee, consisting of Dr O. K. Grimnes, Oslo, Dr J. L. Spaulding, New Jersey and East Lansing, and Dr R. S. O'Fahey, Bergen.

The present study is not a tribal history; the Jaʿalī nomads for example are largely left out, and no attempt has been made to include all aspects of Jaʿalī society. It is mainly concerned with the transformation of agriculture and trade during the Turkiyya, as the period of the Turco-Egyptian occupation is called.

The reasons for concentrating on the Jaʿaliyyīn are simple and obvious: their history has not yet been studied, they constitute a convenient entity for research, their society and economy resemble those of the northern riverain peoples in general, and their fate under Turco-Egyptian rule has had profound consequences for modern Sudanese history. However, since the Jaʿaliyyīn cannot be studied in isolation from their rulers and neighbours, and since numerous Jaʿaliyyīn emigrated to other parts of the Sudan in this period, the present study has a much wider geographical and historical perspective than just the Shendi region.

The Jaʿaliyyīn referred to above constitute one part of a greater so-called Jaʿaliyyīn Group, to whom most of the Arabic-speaking northern riverain tribes belong and who trace their desent back to an Arab of ʿAbbāsid origin by the name of Ibrāhīm Jaʿal. They number today nearly 10 per cent of the total Sudanese population, and can be found all over the country as merchants, farmers, military men, public officials, holymen, and teachers. The first really big wave of emigration from the north took place during the Turkiyya and the aim of this book is also to uncover the factors of emigration by examining political, economic, and social change at the local level. This perspective will also enable us to throw new light on how the colonial regime sowed the seeds of the Mahdist Revolution. Hence the title of the book.

Acknowledgements

The present study would not have materialised without the support of many individuals and institutions, to whom I would like to express my deepest gratitude. The preparations for the study started in 1977 when I was granted a scholarship by the Egyptian Ministry of Culture to study Arabic in Cairo. In the period 1978–82 I received a research fellowship from the University of Bergen. In the autumn of 1978 grants from Nansenfondet and Meltzers Høyskolefond enabled me to spend three months in the National Records Office (NRO), Khartoum, and in the Sudan Collection of the Khartoum University Library. Field work was carried out in January–May 1980, thanks to a grant from the Norwegian Research Council (NAVF). A trip to the Public Record Office, Kew, and the Sudan Archive, Durham, in May–June 1979 was paid for by the University of Bergen. Finally a grant from Nansenfondet enabled me to return to Shendi in 1984 in connection with a follow-up study on the sale of land.

As for individuals, my thanks go first of all to R. S. O'Fahey who introduced me to Sudanese history and supervised my doctoral work, and who has been a source of encouragement to the present day. Thanks are also due to J. L. Spaulding for commenting on earlier drafts and for his many thought provoking ideas. Special thanks go to R. Hill, a veteran in Sudanese history, for his comments and encouragements. P. M. Holt has also been helpful in the early stages. I have also profited from discussions with H. R. Pierce (who also introduced me to the world of word processing), L. Kapteijns, P. Doornbos, L. Manger, G. Sørbø, Ṣalāḥ al-Shāzalī, Bashīr Ibrāhīm Bashīr, Muṣṭafā Bābiker, ʿAlī Ṣāliḥ Karrār and many others. In Khartoum I enjoyed the hospitality of L. Kapteijns, P. Doornbos, S. Munro-Haye, and A. Kleppe, for which I am very grateful.

I am particularly indebted to M. I. Abū Salīm, the Secretary General of the National Records Office, Khartoum, for permission to consult the archive in 1978, 1980, and in 1984 and for permission to do field work through the Board of Anthropology. In 1980 Abū Salīm found me an assistant from his staff, Saʿīd al-Fakī ʿAlī, who accompanied me to Shendi and al-Matamma. In spite of different backgrounds, we became very good friends. I am greatly indebted to him.

Thanks are also due to S. H. Hurreiz at the Institute of Folklore in

Khartoum, who allowed me to consult their material of Jaʿalī folktales. Extracts were translated for me by Al-Rayyaḥ al-Ḥājj al-Makkī.

In Shendi and al-Matamma I owe a lot to many people, not only those who provided information and documents, who are listed elsewhere, but also to all those who became my friends and made me part of their daily life for a few months. Aḥmad Ibrāhīm al-Salāwī, branch manager of the Agricultural Bank, whom I met first in 1978, most kindly invited me to stay in his house in 1980 and allowed my assistant to stay in the bank's resthouse. Furthermore I was invited to have my daily breakfast and lunch with him and his colleagues and friends.

A letter from al-Shāzalī introduced me to the Shāfi family in Shendi, whose pharmacy became a regular meeting-place for discussions, planning, cold water and tea. They most kindly invited me to stay with them when I returned in 1984 and in 1987. Without forgetting the others, I must particularly mention Mīrghanī and Hāshim who did their utmost to bring me into contact with informants and possible owners of documents. Thanks to them I came in contact with Sulaymān, the last surviving son of ʿAbd Allāh Bey Ḥamza, in al-Matamma. Mīrghanī died at the end of 1987 and I lost one of the best friends I ever had.

Sulaymān ʿAbd Allāh Bey and his family opened a new world to me in the form of the private papers left by ʿAbd Allāh Bey. I am therefore exceedingly grateful for their permission to photograph a large part of the collection and to do research on them.

I am also grateful to ʿAlī Ṣāliḥ Karrār, ʿAwaḍ ʿAbd Allāh Radaf, and J. N. Bell who joined O'Fahey and myself in our weekly Arabic documents seminars.

Most of the printed material consulted has been obtained from abroad through the University Library in Bergen, to whose staff, and to Kari Nordmo in particular, I hereby extend my sincerest appreciation. In the same way I would like to acknowledge the services rendered by the staff at the Sudan Archive, Durham, and by A. Fierro at the Bibliothèque Nationale de Paris. Mrs Ryder provided me with a copy of a typescript by her late husband, for which I am also very grateful.

Thanks are due also to Mrs J. K. Ellingsen at the Department of Geology, University of Bergen, for drawing the maps. I must also express my gratitude to the Norwegian Research Council for their generous subsidy towards the publication of this book.

Finally I must acknowledge my debts to my parents, my wife and children who put up with me over these years, both when I was absent on field work or just absent of mind. Special thanks goes to my wife, Sunniva, who typed the doctoral manuscript.

Abbreviations

w.	*walad* (pl. *awlād*), son, son of
b.	*ibn* (pl. *abnā'*, *banūn*), son, son of
bt.	*bint* (pl. *banāt*), daughter, daughter of

Weights and measures

The following tables list the measures encountered in the text. However, as these often varied from district to district, the figures must be regarded as approximate, and relating to the Northern Sudan only.

Measures of length

dhirā'	58 cm
'ūd	3–4 *dhirā'* = 174–232 cm
qaṣaba	3.55m (Egyptian measure), reduced to 3m in the Sudan
ḥabl	8 *'ūd* = 13.92–18.56

Square measures

Traditionally square measures were used to measure land in the rain-fed savanna areas only, conducted by a professional stone-thrower.

jad'a 64 *'ūd* x 64 *'ūd* = 12,401–22,406m^2, of which the last figure is the most common, that is 5¼ *faddān*.

Egyptian square measures

The size of the *faddān* was decreased in the nineteenth century until it arrived at:

faddān 24 *qīrāṭ*^{2} = 3331/3 *qaṣaba*^{2} = 4,200.79m^2

In the Sudan the official size of the *faddān* after 1857 was fixed at 400 square *qaṣaba*, and the *qaṣaba* was reduced to 3m which gave a *faddān* of 3,600m^2. (Chélu (1891), 108; Hartmann (1863), 220 and Anhänge, 26).

List of weights and measures

Measures of capacity

The following measures give average size as there was much local variation.

ardabb	180 litres
wayba	40 litres
murabba'	20 litres
midd	5 litres

Measures of weight

waqiyya	12 *dirham* = 1.32 ounces = 37.44 g
raṭl	12 *waqiyya* = 449.28 g
uqqa or *wuqqa*	400 *dirham* = 1.248 kg
qanṭār	100 *raṭl* = 44.928 kg

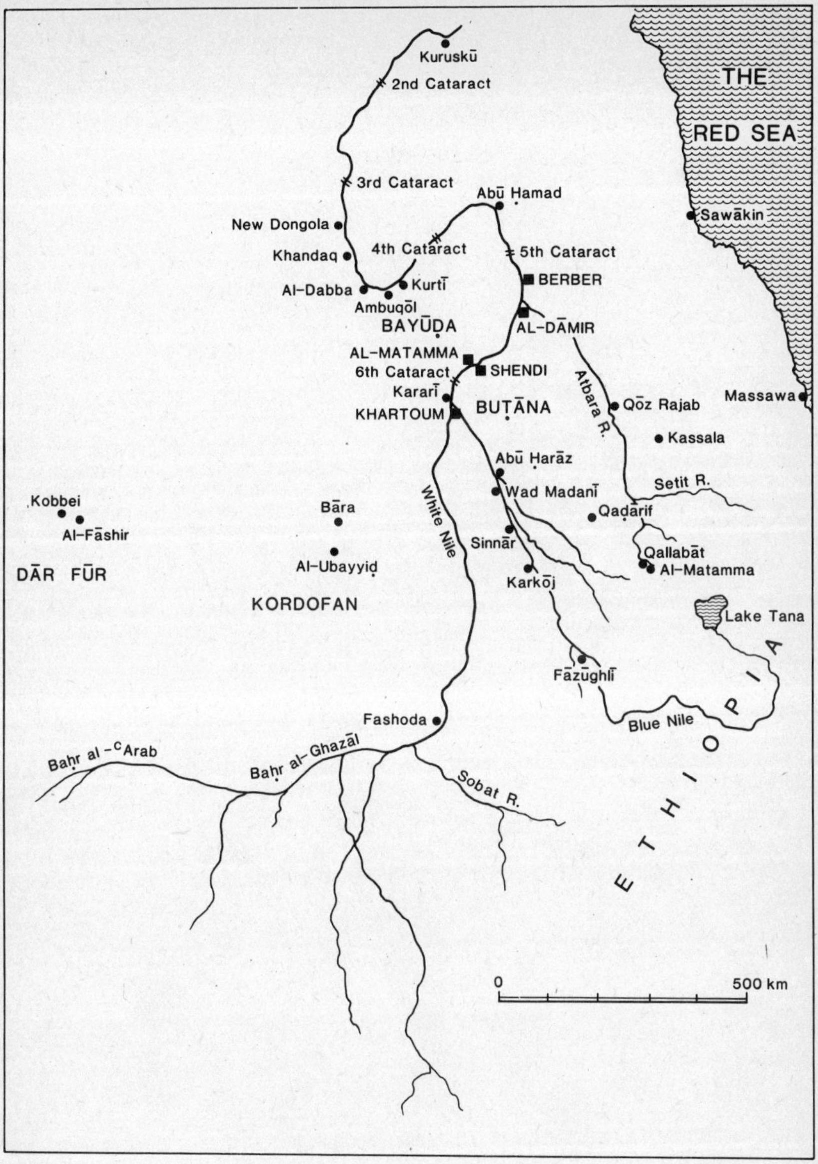
Kuruskū
2nd Cataract
THE
RED SEA
3rd Cataract
Abū Hamad
New Dongola
Sawākin
Khandaq
4th Cataract
5th Cataract
BERBER
Al-Dabba
Kurtī
Ambuqōl
BAYŪDA
AL-DĀMIR
AL-MATAMMA
6th Cataract
SHENDI
Atbara R.
Massawa
Karari
KHARTOUM
BUṬĀNA
Qōz Rajab
Kassala
Abū Ḥarāz
Wad Madanī
Setit R.
Kobbei
Bāra
White Nile
Qadarif
Al-Fāshir
Sinnār
Qallabāt
Al-Matamma
DĀR FŪR
Al-Ubayyiḍ
Karkōj
KORDOFAN
Lake Tana
Fazūghlī
Fashoda
Blue Nile
Baḥr al-ᶜArab
Baḥr al-Ghazāl
Sobat R.
ETHIOPIA
0
500 km

The Sudan in the nineteenth century

Introduction

GENERAL BACKGROUND

The Shendi region lies between the more fertile savanna to the south and the desert to the north, and receives an annual rainfall of about 100–50 mm. It is part of the semi-desert Sahelian borderland of the Sudanic Belt extending all the way across Africa south of the Sahara. Permanent cultivation is possible therefore only on the banks of the Nile, but whenever the rainy season (June–September) is good, cultivation of grain is possible in the inland depressions and watercourses (*wādī*), of which there are many on both sides of the Nile. The surrounding steppes are the homeland of the nomads who herd cattle, sheep, goats and camels, and engage in *wādī* cultivation.

The area under study, also called the Shendi Reach, lay within the heartlands of the ancient Cushitic civilizations and formed the core of the kingdom of Meroe. The remains of the city of Meroe, which flourished between 500 BC and 300 AD, including pyramids, palaces, temples, baths and huge mounds of iron-slag, can be seen not far from present-day Shendi. In the fourth century, Meroe succumbed to attacks from Axum, and by the end of the sixth century the successor kingdoms of Nobatia and Makuria (Dongola) in the north and Alodia (Ar. ʿAlwā) on the Blue Nile, had adopted Christianity.

In the seventh century the Arabs occupied Egypt, but made no sustained effort to conquer Nubia. However, Arabs and Islam penetrated slowly up the Nile and across the desert from the Red Sea and in 1323 the first Muslim king ascended the throne of Dongola. Further south Alodia was wiped out by the semi-Arabised and semi-Muslim forces of the Funj and the ʿAbdallāb, which resulted in the establishment of the Funj sultanate of Sinnār in 1504. This kingdom was to dominate the Nile Valley, with its several principalities and nomadic tribes, until the submission of the last Funj sultan to Ismāʿīl Pasha in June 1821.[1]

During the political, cultural and religious upheavals in the fourteenth and fifteenth centuries, new constellations appeared on the scene along the Nile; those were the so-called Arabised Nubians. The most important was the Jaʿaliyyīn Confederation or Group, who claimed descent from the uncle of the Prophet, al-ʿAbbās, and were thus regarded as ʿAbbāsids in the

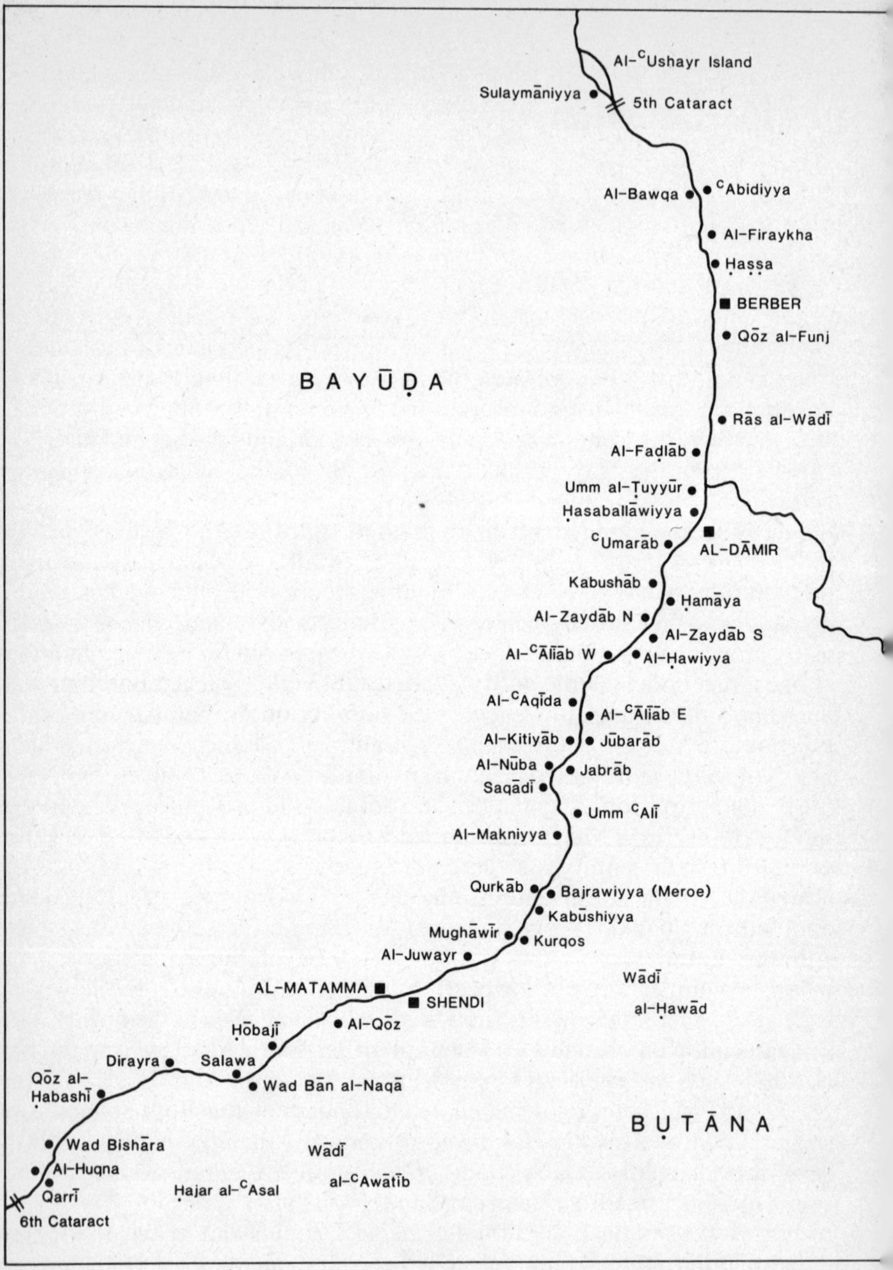

The Shendi Reach

Sudan. In this process of cultural and ideological reorientation the Funj discovered that they in fact were descended from the Umayyads. Arabs undoubtedly emigrated to the Sudan and married into Nubian families, but they were of diverse tribal origin and too few in number to change the ethnic character of the riverain Nubians. Thus the adoption of Arab pedigrees and the Arab language must be seen within a socio-cultural and political context. Closer to the Egyptian border the Nubian language is still predominant and the people generally do not claim Arab ancestry.[2]

The ecology of the Shendi region and most of the Nubian Nile Valley in general and the available technology have limited the range of economic adaptations to basically two: irrigation agriculture and animal husbandry. There was considerable overlapping between the two sectors, particularly among the peasants who also kept some animals. Cattle provided vital motive power for the water wheels (*sāqiya*). There were also additional occupations such as fishing, smithing, craft production, camel-driving, and the highly attractive profession of trading.

The scarce and unequal distribution of resources must have forced people to search continuously for other ways of making a living, such as long distance trading and the ancient Lower Nubian preference for household service in Egyptian cities. It also led to competition and rivalries between peasants and nomads which disturbed the normal relations of cooperation and economic exchange. Nomads such as the Shukriyya, the Baṭāḥīn, and the Bishāriyyīn were aware of the vulnerability of the peasants and were often involved in raiding the riverain peasants and stealing their cattle which were needed for irrigation.[3]

The Jaʿalī towns of Shendi, al-Matamma and al-Dāmir housed institutions and activities which distinguished them from the villages and the camps. Although many urban inhabitants were engaged in cultivation and herding, the characteristic feature of towns was the presence of professional traders, brokers and craftsmen, men of religion and law, the political elite with their followers, servants, slaves, officials and soldiers.

Long distance caravans crossed their land or followed the Nile, and prolonged halts at places like Shendi created much activity. The kings and chiefs encouraged caravans to come and offer their goods in exchange for local products, favourable treatment and protection. Muslim pilgrims from the increasingly Islamised Sudanic Belt used the same routes. Thus an ambition to travel as traders or Muslim teachers or holy men, *fakīs* (Ar. *faqīh*, Sud. pl. *fuqarā'*, class. Ar. pl. *fuqahā'*), took the Jaʿaliyyīn and others from the Northern Sudan to foreign lands, Kordofan, Dār Fūr, Wadai and further west, or to the Upper Blue Nile and Ethiopia and to Egypt. Once a network of kinsmen had been established, it became easier for subsequent generations to travel abroad. The motives for travelling and migration were, of course, many. In a man's lifetime a need for extra income could arise on several occasions, and a few years of trading in the diaspora could solve such temporary crises. Thus the causes and motives of emigration make up a complex picture.

The migration of the Jaʿaliyyīn has brought, and still brings, Islam, the Arabic language and Northern Sudanese culture to the remotest areas of what is today the Democratic Republic of the Sudan, and even beyond. Islam gained a firm footing among the Jaʿaliyyīn Group and famous Quran schools (Sud. Ar. *khalwa*) attracted students from both near and far. Among the Jaʿaliyyīn proper, with whom this study is mostly concerned, the town of al-Dāmir, established by the family of the Majādhīb, had a particular reputation as a seat of learning and sanctity.[4]

Fakīs were (and are) highly respected among Sudanese Muslims, and those believed to have possessed the gift of performing miracles (Ar. *karāma*) were regarded as saints (*walī*, pl. *awliyā'*) and domes (*qubba*) were erected over their graves. *Qubbas* of Jaʿalī saints can be seen both along the Nile and in the diaspora, regularly visited by people in distress in search of saintly intervention.

THE SOCIO-POLITICAL CONTEXT

We are concerned here with agriculture and trade and the changing political circumstances under which these sectors had to operate. The socio-political structure of the Jaʿaliyyīn proper on the eve of the Turkiyya was characterised by a hierarchy of slaves, commoners (peasants and nomads), merchants, nobles and the king. Cutting across this vertical structure were horizontal ties of family, kinship, and religious brotherhoods. Each tribal section had their notable families and for generations the dominant section (the Saʿdāb) also provided the royal family.

The village communities were made up of peasant households. Differences between households in terms of wealth, status and power were reflected in the unequal distribution of land, water-wheels, animals and slaves. Those who were well off aspired to the position of village chief, while the more affluent were either engaged in trade or belonged to the nobility, who did not engage in manual labour on their farms or estates but were preoccupied with tribal politics, administration and war.

The private estates of the nobles, including that of the king, were either inherited through the family line or granted to them as private demesne by a superior lord such as the sultan of Sinnār, depending on the official status of the land holder. Part of the king's demesne consisted of the *kursī* (or *ṭāqiyya*) lands which apparently followed the office rather than the person. The estates were cultivated by slaves or by local peasants (as part of their corvée duties or under a free *teddān* contract) or leased to religious families. The notables were also heads of provinces, districts and villages with the duty of keeping law and order, supervising market places and caravans, collecting dues and taxes, and encouraging new settlers in their territories.

The kingdom of Shendi, though basically a tribal chiefdom, *mashaykha*, can also be viewed as a district within the northern province of the Funj sultanate. Thus the Jaʿalī king was both a tribal chief by right of inheritance and a centrally appointed governor based on loyalty to and marriage ties with his superior lord, and expressed in the payment of tribute. A tribally and administratively defined territory was known as a *dār*, 'homeland'. Thus the kingdom of Shendi comprised the *dār* of the Jaʿaliyyīn or at least a major part of it. The Funj sultanate consisted of numerous tributary *dārs* along the Nile and in the savannas.

The Funj sultanate of Sinnār has been defined as a feudal state and many features would seem to point in that direction. The tribal unit, the *dār*, and ultimately the state may be seen, however, as the supreme landlords rather than any individual persons. Both private (along the Main Nile) and common possession and use of land (in the savannas) could be found. By right of birth and membership in a tribal unit, the producers obtained access to land and pastures and remained in possession of the means of production. The surplus extracted from them can therefore be regarded as a form of precapitalist rent or tax/rent which does not *necessarily* require feudal relations. This was so because theoretically the peasants used land belonging to the *dār* or the state rather than belonging privately to any feudal lord, except in the case when peasants farmed the private estates of noblemen. Therefore the surplus was extracted directly by the state, sometimes by both local and central tax-collectors, and less frequently indirectly by way of feudal rent. The peasants were to some extent unfree, not because of serfdom, but because a part of their labour belonged by right to the state.[5]

The principle of the *dār* applied also, of course, to the savannas, where the land, both pastures and cultivated plots, belonged to the nomadic group in common. Peasants and others from outside who obtained permission to clear a field and cultivate it, paid annual rent to the tribal shaykh, but did not obtain ownership of the fields.

Along the Nile land was scarce and the village land was divided among the cultivating families, who became recognised as joint owners and who pooled resources and labour and shared out the produce according to input. Membership in a family and a village entailed rights to a share in the produce of the allotted land. However, it is possible to indicate a slow movement from shares in the produce to shares in the fields themselves prior to the Turkiyya, to the extent that land could sometimes be sold, mortgaged, bequeathed, given as bridewealth, and established as pious foundations. Vacant land could be granted by the sultan or the local king to favourites as private farms against the customary dues and taxes. Landed grants to holy men (*fakīs*) were in most cases exempt from taxation.

From early on the people along the Nile have engaged in trade and crafts as a means of supplementing household incomes as well as full-time occupations. Most people found time and opportunity for such activities only in the slack seasons, but gradually an increasing number embarked upon a full-time career in trade, in regional centres such as Shendi or outside their homeland, in the diaspora, leaving cultivation to the elders, the womenfolk and slaves. The spectacular growth of Shendi and al-Matamma at the end of the eighteenth century is a reflection of this development. Thus it became more common for peasant families to have one or more members in trade and in the caravan traffic as camel drivers for shorter or longer periods. In spite of the great differences in outward appearance and ideological orientation, there were many ties that bound the agrarian and commercial sectors to each other outside the realm of pure business. The growth of merchant capital drew heavily upon the agricultural sector and soon turned into a dominant force through commodity circulation and more so through the system of moneylending, credit and crop mortgages.

Historical studies on the nineteenth century, few though they are, have tended to concentrate on the political and administrative elite and the issue of slave trade, probably because the relevant sources are more accessible than those on social and economic conditions. However, with the increasing focus on indigenous documentary sources, a new dimension has been introduced. Encouraged by this development and the availability of relevant documents, including my own findings in 1980 and 1984, an attempt has been made here to utilise such sources, together with other material, in order to explore a new field, namely local economic history during the Turkiyya. One example of what local Arabic documentation can yield is the outline of a merchant's career and business interests.

The period under discussion will hopefully attract a wider audience than those interested in the Sudan *per se*, as it represents an early case of colonial rule of a part of Sub-Saharan Africa by a foreign power. The description and analysis of the subsequent political and socio-economic changes in a locally defined area should have comparative interest.

For the Sudan the period was the most decisive in its modern history, even more so than the Condominium period (1899–1956), which in many ways may be regarded as a successor state. Thus the Condominium is known as al-Turkiyya al-thāniya, 'the second Turkiyya'. The legacy of the Turkiyya reached far beyond the fall of Khartoum in January 1885.

1

The Jaʿalī Kingdom of Shendi and its destruction

The Jaʿaliyyīn Group claim to descend from al-ʿAbbās, the uncle of the Prophet, through one Ibrāhīm Jaʿal or Juʿal. Leaving aside the Jaʿalī tribes of the White Nile and Kordofan, whose names are derived from the root *j.m.ʿ.*, 'to gather', or 'collect', and the Danāgla of Dongola, who should perhaps not be rated among the Jaʿaliyyīn at all, we are left with five major riverain Jaʿalī tribes. The Shāyqiyya (roughly between Kurtī and Ḥōsh al-Jurūf), the Manāṣīr (Ḥōsh al-Jurūf to Ḥawīla Island), the Rubāṭāb (Ḥawīla to ʿUshayr Island), the Mīrafāb (from ʿUshayr to the Atbara River), and the Jaʿaliyyīn proper (from Atbara to the Sixth Cataract). Although informants may today admit that their Arab ancestors married Nubian women, the genealogical tree of the Jaʿaliyyīn is a 'deliberate attempt to ignore the Nubian sub-stratum that the Arab immigrants had submerged'.[1]

Interpretations of the meaning of Ibrāhīm's nickname Jaʿal or Juʿal may throw some light on this question. The most common interpretation is that it stems from *j.ʿ.l.*, 'to make'. Ibrāhīm is said to have 'made' or incorporated people hit by famine into his own people by giving them food, shelter and protection.[2] Another and less well-known tradition links his nickname to the colour of his skin. It is said that he was very black and that his grandmother used to call him 'Juʿal', a black beetle.[3] There are, furthermore, many traditions relating to the early relationship between the Arabs and the Nubians, but a study of how the Nubians became Arabs lies beyond the scope of this study.[4]

At the beginning of the sixteenth century, when the Funj were consolidating their newly founded kingdom (Sinnār) on the Blue Nile, there are indications that a tribe by the name of Jaʿal was living below the Sixth Cataract, ruled by a king whose Arabic nickname was Abū ʿAqrab, literally 'father of a scorpion'. His authority reached far into the Bayūḍa Desert, but he was at the same time subordinate to the Funj king, who sent orders to him to convey the traveller David Reubeni to the borders of Dongola in 1523.[5]

Some traditions maintain that the Jaʿaliyyīn lived in Kordofan when the riverain Nubian kingdoms disintegrated, upon which they moved in and as it were took over the political institutions of the Nubians. It may, therefore, well be that the kingdom of Shendi antedates the appearance of the

Ja'aliyyīn and Islam. According to the same traditions, the first Ja'alī king was Sa'd Abū Dabbūs, 'father of a mace', who ruled towards the end of the sixteenth century. He is said to have inherited the right to the kingship from his maternal grandfather, 'Adlān, king of the Nubians, but had to take it by force, hence his nickname, from one 'Abd al-Dā'im.[6]

Sa'd Abū Dabbūs founded the Sa'dāb dynasty which apparently exercised a continuous authority over the Ja'aliyyīn until the latter half of the eighteenth century. The Sa'dāb rulers were subordinate to the Funj king through his governor of the northern province, the king of Qarrī, a relationship which is reflected both in their titles and tributary obligations. They were normally titled *arbāb* (pl. *arabīb*), or sometimes *amīr* (pl. *umarā'*), meaning chief, commander or simply nobleman.[7] Towards the end of the eighteenth century, when the Funj were weakened, the rulers of Shendi took the title of *makk* (pl. *mukūk*) i.e. king, and became more reluctant to pay tribute.[8] However the Ja'aliyyīn were unable to unite since the internecine struggles between their overlords split them into two opposing groups headed by the Sa'dāb and the Nimrāb (the Awlād Nimr or the sons of Nimr) respectively.

In 1762 the Funj sultan was deposed by his vizier Muḥammad Abū Likaylik of the Hamaj people, who put a puppet ruler on the throne. This event inaugurated the final decline of the sultanate.[9] The 'Abdallāb king of Qarrī opposed the Hamaj viziers, as did also sections of the Ja'aliyyīn, but the the Sa'dāb were apparently divided over the issue. In the 1770s and 1780s, a Sa'dābī, Sa'd w. Idrīs II, was fighting in Kordofan on the side of the Hamaj vizier at the same time as his nephew Idrīs III w. al-Faḥl was ruling the Ja'aliyyīn of Shendi. His mother, Bruce's 'Sittina', had a prominent position in Shendi in 1772. At the time Bruce noted that the people of Shendi expressed much fear and consternation at the thought of the return of the Sa'dāb and Hamaj forces from Kordofan.[10]

Sometime around 1780, a branch of the Nifī'āb, the Awlād Nimr, came to power.[11] They took advantage of the weak Idrīs III w. al-Faḥl, who was subsequently killed by the Kawaḥla, and the absence in Kordofan of the other Sa'dābī leader, Sa'd w. Idrīs II, and obtained the support of the 'Abdallāb through a marriage alliance. Thus Muḥammad w. Nimr al-Kabīr broke away from the Sa'dāb demanding the *makk*-ship for himself, and married a royal woman from the 'Abdallāb around 1780. She bore him a son, who was to be the famous *makk* Nimr.[12] A land charter issued by Muḥammad w. Nimr in Shendi in 1794 implies that he was in full control of the place.[13] It can therefore be assumed that when Sa'd and his son Musā'd returned from Kordofan they were compelled to settle in al-Matamma, a Sa'dābī stronghold.

Makk Sa'd died around 1800 and his death was followed by clashes between Musā'd and Muḥammad w. Nimr which entailed the intervention of the Hamaj, the patrons of the Sa'dāb. The right-hand man and brother of the Hamaj vizier, 'Adlān, was sent north with a force to Wad Bān al-Naqā.

There he wrote to Muḥammad promising him the *makk*-ship if he would come to negotiate. This took place in the year 1800 (towards the end of 1214 H or the beginning of 1215 H) and is laconically referred to in a contemporary document, which states that it (the document) was written (a short time) after the coming of 'Adlān to Shendi and the seizure of Muḥammad w. Nimr.[14] The Nimrāb were captured by surprise; apparently only the young Nimr and his uncle Sa'd were able to escape. Another son of Muḥammad, Idrīs, was ransomed by his mother for 300 *waqiyyas* (ounces) of gold.[15] Before he returned to Sinnār with his prisoners for their execution, 'Adlān appointed Musā'd as king of the Ja'aliyyīn at Shendi. In the meantime Nimr took refuge with the Baṭāḥīn and friendly Ja'aliyyīn such as the Nifī'āb and the Nāfa'āb at Abū Dilayq oasis in the Butāna. There Nimr also gained the support of the Baṭāḥīn nomads and in 1216/1801–2, when the Hamaj were engaged in Kordofan, he and his party launched a major attack on Shendi.[16] The Sa'dāb were forced on the defensive, but as in earlier conflicts, the Majādhīb of al-Dāmir intervened to bring about a peaceful settlement. The kingdom was divided, so that Musā'd received al-Matamma and the west bank and Nimr was to rule Shendi and the east bank. This was the political situation when the Turco-Egyptians arrived in 1821.

The actual territory over which the Ja'alī *makk* exercised effective authority cannot be accurately determined. In Bruce's day, the official boundary in the south between the territory of the Shendi and that of Qarrī was at Ḥajar al-'Asal or Ḥajar al-Sarrarīk. This was confirmed by Burckhardt forty-two years later and by subsequent sources, including informants in Shendi in 1980. In the north (downstream) Shendi's authority bordered *de jure* on the Atbara River, but al-Dāmir had long since asserted its independence when Burckhardt passed through in 1814. After a march of nine hours from al-Dāmir, he came to Ḥamāya village, which 'forms at present the northern territory of Shendy'.[17] In the same area, he passed through the area of the Mukābrāb, a section of the Ja'aliyyīn, who were also independent, living partly upon the produce of their fields and partly upon robbery. 'Travellers unaccompanied by one or more of the Fakys from Damar, are sure of being stripped by them.'[18]

On the opposite bank of the Nile across from al-Dāmir was the territory of Dār Ja'al, probably with the Masallamāb as the core population. Its last village upstream was 'Ālīāb (west) and the first village of Dār Shendi was Ḥalāwiyya.[19] After the split between the Sa'dāb and the Nimrāb, the Masallamāb paid tribute to *makk* Nimr or to *makk* Musā'd according to circumstances, but preferably to the first. In addition, there were also other minor tributary *makks* established in such villages as Kabūshiyya and Makniyya.[20]

The administration of the kingdom was, at least under *makk* Nimr, a family enterprise with the ultimate authority in the king's hands,

> The government of Shendy is much to be preferred to that of Berber, the full authority of the Mek is not thwarted by the influence of powerful families,

> which in these countries leads only to insecurity, nor has he adopted the system of rapacity which makes Berber so justly dreaded by strangers. His absolute power is owing to the diversity of the Arab tribes inhabiting Shendy none of which is strong enough to cope with his own family and its numerous branches.[21]

Members of the royal family were appointed governors of sub-districts and villages; thus the village of Jibayl was administered by a relative of the *makk*.[22] The *makk* himself and the numerous *arabīb* had landed estates in various places along the Nile and on islands, which enabled them to enjoy a lifestyle suitable for a nobility in the service of the Funj sultan. In spite of the numerous courtiers, whose names appear upon official documents and charters, a central bureaucracy hardly existed in Shendi.

> I did not hear of any subordinate offices in the government of Shendy, and the Mek seems to unite all branches of authority in his own person; his relatives are the governors of villages; and his court consists of half a dozen police officers, a writer, an Imam, a treasurer and a bodyguard formed principally of slaves.[23]

The *makk* disposed of few firearms, but the strength of the kingdom rested primarily on its cavalry, 'which decides the fate of all battles he [the king] had to fight with his enemies'.[24] From Shendi itself, the king could raise from 200 to 300 horsemen. The townsmen preferred stallions, while Jaʿalī nomads rode mares.

The authority of the king did not stretch far from the Nile; the nomads of the Buṭāna and the Bayūḍa semi-deserts, except the Jaʿalī nomads, paid their tribute directly to the governor of the northern Funj province, the ʿAbdallābī king (*mānjil*) of Qarrī. The king of Shendi was not allowed to tax caravans going from Sinnār to Egypt, as most of the commodities probably belonged to the Funj sultan; towards other caravans he acquired a freer hand.

The riverain principalities and *dārs* such as Shendi and Berber constituted the district level of the pyramid of authority which had its apex at Sinnār. The political hierarchy from the sultan via the provincial *mānjils* to the local *makks* and shaykhs was cemented through marriage alliances, whereby royal and noble women were transferred downwards in exchange for gifts, tribute, allegiance and political support. There were often several claimants to the thrones and this enabled the overlords to exact rich gifts and promises of loyalty and subordination before the candidate was chosen. The danger of being deposed and replaced by a more cooperative candidate was apparently not an empty threat, as is shown by a well-documented case from Berber.[25]

With the rise to power of Muḥammad ʿAlī Pasha in the first decade of the nineteenth century, Egypt's relations with the Sudan changed decisively. The Ottoman Turks who had ruled Egypt from 1517 had been eager to maintain commercial links with Sinnār and Dār Fūr and only occasionally was the actual occupation of the sources of gold, slaves, ivory, feathers and camels seriously contemplated.[26] Muḥammad 'Alī, vastly ambitious, did not hesitate to make such plans and to send spies to the area. For him, state-building and industrialisation at home and expansion abroad, were two integrated aspects of the same process towards making Egypt an independent and strong state on an equal footing with Europe. During his campaigns in the Ḥijāz in Arabia, Shendi had become a vital supplier of camels, but insecurity along the Nile caused much damage to the regular traffic to Egypt. The same applied to the *darb al-arba'īn* or 'Forty Days Road' to Dār Fūr which was closed for several years. Great disorder had interrupted the inland trade, according to English,

> His Highness the Viceroy, in consequence, determined as the most effectual means of putting an end to these disorders, to subject those countries to his dominion. Four thousand troops were accordingly put under the command of Ismael Pasha, the youngest son of the Viceroy, with orders to conquer all the provinces of the Nile, from the second cataract to Sennaar inclusive.[27]

The army was set in motion in the autumn of 1820. The Mamluks fled further south and it was only the Shāyqiyya who offered any serious resistance.[28] The two leading kings of the Shāyqiyya, Shawīsh (Shūsh) and Ṣubayr, were brave warriors who could muster some 6,000 armed men, but still they lost in two bloody battles. The ears were cut off those who were or appeared to be dead and sent to Cairo. It is said that Muḥammad 'Alī paid 50 piastres for each pair of ears, but in a letter to his son, Ismā'īl Pasha, he makes it clear that this affair had alienated the Shāyqiyya. It had been his son's duty to spread justice in order to gain the affection and trust of the people.[29] After heavy losses, Ṣubayr surrendered but Shawīsh fled to the vicinity of Shendi, ravaging the country as he went.

From Dār al-Shāyqiyya the Turkish army crossed overland to Berber whose ruler, *makk* Naṣr al-Dīn, surrendered. It is said that he had already been in contact with Muḥammad 'Alī, hoping for support in his rivalries with the other Mīrafābī *makk*, 'Alī *w*. Tumsāḥ, who resided on the west bank. The background to this division was that in 1818 Nimr and Musā'd had united and invaded Berber and put Tumsāḥ on the throne while Naṣr al-Dīn was on pilgrimage.[30] The latter fled to Egypt and is said to have returned with the invading army in 1820, but that has not been confirmed. The eye-witnesses, English and Cailliaud, say that he made his submission on the arrival of Ismā'īl Pasha. According to Caillaud it took place immediately, but English says that it happened several days afterwards, even after the submission of *makk* Nimr, a delay which was due to illness.[31]

Ismā'īl Pasha rested some time in Berber while he waited for the submission of *makk* Nimr. He had earlier sent a merchant as a messenger to Shendi, and he now returned with letters from the king and with messages from certain religious leaders and merchants of that area.[32] On 12 March 1821, a son of *makk* Nimr arrived in Berber with valuable presents announcing the submission of Shendi. Ismā'īl Pasha thereupon sent one *diwān efendī* (a title rather than a name) to Shendi to arrange the terms of peace with the *makk*. He was also to assure the Shāyqiyya there of the general amnesty offered to them if they surrendered.[33] On his way to Shendi he met Nimr and together they arrived in Berber on 22 March: 'The makk of Shendi was accompanied by a considerable suite, and two most beautiful horses, intended as presents to the Pasha. On being introduced to his Excellence, he kissed his hand, and pressed it to his forehead, and told him that he had come to surrender himself and his country to his favour and protection.'[34] He arrived in a kind of sedan chair (*palanquin*), says Cailliaud, carried by two camels. His robe consisted of two large shirts and an overcoat covered his shoulders. On his head he wore the traditional pointed cap, the *ṭāqiyya*. English, a firm believer in the campaign, thought that Nimr was graciously received, whereas Cailliaud observed that he was coolly received by Ismāʿīl who offered his guest neither coffee nor a pipe. Three days later he left for Shendi after having promised to provide Ismāʿīl with camels.[35]

In the meantime Muḥammad ʿAlī urged his son to move on and complete the campaign. It was therefore decided to strike camp and move to Shendi, where they encamped on the west bank on 9 May 1821. The Jaʿaliyyīn had apparently accepted Nimr's submission without protest. There were no signs of ʿAbdallāb, Funj or Hamaj resistance as yet, but the Shāyqiyya were nervous and threatened resistance. After a while, however, Shawīsh offered his submission and entered into the service of the occupiers, an alliance which many people of the Turkish Sudan came to fear and to hate. *Makk* Nimr, whose house, noted English, was built of no better materials than those of his people, differing only in size, presented Ismāʿīl Pasha with several hundred camels upon his arrival. In spite of the apparently disciplined atmosphere, a dangerous incident occurred when four soldiers were killed in a village, probably after trying to confiscate durra (sorghum) from the peasants, thus triggering off a major raid on the Jaʿalī villages, which was only brought to an end after Nimr's intercession.[36]

Ismāʿīl Pasha decided it was unwise to leave Nimr and Musāʿd behind when he moved south, so he ordered the two kings to accompany him. When Linant de Bellefonds came to Shendi in November 1821, they were still in Sinnār, but on his way there, Linant met both returning home in the beginning of December.[37]

Ismāʿīl Pasha spent more than a year in the south, looking for gold in the Fāzūghlī area. In the meantime Kordofan was conquered by an army under the command of the Viceroy's son-in-law, Muḥammad Bey the Daftardar. Along the Nile the Turks, as the invaders were called, started to introduce the new taxation system. Linant noted that the inhabitants of Shendi found themselves obliged to sell their belongings in order to pay the large tax demands. Rumours of revolts were often heard in Shendi also after the return of *makk* Nimr. The latter, however, is reported to have assured the Turks that he was not contemplating fighting them, as in his opinion,

Muḥammad 'Alī would only send a larger army against him and he would be ruined.[38]

However, tension was increasing among the peasants; violence and, in despair, emigration spread as the armed tax-collectors travelled around to acquaint the people with the new taxes and to collect them. A desperate move could be expected at any moment. On his way northwards in the autumn of 1822 (Ṣafar 1238/October–November 1822), Ismā'īl Pasha could not fail to notice the early effects of his economic policy. When he reached Shendi in his boat, he disembarked and demanded to see the *makk*. At the following meeting he is said to have asked Nimr and the other chiefs for tribute to the value of about 100,000 dollars in cattle, slaves and in cash. When Nimr explained to him his inability to comply with his demands, the Pasha struck him across the face with a pipe. Traditions say that Nimr wanted to kill Ismā'īl on the spot, particularly after an insulting remark about his daughter, but *makk* Musā'd who was also present, managed to calm him down, talking to him in the language of the Bishāriyyīn, Tu Bedawie.[39]

Later that same day Ismā'īl and his men were invited to spend the night ashore (17 Ṣafar 1238/3 November 1822). Covered by darkness, the people started to gather durra stalks which they stacked around Ismā'īl's lodgings. When the work was completed, the dry stalks were set alight and Ismā'īl and his men were burned to death.[40]

News of the burning of the Pasha spread like wildfire; revolts immediately broke out along the Nile, the invaders were hunted down and killed as far south as Wad Madanī, which, however, did not fall, and as far north as Atbara, where the province governor, Maḥū Bey, had a difficult time defending Berber against the furious Ja'aliyyīn. The Daftardar hurried from Kordofan to the Nile with orders to bring the rebels to justice. After an initial period of violent repression along the Nile, a meeting was arranged in al-Matamma between the Daftardar and some Ja'alī notables (Nimr and Musā'd had retreated into the Buṭāna). The talks were, however, interrupted by a sudden assault on the Daftardar, who was nearly killed in the incident. From that moment the Turks showed no mercy in dealing with the Ja'aliyyīn. After burning parts of al-Matamma they crossed over to Shendi which was thoroughly looted and burned. Moving into the countryside, the Turks went as far as al-Dāmir where the mosque was burned before they turned south, inflicting harsh punishments everywhere.[41]

Apparently at first no serious effort was made to hunt down *makk* Nimr, but when rumours reached the Daftardar that Nimr was about to return to Shendi, he decided to march into the Buṭāna. Battle was joined at al-Naṣūb in Shawwāl 1238/June–July 1823 which Nimr lost. However, whereas *makk* Musā'd was subsequently killed by the Turks, *makk* Nimr and his family and followers escaped and made their way to the Ethiopian borderlands where they established a kind of buffer state on the Setit River. From this stronghold, largely outside the reach of the Turks, they harassed the Turks and offered shelter and protection to refugee Jaʿaliyyīn of all categories until the 1860s.

The punitive expeditions of the Daftardar, who was still encamped on the west bank downstream from al-Matamma in the winter 1823–4, dealt a heavy blow to the Jaʿaliyyīn, both materially and culturally and through the decimation of the population. Thousands must have lost their lives, many escaped and emigrated more or less for good, some were enslaved and branded and sent to Egypt. Although many of the latter found their way back, after being released by Muḥammad ʿAlī, some stayed on in Cairo and their descendants were seen in Ḥōsh al-Jāmūs in Cairo by Shuqayr in about 1900.[42] For those who stayed behind in Dār al-Jaʿaliyyīn, as well as for those who escaped or emigrated, colonial rule had begun with a grim baptism.

2

Shendi's economy on the eve of the Turkiyya

Contemporary descriptions of Shendi prior to the Turkiyya survive only for the years 1772, 1814, and 1821–2, but together they offer a vivid picture of the town and the market.[1] Earlier travellers except perhaps David Reubeni in 1523, seem to have crossed the Nile further south, usually at Qarrī where there was a quarantine station on the west bank.[2] De Maillet's reports from 1692 onwards, as well as the accounts left by Poncet, Krump, Brevedent and other missionaries, doctors or ambassadors travelling around 1700 all show that the caravans left the Nile in the Manfalūṭ/Aysūṭ region in Egypt.[3] After passing along the valley of al-Wāḥ (Ar. 'the oasis'), they reached the oasis of Salīma, where the Dār Fūr caravan turned south-west and the Sinnār caravan turned south-east and reached the Nile at Mūshū. The caravans then passed by (Old) Dongola on the east bank. At al-Dabba, Ambuqōl or Kurtī they left the Nile again and crossed the Bayūḍa to Dirayra opposite Wad Bān al-Naqā. Following the Nile on the west bank, they then crossed at Qarrī near the Sixth Cataract.[4]

Qarrī was the seat of the ʿAbdallāb *mānjil* or governor of the northern Funj province. Caravans from Egypt had to pay customs there, usually in luxury items and in cash. Those who were not *jallāba* (sing. *jallāb* or *jallābī*), itinerant or caravan traders, of the king of Sinnār, were thoroughly searched.[5]

About seventy years later, Bruce noted that there had been a second crossing point at Dirayra in Dār al-Jaʿaliyyīn, but the insecurity of the area had made it unattractive. Bruce on his way north from Sinnār had been advised to cross at Qarrī and not to take the less frequented route through Shendi and Berber, where only Heaven could be relied upon for protection.[6]

The origins and early history of the town of Shendi is unknown. Since it is believed to be the burial place of the first Saʿdābī king, it could well have existed in the sixteenth century. Urbanisation has a long history in the Sudan, connected with both administration and commerce. In the context of the Nile Valley, Shendi and its sister-town al-Matamma are located in a relatively fertile and well-populated area. Shendi could therefore have grown out of an earlier village; in fact, Shendi retained many 'village' features. However, its geographical position as a meeting-point of caravans, at least during more peaceful periods, as well as its function as the seat of a local king, were factors which turned the town into a major trading centre.

For the same reasons, shifts in political power or changes in regional and international caravan networks decided the fate of many potentially prosperous towns. Qarrī, for instance, was built to function as a political centre as well as a customs station and ferry crossing. Apparently it had little trade of its own, although it competed with Shendi as a caravan entrepōt. The surrounding countryside was poor. In the mid eighteenth century for both political and commercial reasons the ʿAbdallāb deserted Qarrī in favour of Ḥalfāyat al-Mulūk, near present-day Khartoum North.[7] When Bruce visited the place in 1772, Qarrī consisted of some 140 houses and served only as the main crossing of the area, whereas Ḥalfāya, the new capital, had grown into a small town of 300 houses, and was famous for the production of cotton cloth.[8] Ḥalfāyat al-Mulūk retained its primacy until the arrival of the Turks, but Qarrī decayed and was only a heap of ruins in 1821.[9] The growth and decline of urban centres thus intimately depended on a subtle combination of socio-economic and political factors. That was also, of course, true for the Turkiyya.

The population structure of towns like Shendi, the varieties of occupations and the types of commodities exchanged there, indicate that such markets served local as well as regional needs. This situation may be contrasted with market towns further west, such as Kobbei in Dār Fūr and Nimro in Wadai. There the political centres were physically separate from the commercial centres and the latter were largely populated by professional traders of foreign origin, mainly *jallāba* from the Nile.[10] Thus Kobbei market was mainly of interest to the king and the ruling elite, as both the prices and the types of goods offered there worked to exclude the local peasants and nomads. Shendi and al-Matamma recruited local traders to the internationally-oriented occupation of *jallāba*, many of whom operated in Kobbei.

THE TOWN AND THE MARKET

In 1772 Shendi was a large village or a small town consisting of about 250 houses,

> which are not all built continuous, some of the best being separate, and that of Sittina's [the royal palace] is half a mile from the town. There are two or three tolerable houses, but the rest of them are miserable hovels, built of clay and reeds.
>
> The caravans from Sennaar, Egypt, Suakem and Kordofan, all were in use [*sic*] to rendezvous here, especially since the Arabs have cut off the road by Dongola and the desert of Bahiouda.

Bruce assures us that Shendi was once a town of great renown. At the time of his visit the market was not a scene of great abundance, yet the prices were lower and the quality better than in Sinnār. Fuel, however, in the form of wood was much dearer and the people used to burn camel dung. The miserable appearance of Shendi was attributed to political disintegration and the reduction of regular large-scale caravan traffic between Sinnār and Ethiopia in the south and Egypt in the north.[11]

The problem remains, however, to find out when the decline started, how long it lasted, and which routes and towns were most affected. In the same decade and particularly after Dār Fūr gained control of Kordofan in about 1785, al-Ubayyiḍ became an important commercial centre in that province. This development may well be connected with the times of trouble in the Nile Valley when commodities began to be transported directly between Dongola and Egypt via the Wādī al-Milk thus bypassing Shendi.[12] Whenever the Bayūḍa was made unsafe by the Ḥassāniyya and Shāyqiyya, the Cairo-Sinnār-Ethiopia caravans had to pass along the Nile, after crossing the Nubian Desert in the east from Upper Egypt to Abū Ḥamad north of Berber. However, although a peaceful Bayūḍa enabled particularly the sultan's caravans to cross directly between Kurtī and Dirayra/Qarrī, as we have seen, a more easterly route from Tanqāsī through the Wādī Abū Dōm and the Jilif Mountains to al-Matamma and Shendi was also in use as it was shorter and provided more water on the way.[13] Finally unruly elements among the Jaʿaliyyīn themselves often scared away caravans from Shendi, probably a reflection of the recurrent political impotence of their king and the waning superior authority of the Funj sultanate.

With the decline of Sinnār's control over the northern districts, private merchants took the opportunity to break into the royal monopoly and take their own caravans to the most profitable markets. At the same time there was an influx of merchants from Egypt and Sawākin. The Jaʿaliyyīn, Danāgla (pl. of Dongolāwī) and the Shāyqiyya were quick to take advantage of the new trends, establishing commercial links with Kordofan, Dār Fūr, Egypt and the Red Sea Coast. Many of them settled in the trading diasporas both to trade and cultivate. Thus the negative effect on security of declining central control was largely balanced by the growth of independent free trade, and this may account for the remarkable growth of Shendi between 1772 and 1814.

By 1814 the picture of Shendi in decay had changed completely. The caravan route through the Nubian desert controlled by the ʿAbābda and the Bishāriyyīn camel nomads, had become the major route, also because of the presence since 1811 of the Mamluks in Dongola. In Berber the village of Ankhīra (also known as al-Mukhayrif)[14] had replaced Qōz as the principal place. As in Shendi and other market towns, the caravans preferred to enter Ankhīra at night to evade public and official notice. It was also customary among the *jallāba* to establish themselves in the houses of important people to gain their protection.[15] The village of Qōz al-Sūq was still there; the other two important villages were Qōz al-Funj and Ḥaṣṣa. The name of Berber applied only to Ankhīra. As for al-Dāmir further south it had grown into a town of some 500 houses. Shendi, however, was the largest in the Eastern

Sudanic Belt, next only to Kobbei and Sinnār. It consisted of several quarters, divided from each other by public places or markets, and had altogether from 800 to 1,000 houses. The style of the houses was similar to Berber, but there were more larger buildings and fewer ruins. Wide courtyards and high walls were signs of distinction.[16]

Burckhardt (p. 258) says that the market was held in a wide open space between the two principal quarters of the town. There were three rows, one behind the other, of small shops built of mud in the shape of niches, about six feet long by four feet deep and covered by mats. These were occupied by the more opulent merchants, who carried their goods to their respective shops in the morning, and back to their houses in the evening, since the shops had no locks. The smaller merchants sat upon the ground, under a kind of shed (Ar. *rakūba*).

These impressions were confirmed about seven and eight years later, when we learn that Shendi was located about half a mile from the river, that its circumference amounted to 3,500 metres, and that it consisted of about 8 to 900 houses, built of brick and clay, and with a population of 5,000 to 7,000. The residence of the king was larger than average and whitewashed. The houses had small holes in the walls for light and fresh air and water basins were located in the courtyards. Some of the spacious houses were located side by side of courtyards of up to 300 square feet, which served to store the merchandise and keep the caravan camels. Broad and airy streets intersected the town. The immediate environs were sandy and not fit for cultivation.[17]

An important factor in the economic development of Shendi was the growth of al-Matamma on the opposite bank of the Nile. It was described for the first time in 1821 when, according to English, it had a slightly bigger population than Shendi, 6,000 as against 5,000. There were three market places where people exchanged dollars and durra for what they needed. Its development into a town is unclear, but it was apparently connected with its function as a natural crossing station on the Nile as well as its function as a royal seat from the eighteenth century. Its geographical position and commercial potential not only encouraged wealthy merchants to settle there, it also 'exported' *jallāba* to other towns and regions.[18]

Apart from their political rivalry, there seems to have been little actual commercial struggle between the sister towns. It is therefore tempting to assume that they complemented each other in regional and international trade, largely servicing different regions, caravans and customers. A French merchant wrote:

> Al-Matamma, a town noted for its commerce with the interior, has flourished at all times. It is the seat of a chief of the Ja'aliyyīn whose paramount shaykh resided at Shendi on the right bank of the river four miles from al-Matamma, where the caravans from Dār Fūr, Kordofān and Abysinia brought their produce for barter. Gum, ivory, tamarind, slaves, find their outlet at al-Matamma. . . . Sawākin, a port on the Red Sea, carried on a brisk commerce with Shendi and al-Matamma.[19]

Shendi seems to have developed and consolidated its cosmopolitan character in the years leading up to the arrival of the Turks:

> We [Finati] came in the evening to Shendi [Nov. 1821], the capital of the most powerful and populous among the native princes of these parts, called the Melek Nimmer, whose rule extended over a considerable tract on this [the east bank] of the river, and embraced a population amounting to at least 20,000,... our stay, which, as there are more of the comforts and conveniences of life in the town, than in any other that we had met with on this side of Egypt, was prolonged to about fifteen or twenty days, and was spent not unpleasantly. The cause of there appearing to be something more of civilization and luxury here than lower down, seems to be that it is the principal place of halting and rendezvous for the great caravans, whether connected with the Red Sea by Suakim, or with Kordofan and Darfur, and the Negro countries, the merchants generally resting themselves, and even trafficking here, which rendered it (at least before the invasion) a place of comparative opulence.[20]

TRADE AND THE MARKET

Two basic adaptations characterised Dār al-Jaʿaliyyīn, agriculture and pastoralism, with an emphasis on the first. This pattern was also to some extent reflected in the composition of the population of Shendi and their part-time or indirect engagement in agriculture and animal husbandry. The environs of Shendi, except a narrow strip along the Nile, were sandy and deforested. This meant that the inhabitants were in daily need of food supplies from the primary producers of the rural areas. Thibaut noted that, 'The people from the surrounding countryside used to bring their produce: grain, cotton, liquid butter, cord and cotton piece goods woven locally.'[21] In contrast to the peasants, the nomads had a more transitory interest in the market, as the selling of live animals and meat was against their customs. Still, hundreds of camels, horses and cows could be offered for sale on a big market day. The nomads more commonly offered milk, hides, ropes, bags, butter, wild animals, feathers and leather goods in exchange for commodities such as grain, clothes and spices. The camel owners could in addition earn an income by hiring out their camels to the *jallāba* and by acting as guides and camel-drivers.

It may be assumed that a large proportion of Shendi's inhabitants gained their livelihood from market related activities. It was the market which tempted both Jaʿaliyyīn and foreigners to settle there. Thus the market place came to create its own norms of behaviour and idioms of communication, often in conflict with traditional cultural norms. Among the foreigners, the Danāgla were the most numerous. They occupied a whole quarter of the town, 'but their nation is less esteemed than any other'.[22] They seem to have exercised a monopoly over the brokerage business in Shendi. In Berber the Danāgla specialised in dates and tobacco, while their wives and slaves made the best *būẓa* (*marīssa* beer made of fermented durra). Visitors (*jallāba*) and residents of the same ethnic or geographical origin and/or religious affiliation used to live and work together, both in the town quarters and in the market.

Fundamental to Shendi market were the artisans and craftsmen who frequented it. Crafts were fairly well developed to satisfy local as well as regional and international demands. Blacksmiths, locksmiths, silversmiths, tanners, dyers, potters and makers of palm leaf mats and baskets, shoemakers and carpenters operated in the market, where they manufactured their goods and offered them for sale. The fact that their number increased, notably on the big weekly market days of Friday and Saturday, illustrates two important aspects of the craft industries. First, the craftsmen were to a large extent villagers and nomads who did not live in Shendi but combined their skills with primary production in the countryside. Secondly, the rural market for craft products was limited both because of limited purchasing power and because household production sought to be as self-sufficient as possible, thus limiting the market for professional full-time craftsmen.

> If a house is to be built, the owner, his relatives, and slaves, with a few labourers, execute the masonry, and the carpenter is only called in to lay the roof and make the doors. Like the Bedouins of the desert, these Arabs are their own artizans upon all ordinary occasions. There are no [professional] weavers in Shendi, but all the women and grown up children, and many of them men, are seen with a distaff constantly in their hands, spinning cotton yarn, which they sell to the people of Berber. . . . Cotton is cultivated in the neighbourhood.[23]

The institution of work-parties (*nafīr* or *faza'a*) mobilised neighbours and relatives in both towns, villages and camps for construction purposes and in connection with labour-intensive agricultural tasks. Such social and economic factors did not encourage a rapid development towards professionalisation. Even in the field of commerce, the average trader was also often involved in the production of the goods he offered for sale. Seen from another angle, a peasant or a nomad had to acquire a whole set of 'sub-skills', which at intervals could become their major occupations. This meant not only making tools, utensils, and other necessities, but also marketing them in a market such as Shendi. Burckhardt observed that 'the country people bring to the market mats, baskets, ox hides, and other skins, coarse pottery, camel saddles, wooden dishes, and other articles of their own manufacture, etc. About a dozen shoemakers, or rather sandal makers, from the country work for these two days in the market, and will make a pair of sandals in an hour's notice.'[24] Furthermore, leather sacks were sold for the transportation of baggage and merchandise, and baskets for durra, gum arabic and salt. The blacksmiths repaired from the rural areas to Shendi only on the big market days, where they made and sold two-edged knives which were (and are) carried above the elbow. Various wild products were also bought to Shendi by the rural population, such as ostrich feathers, crocodile flesh and skin, some fish, hippopotamus skin, wild donkeys, wild goats, honey, wood, giraffe skin, etc.

The largest number of rural visitors to Shendi were peasants and nomads who came there in order to supplement their household consumption. Some, like the Jaʿalī cattle nomads of the Atbara River, might have travelled for three to four days to reach Shendi, but most visitors of these categories came from districts closer to the town.[25] On the main market days several thousand people used to visit Shendi, in striking contrast to the daily markets directed towards satisfying the day-to-day requirements of the residents. The economic ties between town and village were also largely dependent upon the small-scale traders who bought farm produce in the villages and brought it to Shendi to be exchanged for goods or cash according to the preferences of the villagers. As the population of Shendi grew, the supply of food became more difficult, until it became a royal concern. By the second decade of the nineteenth century, if not before, the *makk* of Shendi hired merchants to import durra from the rainland areas of the Blue Nile.[26] It was primarily the caravan traffic that made the heaviest demands on the local market's capacity to supply food.

The daily markets offered less in terms both of the quantity and types of goods. The butchers sold beef and camel meat which were provided daily, and pieces of roasted fat were sold to the nomads in the neighbouring shops. Every morning nomad girls brought fresh and sour milk to the market to be exchanged for durra, three measures of milk for one measure of durra. They also sold boiled chickpeas and *turmus* (lupine) for breakfast. Retail dealers sold Sinnār tobacco, pipes, natron from Dār Fūr and salt from the Buwayda hamlets downstream from Shendi. Other traders exposed for sale dried *bāmiyā* (okra), red pepper, onions, and *mulūkhiyya* (Jew's mallow). The most frequented shops were apparently those of the grocer and the druggist where one could buy cloves, pepper, cardamoms, and tamarind. Other articles were sandalwood from India, fenugreek from Egypt, various kinds of gum, *shishm* from Dār Fūr, a small black grain used as eye medicine, antimony, cinnamon used against fever and dysentery, and so on. Some articles were destined for markets further away, only passing through Shendi, while articles like salt, cotton yarn and cloth, horses, camels, mats, bags, hides and whips were export products of Shendi area itself.[27]

A colourful and heterogeneous body of entrepreneurs, middlemen, brokers, craftsmen and caravan *jallāba* were active in their respective niches of commerce. Wholesale transactions in connection with the coming and leaving of caravans and other big business tended to become conducted through brokers and in private locations outside the busy market place.[28]

SHENDI AS AN ENTREPÔT

The complex structure of Shendi's market may largely be attributed to its function as an entrepōt in regional and international trade, through which its domestic economy came into contact with the outside world. Al-Matamma and al-Dāmir were also visited by great caravans, but they could not function as the final stations or first starting point on the same scale as did Shendi. When *en route*, the caravans passed the villages along the Nile and the nomadic camps in the deserts. Jaʿalī traders and camel-drivers would hurry home to visit their families and friends and bring money and presents.[29] Whenever a caravan halted, the people of the neighbourhood would come and offer their produce and manufactures in exchange for medicines, spices, utensils and so on. Occasionally, the caravans would be raided and robbed by local groups. For this reason they tended to be armed and to form large caravans. The caravan leader, *khabīr*, was responsible for the safety of the caravan, both in terms of fighting off robbers as well as finding the waterholes throughout the deserts. If not actually related to the local nomads, he at least had to be on good terms with them to obtain safe passage through their domains. The route across the Nubian desert was in the hands of the ʿAbābda camel nomads who could provide camels and *khabīrs* for the whole way between Shendi and Egypt. Their rivals, the Bishāriyyīn camel nomads, controlled the route between Berber and Sawākin.

The exports mentioned above which Shendi could offer do not by themselves explain the growth and prosperity of the town. Here the contribution of the long-distance caravan traffic was decisive, and particularly the fact that Shendi became the point where so many caravans stopped and exchanged their commodities before returning. This meant that many customers, brokers and merchants were waiting to exchange their commodities with the next caravan going in another direction. Hundreds of pack animals needed forage every day, equipment had to be renewed, including sacks, ropes and bags. Whenever a caravan did not find customers for its commodities, it would have to wait for the arrival of other caravans in Shendi. Sometimes it could take weeks before the *jallāba* from Egypt were able to find buyers for all their imports or find profitable articles for their home markets. On such occasions they could decide to move on to Sinnār, where Egyptian and Red Sea goods would be more popular and fetch a better price. On the other hand, when the market of Berber was active, caravans might stop and return northwards from there, without risking the journey south to Shendi.

Some of the Shendi merchants possessed substantial wealth, but it is unclear to what extent they engaged in wholesale business. The Danāgla brokers mediated big transactions but were generally not in a position to buy quantities of commodities for resale later. They associated with the merchants, discussing the prospects of the arrival of the next caravan, how many slaves it would bring and what it would buy.[30] The king himself was also active in the market through his agents, having the right of pre-emption as well as the right to offer his own commodities to the *jallāba* before the others could enter into serious business. Each caravan was also obliged to pay a market due to the king and bring him precious gifts. No wonder he regarded the merchants as his friends.[31]

When a caravan finally arrived, the royal agents, merchants and brokers flocked to its quarters. Bargaining, which would be conducted by barter or money exchange, was prolonged because of the lack of fixed prices. Little or no long-term credit was extended on such occasions since there was always the risk of debt evasion. In 1772 Bruce had to pay the debts of a co-traveller who was arrested for such evasion in both Shendi and Berber.[32]

THE COMMODITIES

Caravans from the four main directions traded in Shendi, from Egypt via Berber (earlier also via Dongola), from Sawākin via Berber or Qōz Rajab, from Ethiopia and Sinnār, and from Dār Fūr and Kordofan. Smaller caravans also came from Dongola, the Atbara and the Buṭāna.

> The principal articles imported from Egypt are the Sembil [*sunbul*, i.e. spikenard, *Spica celtica*] and Mehleb [*maḥlab*, an aromatic weed], both of which are in great request, and usually sold together, the loads of which are called Zamele (زاملة) [*zāmila*, lit. 'a camel-load']. Every respectable merchant coming from Egypt brings with him two Zameles. The Zamele is easily disposed of, in whole sale, to the Sennaar merchants [in Shendi], who give in exchange dollars, Dammour [*dammūr*, cotton cloth] and slaves . . . These drugs are here at least 250 per cent dearer than in Cairo. The Egyptians sometimes push on as far as Sennaar, if they cannot find a ready sale for their Zamele at Shendy.[33]

Pieces of *takkiyya* (pl. *takākī*, strips of cotton cloth) from Egypt were bought principally by the Kordofan merchants. White cotton stuffs were bought especially for the great people in Sinnār. Beads of various colours, material and qualities were imported from Egypt and used as currencies everywhere, each district having its own particular favourites. The *rīsh* beads from Surat in India via Sawākin were bought exclusively by the Kordofan merchants, as they were in demand as far west as Dār Fūr and Wadai. Cheaper beads made of wood were bought by the poor people. A variety of glass beads were also imported from Venice and Jerusalem.[34] Other articles from Egypt were soap, sugar, linen, sheepskins, coral, paper, and old copper.

According to Burckhardt, smaller caravans set out from Egypt once or twice a month. They stopped to trade frequently, however, so that Egyptian goods could only be found in any quantity in Shendi after the arrival of the big caravans. The departure from Darāw of the major caravan had become irregular however, going south one year and returning the next. This caravan consisted of 300 to 400 men and several hundred camels. On its return, it was joined by 'many Sennaar traders, chiefly agents of the King of Sennaar and his vizier, who are the principal merchants of that place'.[35]

Caravans from Sinnār arrived in Shendi every six weeks or two months; and when they brought durra, their loaded camels numbered between 500 and 600, but normally the number was around a hundred. Durra was also

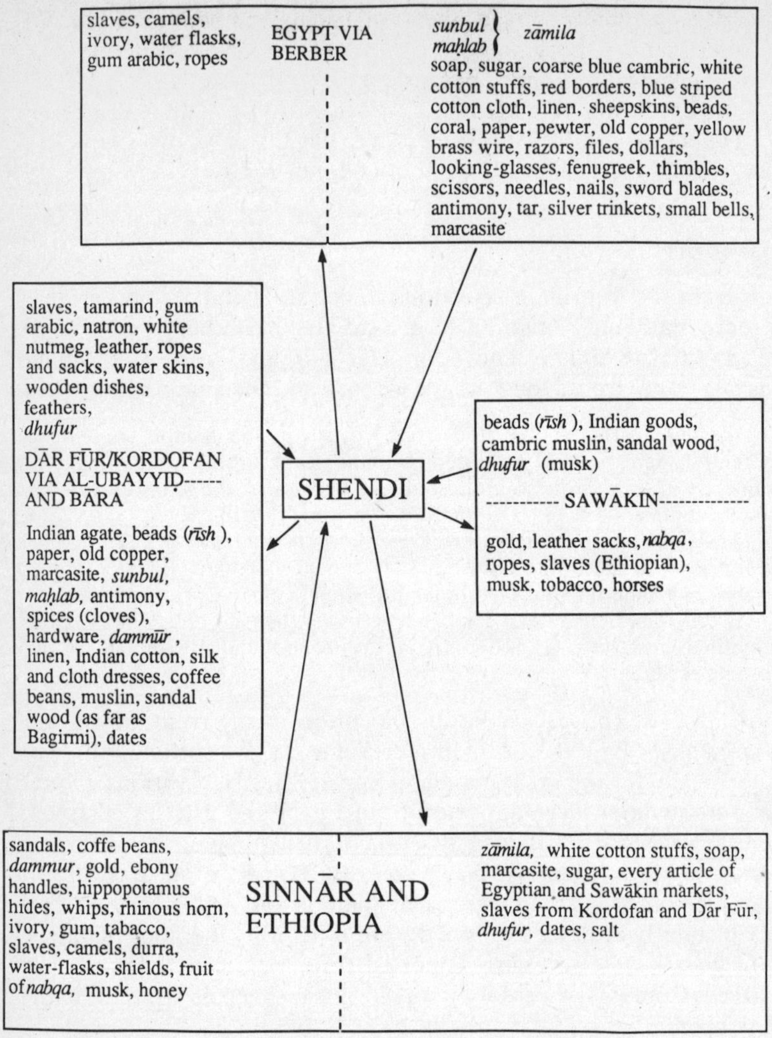

The flow of commodities to and from Shendi in 1814

brought from Abū Ḥarāz, north of Sinnār. On the arrival of such a caravan, the price of durra often fell from a dollar for twelve measures to a dollar for twenty measures. After camels and durra, the main import from the south, probably largely from Ḥalfāyat al-Mulūk, was *dammūr* which served both as a medium of exchange and as a material for *tōb* (Ar. *thawb*) dresses. Gold was another important article. It came from the Banī Shanqūl area near Rās al-Fīl, where it was exchanged for salt from Shendi. In Shendi it was bought almost exclusively by Sawākin merchants, probably for export to India. One *waqiyya* (ounce) was worth 12 dollars in Sinnār, 16 dollars in

Shendi, and 20 in Sawākin. Ivory from Sinnār was bought by the Egyptian merchants. The demand for camels in Egypt, largely because of the Arabian campaigns, led the merchants to bring Spanish dollars to Shendi to buy camels more easily.[36]

Slaves constituted the principal imports from Kordofan. In 1814 the Shilluk had interrupted the trade route between Sinnār and Kordofan, so that Sinnār merchants were obliged to obtain slaves in the Shendi market. They were also cheaper than slaves from the south of Sinnār or from Ethiopia. Burckhardt considered that most of the slaves came from Dār Fūr via Kobbei and al-Ubayyiḍ and not from the southern regions of Kordofan.[37] Caravans from Sawākin led by the Ḥaḍāriba merchants, whose roots went back to Ḥaḍramawt in South Yemen, constituted the most substantial and regular commercial connection. Some of them also visited Sinnār and Kordofan. They supplied Shendi with Indian goods and in return took slaves, horses and gold. Those who went as far as Sinnār, returned also with tobacco.

Not only did slave caravans pass through Shendi, but a large number, estimated at about 5,000, were annually sold in the market or the adjoining private houses. Most of the slaves sold were below the age of fifteen. Those below the age of ten or eleven years were called *khumāsī* ('five-span'), those above eleven and below fourteen and fifteen were called *sudāsī* ('six-span'), and the grownup belonged to the category of *bāligh* ('mature'). A male *sudāsī* with the marks of smallpox was worth 15 or 16 dollars; a male *khumāsī* was 12; a female 15 dollars; a male *bāligh* seldom sold for more than 8 to 10 dollars.[38]

Of these slaves, about 2,500 were bought by the merchants from Sawākin, 1,500 by the Egyptian merchants, while the remainder went to Dongola and to the nomads east of Shendi. The institution of slavery was also widespread among the Jaʿaliyyīn, slaves being employed in the houses and fields and in the herding of animals.

THE TRADERS

The commercial network within which Shendi played such a vital role covered a huge area; direct contacts stretched from the Red Sea to Dār Fūr and from Egypt to Ethiopia; indirect contacts stretched from Spain to the Indian Ocean and west to Lake Chad. In addition there were the pilgrim routes that also passed through Shendi and thus contributed to its trading activities and cosmopolitan character. Consequently the ethnic composition of the merchant community was very diverse. But the use of Arabic as a *lingua franca* and a common if rudimentary knowledge of Islamic commercial law provided a common basis for communication and transaction. Burckhardt saw no trader from countries to the west of Bagirmi. The Egyptians were the most numerous foreign merchants visiting Shendi. The Ḥaḍāriba merchants from Sawākin were also frequent visitors. A few merchants from Yanbuʿ in Arabia occasionally came with the Egyptian or Sawākin caravans. The odd Turkish merchant found his way to Shendi. However, the majority of the merchants frequenting Shendi or staying there, were naturally of Sudanese origin.

Although Upper Egyptian *jallāba* probably had been the dominant element in the Sinnār–Egypt trade in the sixteenth and seventeenth centuries, being joined by Syrians and North Africans, Sudanese *jallāba* took an increasing part in the eighteenth century, at first as royal merchants.[39] They were of Nubian, Arabised Nubian and camel nomad origin. The latter were required to provide camels, guides and safety. According to De Maillet's reports from 1692 onwards, merchants from Ethiopia did not visit Cairo directly. Rather they sold their goods to the people of Nubia, the 'Barbarins', who then took them to Cairo. Every year a caravan left Sinnār for the journey to Cairo, bringing gold dust, ivory, ebony, civet, ambergris, ostrich feathers, various gums, and numerous other commodities. The caravan also used to bring 2–3000 black slaves, each one being worth on the average 200 pounds. The lack of decent clothes and the miserable appearance of the *jallāba* contrasted profoundly with the riches they carried with them. He says also that the Nubian caravan arrived in Egypt twice a year. It departed from 'Gary', which may be Qarrī but is more probably Mūshū since it was located to the north of Dongola, where the merchants from Sinnār, and those from Gondar, the capital of Ethiopia, and many others from various parts of Africa, used to come together before they plunged into the desert.[40]

The market orientation of the Jaʿaliyyīn on the eve of the Turkiyya was thus the result of a long history of contacts with the outside world reinforced by the relatively limited agricultural resources along the Nile. The search for means to supplement their peasant economy led many into trade and to temporary or permanent emigration. Nubians have for centuries found jobs as servants in Egyptian towns. In the market towns throughout Sinnār and Dār Fūr, the number of riverain *jallāba* grew in proportion to the size of the respective markets. Towards the end of the eighteenth century, the main market town of Dār Fūr, Kobbei, was populated mainly by foreign traders, who operated in Egypt and the Nile Valley. They were Egyptians, Tunisians, Tripolitanians; others came from the Nile Valley and Kordofan, all of them being known as indefatigable in commerce.[41] Browne attributed the migration of the riverain people (the *nās al-baḥr*) to political instability at home. In Dār Fūr the riverain *jallāba* were the main force in opening and travelling the direct route between Dār Fūr and Egypt, *darb al-arbaʿīn*, or the 'Forty Days Road'. The Dār Fūr *jallāba* were in fact the most creditworthy in Cairo, many of them were closely associated with royal trade.[42] The sultans of Wadai and Dār Fūr employed riverain *jallāba* in their external trade, which meant that the latter enjoyed particular prestige, privileges and protection in those areas. A Dongolāwī had been the principal agent of the Dār Fūr sultan in Wadai before he fled to Egypt.

Browne also mentioned a village, Ḥillat Ḥasan, inhabited by Danāgla and under the headship of a former *khabīr*.[43] (In Chapter 6 the career of a *khabīr* family, a branch of which moved back to the Nile, will be examined.)

The precise ethnic origin of the Sudanese *jallāba* frequenting the various markets is not always clear in the sources. However, two tendencies in the formation of networks have been noted. First, there was a tendency by ethnic groups to spread to several markets which were bound together by trade routes. Secondly, 'sector specialisation' dominated, which meant that commodities changed hands several times before reaching their final markets. We learn from Burckhardt that the Kordofan *jallāba* who frequented Kobbei were different from those who went to Shendi; the Egyptians who visited only Shendi were different from those who went all the way to Sinnār; and the same was true for the Sawākin merchants. The nature of this 'difference' is not clear, but can be connected with both place and tribal origin, as well as with capital, commodity specialisation and commercial contacts.

Trade by way of sectors can be illustrated by the slave trade between Dār Fartīt, south of Dār Fūr, and Egypt via the Nile Valley. (Generally, slaves from Dār Fūr were exported on the Forty Days Road.) Slaves from that area were obtained either through barter by the *jallāba* or through slave-raids organised by the Dār Fūr sultan.[44] In Kobbei they were sold to Dār Fūr or Kordofan traders who brought them to al-Ubayyiḍ where they were purchased by other Kordofan merchants (of riverain origin) who took them to Shendi. There they were bought either by Egyptians or ʿAbābda who then took them to Egypt.

PROFITABILITY, CAPITAL AND CREDIT

Despite or rather because of the great risks involved in crossing the deserts and passing through unsafe districts, the possibility of huge profits was always there for those who were lucky enough to arrive safely with their merchandise. The increase in the price of a commodity from one market to another arose from a basic price/distance/hardship ratio. An additional factor was the principle of unequal exchange whereby the buyers were unaware of the price of the commodities in their place of origin as well as of the value in foreign markets of the commodities they exchanged for the imports. The supply and demand factor was also vital as a price regulating mechanism. Thus the price/distance/hardship ratio defined the final profit rate but had less influence on the price level. If the *jallāba* were dissatisfied with the prices offered for their commodities in one market, they could move on to another where they knew or hoped that the prices would be better. Price regulation by local authorities was more concerned with local commodities than with imported or transit goods.

The cost of hiring camels, buying export articles and equipping a caravan made heavy demands upon the capital and profit of the *jallāba*. Often loans, credit and partnerships were contracted in order to get a trading enterprise off the ground. To equip a caravan in Cairo was three times more expensive than to equip it in Berber for the return journey, mainly because in the latter place camels were much cheaper. Heavy duties were exacted in Egypt on the caravans from the south and Muḥammad ʿAlī's monopoly policy, by fixing prices in Cairo, had already started to affect the profit rate in the Sudan trade. In addition came all the presents, bribes, and dues as well as material losses on the road.[45]

Commodities from Egypt were sold in Shendi at double or triple their original cost in Cairo or Darāw. The same applied to Sudanese goods in Cairo. It was therefore most profitable for a merchant to take commodities in both directions, thus making a profit twice. The reason that camels were bought for dollars in Shendi was that the Egyptian *jallāba* did not have time to wait to exchange other commodities for camels. Thus coins were continuously imported, mainly to speed up and simplify trade.

The *jallāba* who traded from Egypt to Shendi disposed of relatively large sums of money, but generally the stock of any single merchant did not exceed 1,500 dollars. The capital needed to buy the export commodities was usually borrowed at a high rate of interest or the commodities were obtained on credit and through various forms of partnership arrangements. The people of Darāw appear to have specialised in the Sudan trade. Darāw families operated as corporate groups; they pledged their property and borrowed jointly in order to trade. The boys were trained from an early age and made the journey twice a year.

It could not have been easy for outside observers to calculate the capital and wealth of the merchants they happened to encounter. Figures should therefore be regarded as approximate. It was also unwise and dangerous to expose one's wealth, thus attracting the attention of local chiefs as well as robbers. If one was surprised by illness and death when travelling, it could mean ruin and misery to family members and creditors. In the first decade of the nineteenth century a merchant left Egypt with about twenty loaded camels. He died in Shendi and his property fell prey to the *makk*, 'and no one has since made a similar attempt'.[46]

The Sinnār merchants who operated in Shendi appear to have been better off than the Egyptians. It was not uncommon to see a merchant with ten camel loads of *dammūr* and a whole gang of slaves. A Sinnār merchant had once bought the entire stock of an Egyptian caravan, consisting of thirty camels; perhaps he was a royal agent.[47]

The most substantial merchants who frequented Shendi were the Ḥaḍāriba merchants of Sawākin, also called the Artega.[48] There were always some in Shendi and the arrival of their caravan was looked forward to with excitement. They were the most assiduous purchasers of goods from the Sinnār and Kordofan merchants. Those who went to Sinnār to buy tobacco for sale in the Yemen were the most popular and enjoyed more credit in Sinnār than any others. This was attributed by Burckhardt to the fact that they were the richest and most numerous, and because they belonged to the best families in Sawākin and were not peasants like those from Egypt or blacks like those from Kordofan. Their popularity with the *makk* of Shendi was based on the fine presents they gave him, and the Egyptian *jallāba* regarded them with growing jealousy.

The *jallāba* who operated from Kordofan to Shendi disposed of modest capital, even those who engaged in slave trade. Among those who operated within the market permanently, there were apparently large differences in capital and access to credit. The Danāgla had out-manoeuvred the Ja'aliyyīn in the brokerage business, but seemingly made little profit out of it. Small stocks also characterised those traders who made a living as middlemen between Shendi and the local villages and nomad camps. The latter, however, were to become effective agents of monetisation and market integration. By converting some of the capital accumulated in the market sector into rural credit, they had found a very strong method to tie ever larger segments of the traditional sector to the market forces.

A characteristic feature of the merchant class of Shendi was the low degree of specialisation; even the most prosperous merchant would also trade in articles of little value. The wealth of a merchant could therefore hardly be deduced from his appearance and the kind of commodities he exposed for sale. The merchants of Shendi were known to lead a modest life, even those who, according to Linant de Bellefonds, possessed incredible riches and had agents in Dār Fūr, Kordofan, Sinnār and Egypt.[49] This modesty in housing, clothing and consumption was in line with the Islamic norms that gained a footing in urban and bourgeois communities with the growth of commerce. It also served to mislead the tax-hungry authorities.

MODES OF EXCHANGE

It lies outside the scope of this study to examine exchange in its various forms throughout the sultanate of Sinnār.[50] Generally speaking, in the Shendi market commodities changed hands either by barter or via medium of exchange, there being no clear distinction as to where barter ended and another mode of exchange took over. Media of exchange ranged from commodity currencies like units of durra or cloth, to beads, gold and various coins of foreign origin.

Barter is believed to be a simple and primitive form of exchange, an institution typical of traditional economies which need little sophistication. This was not the case in the riverain economy. The formal difference between barter and exchange via commodity or monetary units does not lie in the degree of complexity involved but rather in the wider economic scope which a medium of exchange allows for. An economic system characterised by barter and calculation in kind may be said to be oriented towards consumption and the satisfaction of needs.[51] A medium of exchange may ensure a higher rate of exchange, it makes it easier to calculate the relative exchange value of commodities, but it may also allow transactional barriers to crumble to the advantage of professional middlemen and enable the political authorities to better control and tax market activities.

Shendi on the eve of the Turkiyya had reached a transitional stage in which barter dominated in the sectors of foodstuffs and other daily necessities, and where various units of exchange dominated the more profit and luxury-oriented transactions. Locally made units of exchange such as the miniature hoe-like iron pieces of Kordofan and Dār Fūr, the *ḥashshāsha*, did not circulate in Shendi.[52] However, gold lumps and rings were brought to Shendi from Sinnār and were in circulation. The most important coin was the silver Spanish Charles IV dollar (with four columns) and to a lesser extent the Charles III dollar. The Charles IV dollar had higher value than the Charles III, which tempted one Shendi blacksmith to forgery by adding the extra column to the three columns of the latter.[53] The nature of the export/import trade led to a concentration of dollars in the hands of the *makk*, the notables and the big merchants, who apparently reserved them for large transactions rather than for the daily business.

In spite of the restricted circulation of dollars among the commoners, most accepted their function as media of exchange, means of payment, storage of wealth and standard of value. However, the dollar did not become an all-purpose money in a capitalist sense. Its use was largely restricted to the sphere of camels, horses and slaves. In al-Matamma it was the only medium that could buy wheat.[54] After the occupation the people were not ready to accept Turkish and Egyptian coins. Even after the official rate of the piastre and the para in relation to the dollar had been fixed (about 13–15 piastres to a dollar), scepticism was widespread. This reluctance came more from doubts about the content of precious metals than from a general aversion against coins. The more sophisticated merchants, when in doubt, could resort to heating coins to check if the gold or silver content was acceptable.[55] By 1822 and before the revolt of the Jaʿaliyyīn some piastres and paras had started to circulate, but when rumours of military resistance against the Turks were heard, the imported

> money of Cairo was brought to us with 'increased urgency' to be exchanged for dollars, at almost any loss, though the currency of the former had been fixed by the most positive edicts, and the relative value of the two sorts of coin fully established. Hence we inferred that this precaution could only be in contemplation of some sudden change and convulsion.[56]

In Shendi the most important media of exchange were *dammūr* and durra. Together with dollars, they constituted the common currencies from Berber to Sinnār.

> every thing of minor value has its price fixed in Dhourra, which is measured by Selgas (سلقا) [*salqā*], or handfuls. Eighteen Selgas make one Moud [*midd*], or measure: one Selga is as much as can [be] heaped upon the flat extended hand of a full-grown man. It may easily be conceived that disputes frequently

> arise between buyers and sellers from the unequal size of their hands; in such a case a third person is usually called in to measure the Dhourra: ten Mouds are now given for one dollar. If a considerable quantity of Dhourra is to be measured out, the contents of a wooden bowl, or other vessel, is previously ascertained in handfuls, and this vessel is then used.[57]

The other unit of exchange, *dammūr*, was used mainly for shirts, and then called *tōb* or *tōb dammūr*. Two *tōbs* equalled one dollar.

> The Tob Dammour is divided into two Ferde Dammour; the Ferde (فردة) [*farda*] makes a long napkin, used by the slaves to wrap around their waists. The Ferde contains two Fittige, (فتقة) [*fitqa*] which serves for nothing else than a currency; thus I remember to have bought some tobacco with a Fittige. Dhourra is generally the most acceptable medium, as sellers will not always take the Dammour at the real market price, which, moreover, varies on the arrival of every caravan from the south. Slaves, camels, horses, or any other articles of large amount, are paid for in dollars, or Tob Dammour; but the broker takes his commission in Dhourra, which he readily converts into dollars.[58]

The media of exchange mentioned here had clearly acquired the function of standards of value ('fictitious currency'). The durra paid as commission also shows that it could function as a means of payment as well. Similar functions were given to certain popular and suitable imported items such as beads, antimony, cotton cloth, shawls, hardware, spices or pieces of soap. Various regions adopted particular types of bead which thus created 'bead-currency zones'. Travellers and merchants would always take care to bring an assortment of such small items which could easily be exchanged for foodstuffs in the villages and camps, where the women would barter 'almost everything' for antimony, beads, perfumes and utensils.[59]

Contemporary documentary evidence from peasant communities outside Shendi shows how land was becoming evaluated in, and exchanged for, *tōb dammūr* between the 1770s and 1820.[60] A market in land was developing and a locally-made and controlled medium of exchange was used to facilitate this process. Access to *dammūr* was fairly equally distributed, at least in moderate quantities, as it could be produced in the households. The mechanisms whereby some were able to buy more land and others were compelled to sell, were fully developed before the Turkiyya, even if the ethos of the time found it hard to accept the spread of market forces into the fields.

The commercial life of Shendi created an urban and cosmopolitan society which in many ways differed from the neighbouring villages. The people were on average better off there and were able to leave cultivation and herding to others. However, at least the Jaʿaliyyīn living there kept their close ties with the countryside, both for social and economic reasons. The Jaʿalī peasants, on the other hand, were not excluded from the sphere of marketing and trade, but sought deliberately to supplement farm incomes either by offering to exchange farm produce or craft products, or to act as part-time middlemen and camel-drivers. The production of *dammūr* could easily launch an ambitious peasant into the sector of commerce in the slack season. The lucky ones were able to put slaves to work on their farms which enabled them to spend more time trading. The strong market orientation of the Jaʿaliyyīn thus seems to have a long history.[61]

To choose Shendi as the gate into Jaʿalī economy and history, may look strange, but it is justifiable on several grounds. For outsiders it was and is the best place to encounter and observe the broadest spectre of economic activities and capital formation among the Jaʿaliyyīn. The available sources from this period on the Jaʿaliyyīn, as the analysis above shows, are also highly in favour of Shendi. One may, of course, discuss what role Shendi and the other market centres played for the rural population whose concerns were first of all to eke out a living from their farms and flocks. Economically, Shendi was characterised by the formation of merchant capital based on commodity exchange, which gradually spread its influence into the rural areas. The villagers defined their social relations with other community members first of all in a family and neighbourhood context. However, on a broader scale, ideas about the common culture, religion and ethnic background facilitated movements and interactions outside the family network and area of origin. These links to the outside world incorporated marketing operations in such places as Shendi. Most Jaʿaliyyīn did not have to extend their fields of interaction beyond Shendi, but long-distance *jallāba* and emigrants were already incorporating even larger areas into the so-called Jaʿalī diaspora, which in this context may represent the broadest field of orientation and interaction. Shendi was therefore also a gate out into the diaspora. Jaʿalī society was not composed of inward looking, isolated or 'primitive' communities. Their many outside contacts, their open country, their life-giving river and fertile but narrow river banks, their religious history (Pharaonic, Christian and Islamic) contributed to a culture that is both firmly rooted in the Nile Valley and yet open to external economic and cultural impulses.

Economic life in Shendi was not only a result of the caravan traffic but was also a reflection of production and prosperity in the countryside. The present analysis of Shendi will also serve therefore as a yardstick by which to measure economic change during the following period.

In Jaʿalī society and in their economy, the traders had started to establish themselves as a practical link, for better or worse, between the rural and urban communities on the eve of the Turkiyya. These new relations enabled them to convert merchant capital into rural credit and land ownership. A form of patron–client relationship, based on credit and indebtedness, could therefore easily develop between a merchant and a peasant who was not himself able to make it in trade. Thus, while the merchant's position was envied and sought after, he was at the same time scorned and despised as a usurer, whose reward in the life hereafter could only be Hell.[62] Years of famine, for instance, could lead to starvation for many and immense riches for the few, as in the case of the 1813 famine in Berber: 'The most wealthy man of Berber, next to the Mek, was pointed out to me [Burckhardt], with the observation that he possessed about two thousand dollars, which he gained last year, during the famine, by happening to have a full-stocked granary.'[63]

3

The Jaʿaliyyīn under Turkish administration

The imposition of foreign rule set in motion profound changes throughout Sudanese societies and cultures. Before it came to an end it had brought under a single administration for the first time a vast area and numerous ethnic groups, languages and religions. The *dārs* of the Nile Valley and the savannas had been used to the often loose overlordship of the Funj and the ʿAbdallāb. The Turks, however, introduced a quite new concept of government, derived from the Ottoman system of administration. They had come to rule as colonisers, to command obedience, to regulate the affairs of everyone at every level, and claimed a natural right to extract a surplus for the Egyptian treasury.

The term 'Turk' is used here in the colloquial Sudanese sense, as a label for all whom they considered to be connected with the *ḥakūma* or 'government'. This is, of course, misleading as an ethnic label, as is also the term 'Turco-Egyptian', so often used by historians.[1] The foreign rulers consisted of a variety of ethnic elements, such as Greeks, Kurds, Albanians, ethnic Turks, Egyptians, Circassians (some of whom were or had been Mamluks i.e. slaves) and others. Turkish rather than Arabic was their language, and although the Viceroy in Cairo liked to think of the Sudan as Egypt's own possession, the Sudanese saw their new masters as representatives of the Ottoman empire as well as of the great Pasha in Cairo.[2] In one sense the term 'Ottoman' would therefore provide a better description of the rulers. Towards the middle of the period, more Arabic-speaking Egyptians were sent to the Sudan as provincial governors, and in the last years a number of Europeans arrived to take up leading positions, the most famous of whom was, of course, General Gordon.

There are reasons to believe that had the Sudanese been able to unite and mobilise, the invaders would have found it much more difficult, perhaps impossible, to subdue them. The political disintegration had reached a stage where the Turks could easily deal with one group at a time. Some *jallāba* may well have welcomed the new order, since they anticipated better trading conditions with Egypt. The actual conquest mainly affected the Sudanese elites in the first instance; it was only when the Turks began to implement their administrative and taxation policies that the lives of the ordinary people were fundamentally disturbed. The initial resistance of the Shāyqiyya was the resistance of a military elite facing the loss of its hard-won political dominance in the Middle Nile region, of being forced to give up raiding their neighbours and reverting to the work of cultivation, previously left to their slaves.[3] Similarly, the nomads rose against their new overlords when they finally understood their political objectives. They had always been the most independent and self-governing groups under the umbrella of Sinnār, and managed to retain some of their distance from the government also under the new order. Only the 'Abābda camel nomads, living partly in Upper Egypt, but with sections in the south towards Berber and Shendi, collaborated loyally with the Turks from the beginning. They became the backbone of the postal service between Khartoum and Cairo and were given the right to guide and tax the caravans which crossed the Nubian desert along the Kuruskū-Abū Hamad–Berber route. 'As the Sudan was a novel unit of government which did not fit conveniently into the traditional Ottoman pattern of rule, Muḥammad 'Alī met this situation not by inventing a new administrative vocabulary but by giving new values to existing ranks, grades and administrative territories.'[4]

The administrative structure was necessarily fluid in the beginning in order to cope with an unfamiliar environment and the economic priorities and private ambitions of the new rulers. In those days the Sudan was far away from Cairo and the officers posted there seldom went there voluntarily. Many saw their service in the Sudan as a form of compulsory exile, which was made endurable only by the hope of making a quick private fortune. Thus the task of creating a lasting administrative structure under the close supervision of Cairo was not an easy one.

It was the alleged riches of the Sudan that had motivated the conquest. However, the establishment of an elaborate administrative system shows that the Turks had long-term plans of exploitation which went beyond the search for gold and the capture of slaves towards an emphasis on taxation and the export of agricultural and natural products. Thus the *raison d'être* of the Turkish administration was to 'activate' the resources of the Sudan, ostensibly for the benefit of the Sudanese, but in practice for the benefit of the Egyptian treasury. The Sudanese, on the other hand, saw the Turkish administration and development efforts as instruments of oppression and injustice, and alien to most of their traditional religious, moral and cultural concepts. This picture of the government was underlined by its military character with regard to both personnel and methods.[5] Some local chiefs were confirmed in their offices, as at Berber, al-Matamma and Shendi, but their functions and powers were greatly curtailed, and their incorporation into the administration did not modify the general character of the new political order. From now on the real rulers were the Turkish central, provincial and district military governors. There are cases where military and civil authority were separated in an administrative area, as it could happen for instance in Berber Province, but they were exceptions.

THE FOUNDATION OF THE PROVINCE OF BERBER AND THE JAʿALIYYĪN

As Ismāʿīl Pasha moved up the Nile Valley, 1820–1, he posited district governors, *kāshifs*, at major centres. The eight districts (Turk./Ar. *kāshiflik*, later Ar. *qism*) between the Second and Fourth Cataract were grouped together to form the Province (*ma'mūriyya*) of Dongola. The first governor (*ma'mūr*) was ʿAbidīn Bey *kāshif*, who in April 1821 took up residence at al-ʿUrḍī or New Dongola.[6] The districts between the Fourth Cataract and the Nile Confluence were formally united into the Province of Berber and the Jaʿaliyyīn with the appointment of Maḥū Bey Urfalī, a Kurd, as the first province governor. He established himself in Berber in January 1822.

Maḥū Bey, a cavalry officer, was originally sent to the Sudan to take command of al-Ḥalfāya District, just north of the Nile Confluence. Ibrāhīm Pasha al-Wālī, the brother of Ismāʿīl Pasha, who had reached Sinnār with his troops later in 1821, argued that al-Ḥalfāya was arid and close to Sinnār, which meant that it could be administered by a small number of soldiers, for example some seventy to eighty cavalry, whereas districts like Rubāṭāb, Berber, and Shendi represented larger and more populated areas, and needed to be governed by an energetic and powerful man.[7]

On his arrival in January, Maḥū Bey set about organising the new province, appointing new subordinate officers, like the *kāshif* whom he sent to Shendi to replace the first *kāshif* there. He sent a force under Aḥmad Bey to al-Ḥalfāya to suppress unrest there. In February, he encamped with his troops at Shendi, under strict orders from Muḥammad ʿAlī to put an end to the opposition of the nomads both among the Jaʿaliyyīn, the Ḥassāniyya and the Bishāriyyīn. Before leaving Shendi on 3 March, he had two Ḥamdābī chiefs executed in Shendi, after leading a campaign against them.[8]

His task of pacifying the area and guaranteeing its security was given first priority. When his appointment to the governorship was confirmed in the autumn of 1821, he made it clear that in order to do this he needed the reinforcement of Maghārba (North African) cavalry, which was given provided he supplied the camels necessary for their transport. Another major task was to facilitate the transport of slaves, both on the river and over land to Egypt.[9]

Berber Province bordered Dongola Province at or around the Fourth Cataract; Wādī Qamar, Ḥōsh al-Jurūf and Bertī Island have been mentioned in the sources as marking the boundary. In the south the province included the district of Ḥalfāya and bordered on the Nile Confluence. Some years later, perhaps in 1825–6, Ḥalfāya became attached to the Province of Sinnār, and with the establishment of Khartoum Province around 1837, Ḥalfāya was incorporated into the latter. Consequently, from around 1826, the southern border of Berber Province lay somewhere in the vicinity of the Sixth Cataract. Al-Ḥuqna, Wad Bishāra, Ḥajar al-ʿAsal are mentioned in the sources.[10]

In addition to Dongola and Berber, two other provinces were created by the Turks, Kordofan and Sinnār. But whereas the first two communicated directly with Cairo, the latter two were placed in the beginning under the command of the commander-in-chief of the army, the *sar-i'askar* or *sir 'askar*. When Ibrāham Pasha returned to Egypt in 1822, the Daftardar was appointed commander-in-chief of the troops in Sinnār and Kordofan, a position which he held till 1824. He was then relieved by 'Uthmān Jarkas al-Birinjī, who established his headquarters at the junction of the two Niles and thus laid the foundations of the new capital, Khartoum. He died, however, the following year, and Maḥū Bey was secretly asked to move quickly to Khartoum with his troops to take up the position of acting commander of the troops of Sinnār. In the meantime Kordofan was given its own governor and communicated directly with Cairo till 1833.[11]

Maḥū Bey died in 1826 and was followed by 'Alī Khūrshīd Aghā, who became responsible for organising the Sudanese provincial administration as the first governor-general (1826–38). His title was first *Sinnār ḥākimī*, governor of Sinnār. Shortly afterwards the Province of Berber was added to his responsibilities and in 1833 Dongola and Kordofan were also integrated. 'Alī Khūrshīd was now *mudīr* of the Sudanese provinces with the grade of Bey. Two years later, he was granted the title of *ḥikimdār* (lit. commissioner), translated as governor-general, and elevated to the grade of Pasha of the fourth grade. At the same time the title of provincial governor was changed from *ma'mūr* to *mudīr*, and the term for province was changed from *ma'mūriyya* to *mudīriyya*. Henceforth the term *ma'mūr* came to mean sub-governor.

Berber Province was under the governor-general between 1827 and 1843. On the mysterious death of 'Alī Khūrshīd's successor, Aḥmad Pasha Shāmlī (called Abū Widhān or Adhān), in 1843, Muḥammad 'Alī Pasha decided to abolish the *ḥikimdāriyya* and place each province directly under Cairo again. Aḥmad Pasha Maniklī received orders to that effect in January 1844. Berber Province was to be abolished altogether, its northern districts were to go to Dongola and the districts south of Atbara River were to go to Khartoum.[12] Other administrative measures followed. New governors were appointed with the rank of Pasha; the civil and financial staff of the provinces was strengthened, which meant more power to the Coptic *mubāshirs* (chief clerks), *mu'allims* (clerks), *ṣarāfs* (cashiers), and *kātibs* (scribes) on all administrative levels. As in Egypt they were crucial to the smooth running of the government, particularly in the field of accounting and bookkeeping. However, a few months later Muḥammad 'Alī changed his mind about decentralising the provinces and Maniklī was appointed to the position he had been instructed to abolish. Apparently Berber remained divided between its two neighbouring provinces for a few years.

In the following decade, in an effort to improve the political and economic conditions of the Sudan, Muhammad Sa'īd Pasha (Viceroy of Egypt 1854–63), visited the Sudan in 1856–7 and decided to abolish the

Table 1 *The governors of Berber Province, 1822–84*

Maḥū Bey Urfalī	1822–5	governor of Berber, al-Ḥalfāya
Al-Ḥājj al-Amīn	1825–7	
ʿUthmān	1827–8	
Ṣāliḥ	1829	
ʿAlī	1829–32	
ʿAbbās Aghā al-Bazarlī al-Jundī	1832–5, 1836–8	
Ḥalīm Efendī Bey	1838–40	
Nihād Bey	c.1840	
Khuṣraw Pasha	1843	Berber and Dongola
Ḥilmī	1843	
Ḥasan Pasha Rafʿat	1843–6	Northern half of Berber with Dongola
Ḥasan Bey Ḥusnī	1846–?	Northern half with Dongola
Muḥammad Amīn Pasha Arna'ūt	1843–4	Southern half of Berber with Khartoum
Mūsā Ḥamdī	?	
ʿAlī Bey Ḥasīb	1851–2	
Muṣṭafā *kāshif*	1852	governor *ad interim*
Ḥilmī Bey	1854–?	
Ibrāhīm Bey Abū Filayja	?–1857	Replaced by a council of notables
Maḥmūd Bey	1857–9	
ʿAbd Allāh Bey al-Wānlī	1859–62	Berber and Dongola
Ibrāhīm Bey	1863–5	
ʿUmar Bey	1865–?	
ʿAlī Bey ʿUwayḍa	?–1867	
Aḥmad Rāmī Bey	1867	
Ḥusayn Bey Khalīfa	1869–73	Berber and Dongola, 1871–3
ʿAlī Bey Sharīf	1874–5	
Muṣṭafā Bey Murād	1875–8	
Muḥammad Saʿīd Bey Wahbī	1878	
Ibrāhīm Bey al-Sabbān	1878–9	
Muḥammad Maʿanī Bey	c.1879–c.1881	
Firhād Bey Muḥibb	1882	
ʿAbd al-Raḥmān Bey Fā'iz	1882	
Ibrāhīm Bey	1883	
Ḥusayn Pasha Khalīfa	1883–4	

Source: Hill (1951), 87–8.

ḥikimdāriyya again. He was apparently shocked by the bad state of the country and the incompetence of his officials and decided that a form of provincial autonomy and Sudanese participation would be better. Thus he removed the *mudīr* of Berber and replaced him by a council of notables.[13] In Shendi, where 150,000 [*sic*!] people had assembled, Muḥammad Saʿīd made an excellent impression, according to his friend and apologist, Ferdinand de Lesseps:

> This was within the area where his brother had met such a terrible end, and therefore the same country which had suffered most from the vengeance

which followed. The people must have come into the town with a minimum of confidence, but Saʿīd, with two theatrical gestures, won them over. He had a slave-owner chained in public for cruelty to a female domestic, and he caused all the cannons from the fort to be thrown into the river. [They were in fact defective] . . . Saʿīd declared that he would send back to Egypt all the Turkish officials, and would institute self-government through municipal councils, which, since the beginning of the world, have been the chief element of all organised societies. I [de Lesseps] was told to stay a few days in Shendy so as to superintend with His Highness' Ministers, the creation of the councils, which were composed of heads of families appointed by election.[14]

When Muḥammad Saʿīd reached Khartoum he was no longer so optimistic about the possibility of introducing effective reforms, and it seems that after his return to Egypt, things reverted to normal. A new *mudīr* of Berber was appointed later in 1857, and the province was again integrated into the *ḥikimdāriyya* between 1862 and 1869, and between 1873 and 1882. In the years 1869–73, it was directly under Cairo, and after the reorganisation of the provinces following the British occupation of Egypt in 1882, Berber became a part of the *ḥikimdāriyya* of the Central Sudan, including also the provinces of Khartoum, Sinnār, Fashoda (White Nile) and Equatoria (Khaṭṭ al-Isṭiwā).[15] Berber was united with Dongola and Khartoum in the middle of the 1840s, with Dongola in 1859–62 and 1871–3. Between 1869 and 1873 and the early months of the year 1884 the governor was a Sudanese of the ʿAbābda tribe, Ḥusayn Pasha (formerly Bey) Khalīfa.[16]

Because of the state of unrest and rebellion following the occupation, a formal administrative apparatus was established only slowly. Two features were particularly crucial in shaping the political development in the period; the Turks were alien conquerors and never stopped behaving like conquerors, and the hierarchy of personal relations from the Great Pasha downwards which required a steady flow of gifts upwards. The growth of a small bureaucracy in the Sudan never hindered the personal character of government.

The governors and *kāshifs* are to a large extent anonymous figures. A few portraits have survived, however, and we may choose Hoskins' description of a governor of Berber, ʿAbbās Aghā al-Bazārlī al-Jundī, 1832–5, 1836–8. He was in 1833 'a man about thirty, of a stern and yet prepossessing appearance'. He found 'the difficulties of his situation trying and embarrassing', and summed up well the paradox of Muḥammad ʿAlī's policy towards the Sudan, 'I [ʿAbbās] have few friends here' [said he,] 'and many enemies. It is difficult to satisfy the demands of the pasha and not oppress the people. The Government of Alexandria are never content with the amount of the revenue; and yet are enraged if any complaints reach them, although they are the consequence of their own exorbitant demands.'[17] The style varied probably little from one *dīwān* (court) to the next. Local officers tried to copy their superiors and add a little Mamluk panache to their daily routine. When ʿAbbās left the provincial headquarters on his daily visits, he was 'preceded by his guards, armed with guns; then four cowhases [*kavasses*], beating their massive silverheaded sticks on the ground, . . . a substitute for music; the bey himself then followed, on foot or on his charger, having behind him six other guards, with guns, and a crowd of perhaps twenty servants'.[18] The departure and return of the governor were occasions for a show of loyalty towards him on the part of subordinate officials, local shaykhs and household servants. Thus authority was vested in persons rather than in offices and personal loyalty was sworn to every new superior officer. The ultimate source of authority and patronage was, of course, Muḥammad ʿAlī, who though a moderniser in many fields, regarded his officials in the Sudan as irresponsible youngsters whose strict and well-meaning father he thought himself to be.[19]

The district officers, the *kāshifs*, appear more frequently in the sources because of their number and distribution. Pückler-Muskau, in the late 1830s, claimed that the *kāshifs* were the slaves (Mamluks) of the governors, but that has not been verified.[20] The status and authority associated with the office seem to have varied quite a lot. In 1833 Hoskins was very hospitably received by a retired *kāshif* in Shendi, who was still surrounded by followers, servants and slaves, and who organised a Mamluk military show for his guest. However, the commanding *kāshif* of the district who lived in al-Matamma was, according to Hoskins, a stupid fellow who resided in a filthy castle.[21] His name was Ismāʿīl and he was still there in 1837–8 when he was described by Pückler-Muskau and an anonymous French diarist. According to the former, the *kāshif* had come to the area as a young man with the Daftardar, and had occupied the post of *kāshif* for longer than normal. He appeared to be an honest and therefore a poor man, who knew few luxuries in life, being able to offer his guests only sugared water.[22] The French diarist says about the same man,

> Ismāʿīl Aghā told me that he had been *kāshif* of al-Matamma for the last eight years. He is paid 1,000 piastres a year to clothe himself and he receives free rations for himself and forage for one horse. He told me that for a man drawing his pay [it] was a poor allowance. The high cost of living obtains not only here but at Dungula [Dongola] according to various people who have come from there.[23]

The poor lifestyle of the *kāshif* of al-Matamma had not changed radically between 1833 and 1837–8. He had apparently been unable to benefit economically from his position, probably as a result of severe famines, diminishing agricultural production and decreasing revenues. It is more difficult to account for the expensive way of life of the retired *kāshif* of Shendi.

LOCAL ADMINISTRATION

The *kāshifliks* (later called *qism*, pl. *aqsām*) were the first administrative units created by the Turks along the Nile, and after their incorporation into provinces, they continued to serve as a link between the Turks and the

Table 2 *The* qisms *and* khuṭṭs *of Berber Province*

Qism Manāṣīr No *khuṭṭs*	from Bertī Island to Sulaymāniyya, with al-Salamāt as its centre.
Qism al-Rubāṭāb three *khuṭṭs*	1 *Muqrāt*, from Shamkhiyya to Kurgos Island, with Abū Ḥamad as its centre. 2 *Abū Hashīm*, from 'Aṭmūr (West Bank) to Kuduk (East Bank), with Abū Hashīm as its centre. 3 *Al-Baqayr*, from Kuduk to al-Sinqayr, with Baqayr as its centre.
Qism Berber three *khuṭṭs*	1 *Al-Inqiriāb*, from Sulaymāniyya (West Bank) to Firaykha (East Bank), with al-Bawqa as its centre. 2 *Berber*, from Ḥaṣṣa (East Bank) to Qōz al-Funj (East Bank), with Berber as its centre. 3 *Rās al-Wādī*, from Shiqla (East Bank) to Muqran (East Bank), with Salāma as its centre.
Qism Zaydāb three *khuṭṭs*	1 *Al-Dāmir*, from Muqran to Dayyika (East Bank), with al-Dāmir as its centre. 2 *Zaydāb al-Shimāl* (North, i.e. West Bank), from Ḥasaballāwiyya to Zaydāb, with Zaydāb as its centre. 3 *Zaydāb al-Janūb* (South, i.e. East Bank), from Zaydāb to Jabrāb, with Jūbarāb as its centre.
Qism al-Matamma three *khuṭṭs*	1 *Saqādī*, from al-Nūba (West Bank) to al-Juwayr (West Bank), with Makniyya as its centre. 2 *Al-Matamma*, from Sayyāl Karīm al-Dīn to Nagazū Island, all on West Bank, with al-Matamma as its centre. 3 *Shendi* (East Bank), from Jabal Umm 'Alī to Ḥajar al-'Asal, with Shendi as its centre.

Sudanese. The *kāshif* (later also called shaykh *al-qism* or *qism nāẓirī*) dealt directly, or sometimes through subordinate officials, with the local leaders and people and was responsible to the governor.

The development of the territorial subdivisions and the parallel hierarchy of authority is far more complicated and fluid than it appears at first sight. As was alluded to above, the power and authority of the *kāshif* varied greatly; he could be the commander of 400 troops with the rank of a *sanjaq* (colonel), or he might live almost isolated in the countryside for most of the year, he could act as a councillor, or be the head of a village under the authority of another *kāshif*. The most powerful *kāshif* was probably Sulaymān Abū Da'ūd Aghā, a military commander based at Kararī, who on occasions acted as a deputy governor-general in the absence of 'Alī Khūrshīd Pasha, and who played a leading role in the opening-up of the White Nile.[24]

When Ismā'īl Pasha left Shendi for Sinnār in May 1821, he left a *kāshif* there with a small garrison. Presumably he was responsible for both banks of the Nile, including al-Matamma. After the destruction of Shendi in 1823,

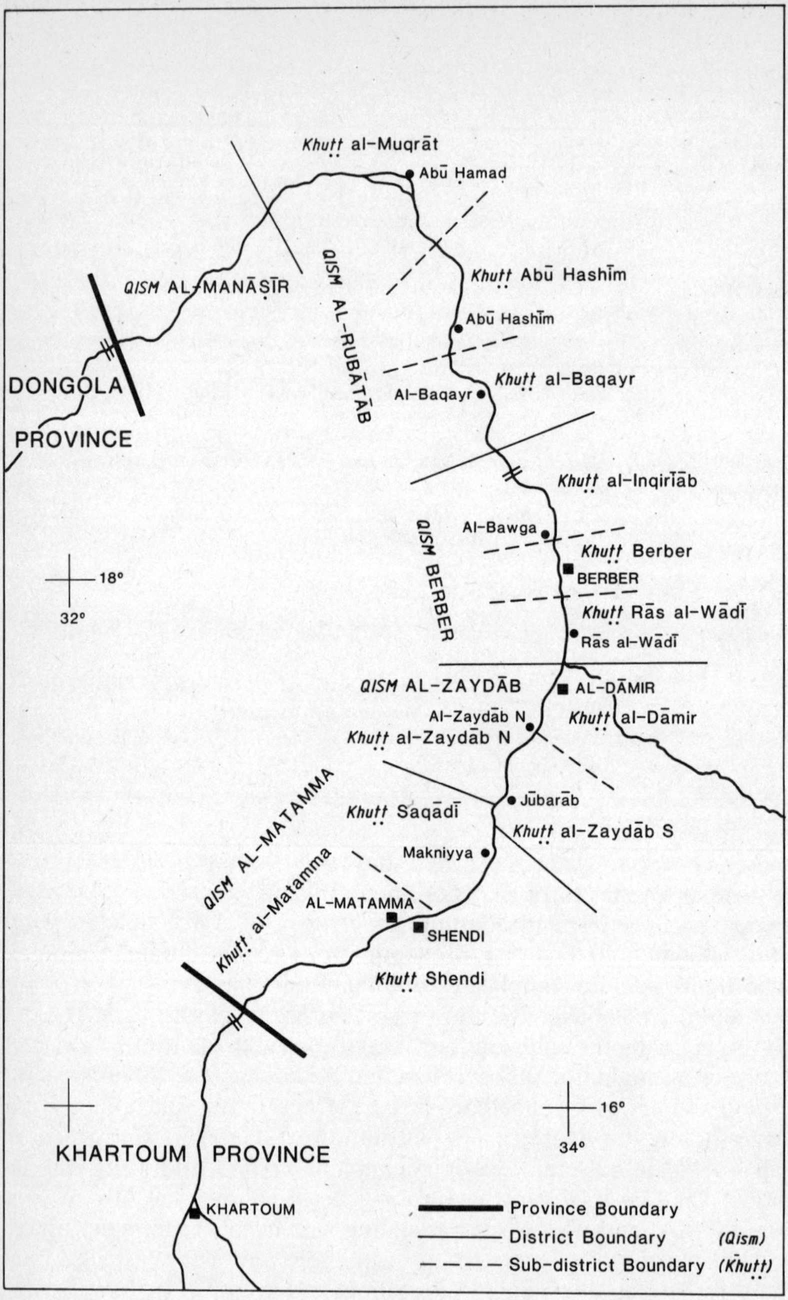

Berber Province, administrative divisions

the district administration was transferred to al-Matamma; thus the district of Shendi and al-Matamma became known as *qism* al-Matamma. From then on, although it was to become a garrison town, Shendi was degraded to a centre of a sub-district (*khuṭṭ, akhṭāṭ*) within the district of al-Matamma.[25]

The district of al-Matamma stretched from Wad Bishāra to between Kitiāb and al-Nūba and included some eighty villages. A *kāshif* is also reported on Kurgos Island, covering the surrounding villages, that is within the jurisdiction of the *kāshif* of al-Matamma.[26] In the early years, the *kāshif* administered his district through the *qā'im maqāms*, who acted as travelling deputies, tax-collectors and heads of villages. In Egypt, the *qā'im maqāms* had similar functions as heads of sub-districts, but in the Sudan they were gradually withdrawn from local administration, to be replaced by Sudanese. From the 1850s onward the title was mainly an army rank equal to lieutenant-colonel. Al-Matamma consisted of three *khuṭṭs*, one of which was Shendi. The *khuṭṭs* were laid down by the governor-general ʿAlī Khūrshīd Pasha.[27] At the bottom of the hierarchy were the village shaykhs. The Province of Berber consisted of five *qisms* and twelve *khuṭṭs*, as shown in Table 2.[28]

As the centre of a *khuṭṭ*, Shendi was the residence of a *hākim al-khuṭṭ*, a *qāḍī* of the religious court (*maḥkama sharʿiyya*), with the necessary staff of clerks. There was a *muʿallim* (accountant) in both al-Matamma and Shendi; both were hanged by Aḥmad Pasha for discrepancies in their books.[29] Shendi was also the residence of the shaykh of shaykhs (*shaykh al-mashāyikh*) of the Jaʿaliyyīn. In addition to these officials and their staffs, some time before 1840 Shendi was made a garrison town, and in 1841 the Ninth Regiment was stationed there. The military commander first moved into the castle of the former *makk* Nimr, but as it was in a very bad state of repair, he changed his residence to the summer palace of ʿAlī Khūrshīd Pasha. The garrison formed a small village on its eastern side.[30]

In about 1851 the commander was one Ḥusayn Aghā, a colonel (*sanjaq*) in the Egyptian army, who had been sent to Shendi by Muḥammad Saʿīd. He apparently spent much of the year in Khartoum and delegated his functions to a deputy. Ḥusayn Aghā's main duties seem to have been to supervise the cultivation of large areas of government land, probably for cash crops. The same or a different Ḥusayn Bey is reported as commander of al-Matamma (*khuṭṭ* or *qism*) at approximately the same time, which only illustrates how difficult it is to arrive at a clear picture of the structure of authority at the intermediate level, when we are left with sources that did not pay much attention to such details.[31]

A widespread feature was the relatively low number of salaried officials. Thus in the final years of the Turkiyya a *kāshif* might be assisted by a treasurer (*ṣarrāf* or *khaznadār*) and a secretary (*kātib*)[32] only. However, in compensation, the army units and irregular soldiers, both foreign and Sudanese, performed administrative duties. In addition came the growing number of Sudanese civil officials, who served the government in various ways.

JAʿALIYYĪN IN THE GOVERNMENT

'The Sudanese participated in local government from the beginning of Egyptian rule, for this was an economic way of keeping order and collecting taxes.'[33] This observation by R. Hill may serve to introduce the following discussion of participation and cooperation in the government. We may also quote G. Warburg who interprets the government's policy towards the local elites in the slightly different way: 'The sixty years of Turco-Egyptian rule were characterized by the government's attempts to undermine the power of the local leadership and integrate it into the new Egyptian administration.'[34] An understanding of the changing status and functions of the riverain elites (elite formation) during the nineteenth century must be based on an analysis of the transformation of the economy. It is possible to analyse the growth of the local elites within the context of the administrative framework described above, emphasising recruitment to government positions. In the case of the Jaʿaliyyīn, their revolt and its repression in 1822–3 eliminated a large part of the traditional noble elite, particularly those linked to the *makks*. Those Jaʿaliyyīn who obtained office of any importance were recruited largely from the periphery of the old elites. The most successful Jaʿalī office-holders based their careers on commercial power and flourished outside their homeland (cf. Chapter 6 and 7). In the area from Shendi and southwards loyal Shāyqiyya were settled as landlords, soldiers and peasants to replace the Jaʿaliyyīn and local officials were recruited from them. However, some Jaʿaliyyīn were also recruited, notably to low-level positions which involved administering themselves, that is as shaykhs, *ḥākims* of *khuṭṭs*, and *qāḍīs*.

Hoskins vividly describes the court of ʿAbbās Aghā, the governor of Berber Province, in 1833.

> The courtiers were arranged on each side according to their respective ranks. On [the governor's] right side was the grand Cadi, in a brown dress, with a green turban (the badge of his having made the pilgrimage to Mecca, and being a sheriff, or descendant of Mahomet). He is a native of this country, and fills the offices of high priest and chief judge. The Bey [or Aghā?] paid him great attention; no doubt on account of his great influence with the people. He was a very jesuitically [sic] countenance . . . Next to this priest was Sheakh Sayd, the chief of the Ababdes . . . His family have held this title from time immemorial: the stamp of nobility is marked upon his high forehead; and there is an expression of dignified mildness in his countenance which commands respect . . . Another, but inferior, Sheakh of the Ababdes was seated next to Sheakh Sayd, in a blue linen dress. Next to the Ababde Sheakh was the Melek Nazr ed Deen. This man was forty years melek or king of this province.[35] . . . he is now a disregarded pensioner (having merely the rank and authority of a katsheff), and no real authority in the extensive province where, at one time his will was law. Several other personages were present, among

> whom were katsheffs, kaymacans, and artillery officers; Sheakh Beshir ... now melek of Shendy, and some sheakhs of the Bishreens. In the centre of the room stood about thirty attendants; ... The Bey was playing at drafts with Sheakh Sayd when we entered ...[36]

The Turks realised that some degree of Sudanese participation in government was necessary to cope with a hostile population. However, authority that formerly rested on traditional power and support was now increasingly dependent upon Turkish political support and military assistance which alienated the Sudanese collaborators from their own people. Appointment to the positions of village and tribal shaykhs was directly controlled or at least sanctioned by the government. These office-holders, although they might find their positions economically rewarding, could easily attract the hatred of their subordinates and at the same time suffer under the unreasonable demands and severe sanctions of their superiors.

Sudanese were also appointed to positions above the purely tribal level, to positions belonging to the new colonial structure. In 1861 the first Sudanese, Muḥammad Bey Rāsikh from near Berber, was appointed to the position of governor-general (of the combined provinces of Khartoum and Sinnār). He was succeeded in 1863 by another Sudanese, the *nāẓir* of the Shukriyya, Aḥmad Bey 'Awaḍ al-Karīm Abū Sinn, who was governor of Khartoum till 1870.[37] The number of such cases was, however, limited. The only field to which large-scale recruitment took place was the army. Many Shāyqiyya joined as irregular soldiers and earned a bad reputation as merciless tax-collectors. Recruitment from among the Ja'aliyyīn was most often through forced conscription. After around 1840, the Ja'aliyyīn were exempted from conscription, largely because of their opposition and the general depopulation of their districts as a result of emigration.[38]

Whereas the authority and position of the nomadic chiefs were largely confirmed in return for the promise of tribute and at least outward loyalty, the sedentary *makks* and shaykhs became virtually redundant. In Dongola Province after the conquest, only the *makk* residing at Arqū Island enjoyed some privileges, such as the rank and pay of a *kāshif*.[39] Only *malik* Shāwīsh of the Shāyqiyya was able to increase his power and privileges under the new regime, till Ahmad Pasha found the Shāyqiyya too unruly.[40]

Cut off from their former sources of wealth and power, many noble families who did not gain the favour of the new rulers were sinking fast to the level of the peasantry. Their impoverishment and political impotence was naturally a matter of indifference to the peasants, who had few reasons for regret. However, there were shaykhs who formulated and passed on complaints and petitions from the peasants to the government and who refused to comply with the demands for more taxes.[41]

Generally, the offices from *kāshif* upwards were filled by Turks. Nevertheless in Dongola Province at least five *kāshifs* are known to have been Sudanese.[42] As for the Ja'alī districts of Berber Province, the sources are less informative. Informants today have some knowledge about the origin of local officials such as *ḥākims* of *khuṭṭs* and both Shāyqī and Ja'alī officials are mentioned.[43] There were, however, in our area some offices created by the Turks to which local people were exclusively recruited, namely the supreme shaykh (of shaykhs) of the Ja'aliyyīn (*shaykh al-mashāyikh*), the offices of sub-district, district and perhaps also provincial *qāḍī* and finally the offices of the secular district courts.

THE SHAYKH AL-MASHĀYIKH: THE CAREER OF BASHĪR AḤMAD 'AQĪD

Initially the Turks realised the crucial position of Sudanese tribal leaders to the extent that they invented the position and title of *shaykh al-mashāyikh* of large ethnic groups such as the Shukriyya, the Kabābīsh and the Ja'aliyyīn. This title was changed to *nāẓir* in the latter half of the Turkiyya. The office-holder was chosen from the shaykhly families of each group, but in the case of the Ja'aliyyīn, where the most relevant families had emigrated or fallen into disrepute, it became all the more urgent to find a loyal leader with a sufficient socio-economic and political basis to fill the gap. Thus Bashīr Aḥmad 'Aqīd was drawn from the periphery of Ja'alī politics into the centre of local events.

We have already met Bashīr in the provincial headquarters in Berber in the company of Turkish officers and Sudanese notables. Hoskins calls him, perhaps not too accurately, *makk* of Shendi, but the expression reflects his high standing. Before the Turkiyya, Bashīr was shaykh of the Masallamāb section of the Ja'aliyyīn. He lived in Umm al-Ṭuyyūr opposite the Atbara confluence; the two other main centres of the section were 'Aqīda and Saqādī, all on the west bank. This territory seems to correspond with Cailliaud's Dār Ja'al, whose border with Dār Shendi lay between 'Ālīāb and Ḥallāwiyya.[44] He is said to have been an intelligent and cunning man, who paid tribute with reluctance and then to Nimr rather than to Musā'd. At one time he apparently married a daughter of *makk* Nimr, which was in conformity with the general system of binding subordinates to overlords.[45] As with the *makk* of Berber, Naṣr al-Dīn, it is believed today that after an attempt on his life by Musā'd for disobedience, Bashīr fled to Egypt where he encouraged Muḥammad 'Alī to conquer the Nile Valley and bring order to the area. When *makk* Nimr had fled and the Daftardar came to Shendi, Bashīr provided the latter with food and equipment and betrayed the Nimrāb and their followers by pointing out their houses.[46] Even if this is only partly true, Bashīr showed himself to be a useful collaborator, it is not surprising therefore that he was chosen, probably already in 1823, to represent the Ja'aliyyīn as shaykh of shaykhs. Rüppell met him in the winter of 1823–4 in the camp of the Daftardar at Qurqab village opposite Kabūshiyya.[47]

Bashīr was a rich man, which enabled him to ransom some of the captive Ja'aliyyīn, otherwise destined for death or enslavement.[48] Despite this, the

Sa'dāb and many other Ja'aliyyīn continued to regard him as a traitor and an illegitimate chief; but the Masallamāb were now strong and the Sa'dāb were weak, as an informant put it in 1980.[49] Based on Turkish support, he used his new position to acquire more wealth in terms of land and camels. He was particularly interested in island land (*jazīra*), the most fertile in the area. His methods are not known, but even for the Turks he went too far in causing unrest among the peasants. In 1826 Khūrshīd went to Shendi to arrest Bashīr and his brother Muṣṭafā, and extorted great wealth from him.[50] Khūrshīd claimed that the property seized from Bashīr had been taken from the peasants without any right, and Bashīr was promptly sent to Cairo in chains. An offer of mediation from the governor of Dongola was denied him. Learning of this, Muḥammad 'Alī sent a special envoy to make an investigation of Bashīr's oppression, but at the same time ordered Khūrshīd to refrain from exercising authority in Berber province and limit himself to Sinnār only. (Berber was still directly under Cairo.) As for the money confiscated from Bashīr, Khūrshīd took 4,500 dollars on one occasion and 5,000 on another; a follower of Bashīr took 500, and Shaykh Khalīfa al-'Abbādī took 5,000.[51]

Apparently Bashīr was reinstated, since in the 1830s protests and complaints against him were again made by peasants whose land he was taking. With many of the peasants in flight, much of the land was either uncultivated or attended to only by women and the elderly or by trust (*amāna*) holders. It was a tempting target for Bashīr. In the 1830s some of the rebellious Ja'aliyyīn were allowed to return; some found their land occupied by the Shāyqiyya and apparently also by Bashīr. By 1835 disputes over land had reached such dangerous proportions that Khūrshīd deemed it necessary to go to Shendi with the Grand *Qāḍī* and the provincial governors to put an end to the crisis.[52]

Bashīr received a salary of 500 piastres per month from the government, according to Pückler-Muskau, who calls him *amīr*. He presumably also shared in the profit made by his wife, a rich lady, who engaged merchants as travelling agents. A large part of his wealth consisted of camels; his biggest herd was in Berber area, near to Dār Bishāriyyīn. He was considered, in spite of the trouble he created, as an ardent follower of the Turks, and was willing to campaign with them as he did in 1833.[53]

However, Bashīr was totally subordinate to the *kāshif* of al-Matamma, who ordered him to accompany and protect Pückler-Muskau to the historical monuments south of Shendi. Indeed Bashīr himself was in need of protection. His predicament is highlighted in a remark by the *kāshif*, that Bashīr was bitterly hated by the shaykhs around Shendi because of his ties with and dependence upon the government and he did not willingly show himself among them without a numerous guard.[54] On the other hand, the Turks could not use an ally who was too unpopular with the shaykhs and peasants. In order to restrict the abuses of Bashīr, the government had to interfere on at least two occasions. The political realities of *qism* al-

Matamma and Shendi town where he took up his residence, worked against Bashīr in the long run. His sources of authority in terms of followers and relatives, land and animals, lay mainly in the *qism* of Zaydāb and *khuṭṭ* of Rās al-Wādī. In Shendi he was separated from his own people.

What happened to Bashīr is as yet uncertain. He is not heard of after 1837. His sons were sent to Egypt to learn agriculture. One of them, Ḥamad, is said to have become *kātib* (scribe or secretary) in the government, and another, Aḥmad, was deputy governor of Dongola in 1857.[55] After Bashīr the office of *shaykh al-mashāyikh* seems to have lost some of its functions among the Jaʿaliyyīn. In the early 1860s the title was changed to *nāẓir*. In the 1870s there are indications which show that the Saʿdāb are back in the tribal leadership again, not as a reward for any loyalty to the Turks, as the events of the early 1880s show, but rather as a result of political necessity.

THE OFFICE OF *QĀḌĪ*

The administration of justice was traditionally in the hands of the Funj sultan, his subordinate shaykhs and *makks*, and a hierarchy of *qāḍīs*.[56] Two sets of law were enforced, the Sharia (Islamic law) and customary law, *ʿurf* or *ʿāda*. In the Turkiyya, the older system of provincial and district *qāḍīs* was preserved and formalised into a hierarchy of religious courts, *maḥkama sharʿiyya*, headed by the Grand *Qāḍī* and Muftī and a Court of Appeal in Khartoum.

> These local Sharia courts possessed in the beginning jurisdiction over a whole range of civil and criminal cases, [but] their powers were rapidly diminished. By the end of the period they dealt only with matters of personal status and inheritance, while through a system of local councils (*majlis maḥalliyya*) set up in 1850, a general civil and criminal jurisdiction devolved on amateur benches of notables and merchants applying customary law.[57]

There was a provincial *qāḍī* in Berber, and there are indications of the existence of subordinate *qāḍīs* for each *qism* and *khuṭṭ* within the province. The *qāḍī* in Shendi had jurisdiction over Shendi sub-district, and he styles himself *qāḍī khuṭṭ* Shendi.[58] In al-Matamma one would expect to find one *qādī* for the *qism* and another below him for the *khuṭṭ*. Unfortunately only the titles of *qāḍī* and deputy *qāḍī* (*nā'ib*) of *khuṭṭ* al-Matamma have been found till now.[59] The earliest contemporary reference to the *qāḍī* in Shendi is to one Aḥmad Jalāl al-Dīn, most probably belonging to the famous Majādhīb religious family in al-Dāmir,

> He mightily entertained me [NN] with roast meat, marisa, and then coffee. This man's ambitions are very modest; he only wants permission to install a couple of water wheels near the town. I tried to get him to consider a visit to Cairo but he protested that he would die of grief if he ever had to leave his native land. He was not interested in my lofty praise of Egypt. This love of country in an old priest seems to me a truly classic example.[60]

On an earlier occasion (10 February 1838) the *qāḍī* had approached Dr Gassier, principal medical officer of the Eighth Regiment, to induce him to speak favourably of him to the next governor-general, Aḥmad Pasha.[61] He is also called *muftī* by the French diarist, a title that is confirmed in legal documents in which his descendants appear. The practical meaning of this title, if it had any, in the local-level court structure of the 1830s is unclear.[62]

The functions of a local *qāḍī* were both public and semi public. Although his criminal jurisdiction was severely restricted from around the middle of the century, he was still in charge of civil matters relating to the family. Like the private *fakīs*, he could be consulted on legal matters and acted as notary, drawing up and witnessing contracts and agreements of all types. The Sharia courts served the Turks in many ways, not because they were open to pressure, but because they gave the regime a shade of legitimacy as formal upholders of the sacred law.

THE VILLAGE SHAYKH

The village shaykh, *shaykh al-ḥilla* or *shaykh al-balad* was retained and incorporated into the Turkish administration at the bottom of the ladder. In the early years some were replaced and lost their functions to the *qā'im maqāms* but it was gradually realised that Turkish interests were perhaps better served by having Sudanese as village heads, and it was naturally more economic.

The shaykh and his family represented a section of the peasantry who were somewhat better off in wealth, power and prestige, although there were wide differences among them. Thus in Dār al-Ja'aliyyīn some villages were headed by members of the royal family; such noble connections carried both power and wealth. The majority of the village shaykhs, however, did not differ much in lifestyle from the peasantry to whom many of them belonged. Representing as they did the leadership and upper stratum of the local agricultural communities, they formed an important link between the Turks and the peasants. Thus the agricultural policies and government orders with regard to the assessment and collection of taxes and so on, were communicated to the peasants and carried out through the shaykh or at least with his assistance.[63] As the difficulties in agriculture and tax collection increased in the Shendi area, the office of village shaykh turned out to be a mixed blessing.

Several of the pre-Turkiyya functions of the shaykh were kept up out of necessity, such as mediating in disputes, assessing and collecting taxes (with the aid of the irregular soldiers), supervising the redistribution of river-bed land, basins and rain land (with the aid of the professional land measurer (*dallāl*) and keeper of the village yard stick, the *'ūd*), organising collective activities, protecting the local market, and providing security and hospitality for itinerant traders and others. Normally the shaykh had access to more land, animals and slaves than the average, and he kept a larger household.

His position secured incomes above the average, but he was also expected to be generous, and provide free lodging and food to visitors. Hospitality (*ḍiyāfa*) was expensive, particularly with the increasing traffic along the Nile in the Turkiyya, and the shaykh could resort to collecting food from the villagers to feed unexpected guests. Passing notables, shaykhs and *makks* with their retinues prior to the Turkiyya and passing Turks and irregular soldiers afterwards, made heavy demands upon the resources of the villagers, both commoners and shaykhs. No wonder that Churi, travelling in 1851–2, in order to stop villagers from fleeing at the sight of their group, had to cry out: 'Do not be afraid; we are not Turks, but will pay you money for everything you bring us!'[64]

It was some time before Jaʿaliyyīn village life recovered after 1823. Social and political disintegration made it difficult to reconstitute the social system and normal economic activities. Some of the vacuum was filled by the Shāyqiyya. But in order to speed up the process of recovery and halt emigration from the Nile, the Turks established a class of shaykhs around Shendi who received monthly government allowances.[65]

Under the Turks, the village shaykh could become more powerful in relation to the villagers in so far as he cooperated with his superiors. Traditionally, his authority had to rest to a large degree on consensus and only to a small degree on force. As a mediator, he had to be acceptable to the majority, if he was not imposed on the villagers by the *makk*. These restraining mechanisms could easily disappear under the Turks for those who were ready to throw in their lot with the rulers. However, the shaykhs lived among their co-villagers, and the Turks were away most of the time, so that the shaykh often found he had to strike a balance between unpopularity with the peasants or with the Turks.[66]

No portrait of a Jaʿalī village shaykh has been found similar to those painted of shaykhs from other areas. Hoskins once walked into the harem of the shaykh of an ʿAbābda village north of Berber,

> without much ceremony, and chatted with his wives and female slaves. . . . The slaves were employed in making basket-work, and the wives reposing on their angoureebs . . . The sheakh was smoking under the shade of some doum trees. . . . The title of sheakh was at one time hereditary in upper Egypt; but the Pasha, in most instances put an end to this mode of transmission; choosing for that honour those that had best suited his purposes. In Upper Nubia [Northern Sudan] he has respected a little more the existing distinctions. There the office of sheakh is still in general hereditary: the eldest son succeeds to the father; and, in default of male issue, the eldest daughter enjoys the dignity . . . [The house of a] less powerful and wealthy [shaykh] consists, generally, of two large rooms, a divan and harem, between which is a pallisaded enclosure, where the flocks are kept, . . . The sheakhs offer us every night angoureebs (bed steads) made of wood and cords, . . . We always go to the house of the sheakh, who meets us with the usual Arab civilities, . . . Some of these sheaks have an air and bearing truly dignified and patriarchal. Their flocks of goats and sheep form their chief ostensible wealth, . . .[67]

Taking into account that the 'Abābda were on the average well treated by the Turks, this particular shaykh was probably better off than his Ja'alī counterpart, but Hoskins' general comments, perhaps with the exception of female village heads, holds good for Dār al-Ja'aliyyīn as well. However, this rather idyllic picture must be contrasted with another, in which the political realities of the position of village shaykh is underlined.

> The *mudīr* is absolute in his province and has the right to remove *kāshifs*, shaykhs and, in short, all who govern under him. He may replace them and give their posts to others who have secretly bought them from him and from whom he compulsorily exacts an agreed sum every year as well as butter, sheep, wheat, durra, and other things, which they are obliged to provide whenever they are asked [to say nothing of presents such as camels and the like] [sic]. If the subordinate does not keep his promise he draws upon himself the *mudīr*'s vengeance. For at the first opportunity the *mudīr* makes him render his accounts and as a result [he is left] [sic] with only his shirt and sometimes also with penal servitude. Every year the governor leaves his seat to make a tour of the chief centres within his jurisdiction. He does this ostensibly to do justice among the peasants who may have a just cause of grievance against their rulers. They never get this justice for he comes actually to sell his favours dearly to those chiefs who are frightened by his threats after the people have complained to the *mudīr* about them. The scared chiefs flock to swell the *mudīr*'s treasure.[68]

The buying of offices was known also before the Turkiyya, but recruitment to the office of shaykh underwent profound changes throughout the nineteenth century, particularly among the Ja'aliyyīn. The methods of obtaining and maintaining an office, and the various conflicting pressures on the shaykh, led to the borrowing of money from the merchants. Debts incurred in this way rebounded on the peasantry in the form of extra illegal taxes. Reforms aimed at improving the conditions in the villages reflected a late awareness on the part of the government that something was wrong. The unsuccessful reforms put forward by Muḥammad Sa'īd Pasha in 1857 included also an attempt to upgrade the authority of the village shaykh in the fields of security, land measurement and tax assessments, as well as formalising his income whereby he was to receive 4 per cent of the water-wheel tax. Furthermore, to induce more confidence in the peasants and the shaykhs alike, the irregular Shāyqī cavalry were not to be used for tax-collecting expeditions any more.[69]

We know virtually nothing about the day-to-day routines of provincial and district administration. The internal documentation was destroyed by the Mahdists. The above presentation gives therefore a rather unjustified static picture derived from the scanty and diverse sources that have been available to the author. It is to be hoped that a thorough search in the Egyptian archives may uncover enough material to fill in the gaps and advance our understanding of the workings of the Turkish administration in the Sudan. In the present context we are more concerned with creating a frame of reference within which we can examine the agricultural, financial and commercial policies. After all, the main objectives of the new administration was to facilitate and carry out the extraction of surplus, from the pre-existing as well as from the newly introduced productions.

A striking feature of the administration in the Sudan was the combination of an Ottoman formal structure with unstable tenures of office, unclear demarcations of authority, and uncertain guide-lines on how to deal with the Sudanese. There were clear racist undertones in the attitude of the Turks. In order to categorise and differentiate the Sudanese and dispense their unequal justice, they used the degree of Islamisation as a yardstick, which meant that only a thin layer of orthodox, 'proper' Muslims, reinforced from Egypt, were to be treated as fully civilised human beings, while the majority, unless they were regarded as allies, deserved no particular pity, as they were either superstitious sufis, pagans or just black slaves. The Turks sonorously and methodically induced fear in the Sudanese population by exposing them to continuous episodes of atrocious acts and barbarous punishments (such as impalement). Even the powerful Kabābīṣh camel nomads feared no one else but the Turks.[70] Thibaut wrote that 'The government turns a blind eye to everything except profit and pays no regard to the consequences of its actions.'[71] This contrast between theory and reality, between official laws and administrative practices, between a declared adherence to economic development and outright plunder, characterised Muḥammad ʿAlī's autocratic administration, but in the Sudan the ambiguousness, capriciousness, nepotism, and patron-client relationships which coloured the system from top to bottom, became all the more harmful as the Viceroys were far away and could not see, and were prevented from hearing about, the negative results of their own demands. Only twice was the Sudan visited by a Viceroy, Muḥammad ʿAlī in 1838–9 and Muḥammad Saʿīd in 1856–7, and in both cases, but particularly in the latter case, they found a country which differed greatly from what had been reported to them beforehand.

4

The transformation of agriculture

THE LOCAL SETTING

The Jaʿaliyyīn gained their livelihood principally from river bank cultivation, with the addition of rainfed desert (*ʿaṭmūr*) cultivation and animal husbandry. They practised a subsistence economy with durra as the staple crop. Small-scale marketing of farm produce and handicrafts through barter went largely towards supplementing the household economy. The subsistence character of the economy was subjected to serious attack during the Turkiyya, but did not change greatly before the introduction of mechanical pump schemes in the present century. Trade was regarded as an activity which under the right circumstances could secure a better and less arduous way of living than cultivation, and the Jaʿaliyyīn are often stereotyped as traders. This conceals the fact that they are and have always been largely riverain peasants.

Those who deserted cultivation for a short period or for ever, resorted to the institution of *amāna*, 'trust', and arranged for their land to be cultivated by others (family members or trustworthy neighbours) and seldom considered selling it. Rather, capital accumulated in trade would in part be invested in water-wheels and more land either back home or in the diaspora. Emigrants continued therefore to keep an eye on their patrimony, lest it should be appropriated by others or sold by family members.[1] Emigrants were still members *in absentia* of the village society, enjoying the same rights and duties as the resident villagers, with obligations to aid relatives and neighbours, to give presents at the various *rites de passage* such as circumcision, and to marry their cousins.

Cultural and other factors have contributed to the Jaʿalī system of values in which land plays so dominant a role. Land ownership is highly prized, but the former employment of slaves and low-status seasonal labour in cultivation, has imbued the self-conscious Jaʿaliyyīn with a dislike for agricultural work. This confrontation between land ownership and the work ethic was observed by the travellers and emphasised by informants, and the British regarded it as a major obstacle to progress.[2]

The land belonging to a family was largely transferred from one generation to the next through inheritance or testamentary bequests, less often through bridewealth (*mahr*). A daughter inherited half of a son's share, according to the Sharia (Islamic Law), which became more rigorously adhered to in the nineteenth century than before. However, the fact that girls might marry non-relatives and even 'strangers' and thereby cause part of the family holding to go to another family, led either to ways of buying the sisters out or to a more strict adherence to parallel cousin marriages. Some folktales suggesting marriages between brothers and sisters have been interpreted as a most extreme theoretical precaution against giving away girls and land to others.[3]

Social and economic life found its form and substance in the village (*ḥilla*), where neighbours were also most often relatives. In the larger villages an open space near the houses of the local traders would be reserved for the market. House types in the Northern Sudan included both flat-roofed mud-houses (*murabbaʿ*), round huts (*quṭṭiyya* or *tukul*) and rectangular shelters of mats (*rakūba*), depending on wealth, domestic stability, regional security, and many other factors.[4] The desert-coloured scenery was beautified by palm trees, vegetable gardens and durra fields along the banks of the river. Except around midday, people would be engaged in various cultivation activities depending on the season. Occasional visits by traders or the passing of larger caravans would stir up extra activity; a trading relative might stop to bring presents or necessities to his family. Some villagers would seize the opportunity to barter foodstuffs and handicrafts for utensils, spices, perfumes, medicines and so forth.

Flat-roofed mud-houses and dried brick houses were associated with the North, being suitable to a climate with little or no rain. Outside this area, such 'Berberine houses', to quote Brocchi, were a sign of northern immigration, traders particularly, and reflected the wealth and position of their owners.[5] Also in the north such houses, with the characteristic court-yard walls (*ḥōsh*) surrounding them, were first built by traders and well-to-do villagers. Thus low status *quṭṭiyas*, *tukuls* and *rakūbas* were far more widespread in the riverain villages than today. In the years of political disturbances before the Turkiyya, mud-houses ceased to be built in the most threatened areas, since *quṭṭiyas* were cheaper to build and the building material could be moved and hidden in an emergency.[6]

The factors affecting the development of house styles cannot be analysed here. Generally speaking, the mud-house predominates in the whole area. The *quṭṭiya* occurs most frequently between the Sixth Cataract and Wad Bān al-Naqā, and decreases in frequency downstream to al-ʿĀlīāb, where it ends. In Shendi there is a high concentration of dried brick houses, but mud-houses form the majority.[7]

Villages were normally situated behind the agricultural land, on the fringes of the steppe or desert, known as the *qōz* or permanent sand dunes. This location reflected both a desire to save cultivable land between the *qōz* and the river, varying most often from a few dozen metres to a kilometre, and to escape abnormal floods and the malaria mosquitos. Settlement morphology was influenced by kinship, geography and economy. The basic type was and is the linear strip village situated along the *qōz*. Its constituent parts were hamlets of relatives parallel to the river and with their respective plots of land stretching down to the river. The second type was the amorphous cluster village which developed at right angles with the strip village as a result of growing families. The third type was the nucleated village, which developed from both the first and the second type, mainly as a result of economic factors as well as socio-cultural preferences. It was characterised by mud-houses, in front of which were private courtyards (*ḥōsh*) surrounded by high mud walls (also called *ḥōsh*), to protect private life. The *ḥōsh* walls of neighbouring houses were connected to encircle whole quarters of the village or town. Facing the main thoroughfares were only long walls and the doors of the individual houses, two for each, one for the male entrance and one for the female (harem) entrance. This style of building was at first most often associated with the merchant class, and hence predominated near the market places and in the towns. Walled courtyards of different material may well have a long history in the Sudan, but they gained a particular socio-economic significance from the eighteenth century onwards as a sign of wealth, prestige and female seclusion in the north, and as a sign of Nubian, Arab and Islamic penetration in the diaspora.[8]

The village's social structure was characterised by varying degrees of differentiation related to ownership of land and animals and commercial wealth. Parallel to this ranking system based on property, people were also ranked according to occupation. Blacksmiths, fishermen and woodcutters had the lowest status among free men. Religious learning and sanctity, expressed in the ability to cure sick people and perform miracles, bestowed great prestige and respect. Family ties with prominent lineages or the ruling elite as well as with holymen, were sources of status and prestige, irrespective of secular wealth. Differentiation according to sex meant among other things a lower status for the women, not only in legal terms, but also with regard to the range of occupations and outdoor activities that could be permitted in an increasingly Islamised society. There are reasons to believe that the position of women became encircled by ever more restrictions throughout the nineteenth century, particularly among the better-off who could afford to clothe and seclude their womenfolk properly. At the bottom of the ladder were the slaves and the half-castes (descendants of slaves and free men). Although slaves benefited from the status of their owner, they were without any rights whatsoever, and for instance in the marriage contracts (*ṣadāq*) they were classified among the animals. Their tasks and services covered a large spectrum. Children born of a slave woman to a free man, were not regarded as free; they could even be sold and fetched higher prices than pure black slaves.[9]

Succession is patrilinial among the Jaʿaliyyīn; there is, however, no primogeniture as such. Daughters have a right in the patrimony according to the Sharia. Marriages were contracted by the senior generation in the light of economic, political and other factors. A man who wanted to marry additional wives at some later stage, negotiated personally with his future father-in-law. A young newly-wed couple might be given the right to use some economic assets, like a plot of land or some palm trees, as a first step towards forming an independent household. However, it was generally the practice that the husband moved to his wife's parents' household and lived there till the first child was born. He could still attend to his own affairs and take part in the cultivation of his father's farm. Upon moving back to his father's farm with his wife and first child, he joined the extended family. His own household was not normally established as an independent unit before the break up of the extended family at the death of his father.

A vital part of the wedding formalities was the writing of the dower contract, *ṣadāq*, in which the husband undertook to transfer specific assets (bridewealth) such as animals, slaves, plots of land or shares therein, other forms of property, jewellery, clothes, and later also cash. A part of the dowry was to be transferred immediately, the rest later. These assets were at least theoretically of some value to the wife in case of the husband's death, divorce, or migration. If the husband initiated divorce procedures, he was obliged to pay out the delayed dowry; if the wife took the initiative, she could not demand the part of the dower that had not been transferred.[10]

THE RIVER AND THE LAND

After passing through the rocky and narrow channel of the Sabalūqa Gorge (the Sixth Cataract), the Nile enters a broader valley with low, fertile banks, basins and islands all the way to beyond Berber. This part of the Nile Valley is known as the Shendi Reach, and the same degree of fertility is not found again before the Nile passes the Fourth Cataract and enters the Dongola Reach with its famous basins. The intermediate area, roughly the districts of the Rubāṭāb and the Manāṣīr, is characterised by stony islands, high banks and little alluvial sediments.[11]

The amount of cultivable land varies considerably within the Shendi Reach, perhaps more today than before, owing to desert encroachment on the one hand and mechanical pump schemes on the other. The acreage that could be cultivated each year in a given village depended on the height of the annual flood, the silt depositions on banks and islands, and on the availability of artificial means of irrigation. The average rise of the Nile could be 8 to 12 metres, depending mostly on the rainfall in Ethiopia and on the narrowness of the local river channel. Excessively low Niles meant famine, and when the opposite happened, water-wheels (*sāqiyas*) and houses could be destroyed and fertile slopes and islands could be washed away or replaced by sand. Some erosion took place also under normal circumstances and islands shifted their locations, but in most cases enough new silt would be left on the surface to enable cultivation. Island soil (*jazīra*, pl. *jazā'ir*) was the most fertile of the area.

The Shendi area belongs to the Sahel belt stretching across Africa from east to west south of the Sahara, and is situated in the most northerly zone where rain has had until recently any agricultural significance; the annual figures use to vary from 100 to 150 mm per year, falling mainly between May and September. The water collects in the many *wādīs* and depressions of the adjoining steppe (*khāla*), where fast-growing types of durra can be sown in July/August and harvested in October/November. Crowfoot wrote in 1911,

> during the autumn months, unless the rains have failed altogether, the interior is actually more populous than the riverside. Before the rains the villagers from the Nile and the Blue Nile go out, where necessary, to repair the little banks (*turus*) which train the waters, and after the rains they live in temporary huts upon their basins and sow and reap before they return to the river.[12]

Despite the geographical variations, a general idea of the topography of the Nile may be obtained from a schematic cross-section of the river and its banks. Theoretically, all the different types of land could be found in a village, but that was not always the case. Thus there was little *sāqiya* land between Ḥajar al-ʿAsal and Salawa while Shendi and Zaydāb areas were particularly favoured by *karrū* land. The presence, number and accessibility of islands also varied considerably from one locality to another.

Naturally the quality of the soil declined the further it was from the Nile, the most fertile being the *jazīra* soil deposited every year during the flood on the islands and the sloping river banks called *jarf* (or *jarif*). The *jarf* or only the lower part of it, is also referred to as *sallūka* land, named so after the digging stick used to cultivate it. The *qayf* is the edge of the permanent bank, marking the division between the *jarf* and the *sāqiya* land. The soil of the latter is called *qurayr* and consists of an alluvial terrace of older silts, from time to time rejuvenated by silt from extra high floods and irrigated by the *saqiya* and the hand-operated lever with a bucket on a rope, the *shadūf*.

The higher ground, called *kurus*, behind the *sāqiya* land, could in certain favourable places in the Shendi area be irrigated by well-*sāqiyas* erected there, the soil being fairly good, probably because it represented ancient river banks. Both the *kurus* and the low-lying grounds (*karrū*) behind it, were particularly common in the Shendi area. The *karrū* soil, although somewhat heavy and clayey, would yield reasonable harvests when watered either by the Nile or by rainwater; artificial means of irrigation being less suitable for this type of land away from the Nile. Canals were dug to facilitate the flow of water to the *karrū* where ridges hindered the water from finding its way to the receding river too quickly. Further away from the river, we have already mentioned the *ʿaṭmūr* cultivation in the numerous *wādīs* both behind al-Matamma and Shendi, shared according to customary regulations between peasants and nomads.[13]

From Dār Rubāṭāb and downstream, with the exception of Dongola Reach, the strip of *qurayr* land became narrower and poorer, and the *kurus* and *karrū* as well as *ʿaṭmūr* cultivation disappeared completely. The value of the islands increased proportionately and on islands permanently above the flood, *sāqiyas* were erected. Similarly the climatic suitability and economic value of the date palm increased towards the north.

THE SYSTEM OF LAND TENURE

Theoretically any form of land tenure may be placed on an absolute freehold to communal ownership continuum. In Northern Sudanese practice, *milk* rights can be placed somewhere on the freehold end of the continuum, while *ḥawz* or *ḥiyyāza* (the prescriptive right to use unoccupied land and ultimately to own it after a period of continuous occupation, usually seven years in Mālikī law), comes somewhere in the middle. At the end, the *kifāyat yad* principle ('enough for the hand'), defined the usufruct right to cultivate communal land according to one's needs and capacity. This latter principle is well known in the rainland savanna, where land was plentiful and access to it was regulated by the local tribe or the political authorities.[14] Along the Main Nile, however, land was largely limited to the river banks and islands, and a consciousness of family ownership of land, particularly *sāqiya* land, was developing before the Turkiyya. The occurrence of land sales at the end of the eighteenth century, though not a widespread phenomenon, indicates that individual rights in specific plots of land was no longer against customary law.[15] However, along the Nile there existed also lands, such as *karrū*, *wādīs*, and sometimes also the *jarf*, in which each village and family had general rights and where access to specific plots was negotiated and redistributed every year.

The Turks accepted claims of ownership of riverain land and issued *ḥujjas* (lit. 'proofs' of ownership) to that effect. They also continued the policy of granting private estates to favourites, redistributing vacated farms, and stimulating the foundation of new villages, but were less willing to grant tax immunities and similar economic privileges. As before the Turkiyya, the local elite were also the biggest landowners, but Turkish officials did not normally buy up agricultural land for private purposes, with some notable exceptions. From 1861, European residents were allowed to buy and possess agricultural land.[16]

In order to simplify the system of land tenure along the Nile with the aid of concepts from more central areas of the Ottoman Empire, the Turks introduced the concept of *mīrī* land i.e. government land, as opposed to freehold, *milk*. They found a situation in which the degree of freehold decreased as one moved away from the Nile. Only the *sāqiya* land and the *jarf* below it seemed to belong permanently to production units, i.e. one or more households. Thus regularly cultivated land was categorized as *milk* and the land which was cultivated only when natural irrigation made it possible, came under the category of *mīrī*. This twofold division of riverain land ownership was highly in favour of the colonial government both for taxation and development purposes. It was taken over by the British after

1898, who added much riverbed land to the *mīrī*, and it has since been a vital instrument in providing land for public agricultural schemes or for individual tenants.

The rights of absentee landowners were also recognised in the beginning, but later on, in order to deter emigrants, their land could be expropriated and sold or leased to others who were willing to maintain the *sāqiya* and pay the tax arrears.[17] The governor of Berber, Ḥusayn Bey Khalīfa, made it clear that the *karrū* of the province was to be regarded as government land, in order to exploit it for cotton cultivation. The riverain peasants pressed for the recognition of their customary rights in the *karrū* and the *wādīs*, but in vain. In the 1820s much of the Ja'aliyyīn's *karrū* land was given by the government to the Shāyqiyya, without any reference to its former owners. The taxes or rather rents demanded from this unstable type of cultivation were felt to be equal to those collected from regularly cultivated land, and therefore highly unreasonable. Thus more Ja'alī peasants threatened to join their relatives in the diaspora.[18]

Private possession of land, water-wheels, animals and the other factors of production was a socio-economic reality before the Turkiyya, but joint cultivation and rights in shares of the produce were still the dominant subsistence principles. The term *sāqiya* applied to both the wheel, the land it irrigated and the production unit, including the owner or owners who gained their livelihood from operating it. We may therefore talk about a *sāqiya* system of production, in which the people belonging to a *sāqiya* defined their ownership rights in terms of shares in the wheel and the land, rather than in physically demarcated plots, and received from the produce according to their number of shares and labour input. One or more households or extended families had joint rights in a *sāqiya*, worked it together, sometimes with additional labour from outside or with slave labour, and shared in the taxes. Only among the better-off and the nobility did it happen that a single household possessed more than one *sāqiya*.[19] At the other end, there were also people who, for various reasons, possessed little or no land, and who did not have shares in a *sāqiya*. However, they might possess other assets, such as expertise, animals, and labour power, which enabled them to negotiate a kind of sharecropping agreement (Nub. *teddān*) with the *sāqiya* owners. Seasonal agricultural labour might also be recruited and remunerated in different ways up to the present time, both among villagers, (former) slaves and nomads.

The present chapter will try to show the central position of the *sāqiya* system (the institutions and labour processes associated with it) in the peasant subsistence economy and how it defined the relations of production.[20] During the Turkiyya, the *sāqiya* system became exposed to systematic pressure from a profit-seeking government on the one hand and from a growing merchant class which looked upon the agricultural sector as an investment target, a source of cheap commodities for exchange, and a recipient of credit against usurious interests. Compared to the Funj period, when the peasant economies were relatively isolated and shielded from the world market, the Turkiyya changed the rules of the game completely. The Turks brought the Nubian Nile Valley within the orbit of the expanding Western economy, represented by the numerous Western merchants, adventurers, geologists, hunters and consuls, who used Egypt as a staging point. The *sāqiya* system, however, refused to compromise with this enormous demand for higher output; it had to operate virtually as before, i.e. according to its own rules, or it would just break down and disintegrate.

PLOTS AND BOUNDARIES; CUSTOMARY LAW UNDER PRESSURE

After the reconquest of 1898, the British were immediately confronted with the issue of land rights, not only claims to private ownership, but also the far more disruptive question of boundaries between plots. The century that was coming to an end had uprooted and scattered many families who were now coming back and claiming their land rights. These might well conflict with the rights of the neighbour, as he interpreted them, as well as with the rights of the new government, as they chose to define them. Much ink was spilled over these issues and it took more than three decades before some clarity was established. However, the numerous disputes and reports offer invaluable material for the study of customary law.[21]

Generally the land holdings were systematically arranged at a right angle to the river, so that each rectangular plot would stretch from the Nile into the steppe or desert edge where they reached useless land known as *ḥajar* (rock) or *jabal* (hill). It was commonly recognised that an owner or group of owners of a *sāqiya* plot had certain locally-defined rights to the *sallūka* below it as well as to the *kurus* and *karrū* behind it. Thus each holding could at least theoretically, consist of all the various forms of land. One reason for this system was the need for access to wood and fodder on the one hand, and access to irrigation water from the Nile which often meant digging a channel through the *sallūka* land to just underneath the wheel. In the Turkiyya it became more common for different people to own the *sāqiya* and the *sallūka* lands, for reasons which will be discussed later, and the first had to compensate the latter by a fraction of the *sāqiya* harvest, the so-called *shaṭībat al-maḍrab* (lit. 'the fraction of the cutting').[22] This division of the *sallūka* from the *sāqiya* became widespread in the Shendi area, where it was customary to add *sallūka* land to the bridewealth.[23]

The main boundary between holdings at right angle to the river was called *fāṣil* (lit. 'border') and was naturally the most important boundary. This is confirmed by documentary evidence in which other boundaries are nowhere so fully described. The northern or downstream *fāṣil* was called *sāfil* and the southern or upstream was the *ṣaʿīd.* When the practice of dividing and demarcating the land of the extended family among the younger generation became common, new *fāṣils* were drawn parallel to and between the original two, and new cornerstones were struck into the ground. Thus riverain land was measured and evaluated according to the distance between the two *fāṣils* of a plot. The distance was sometimes referred to as the *jad'a*, consisting of a number of *'ūds*, which again consisted of a number of *dhirā'* or cubits, varying between three to four to an *'ūd*. The sales contracts, therefore, from the late eighteenth century onwards do not indicate the size of the land in square *'ūds*, but rather in the number of *'ūds* between the two *fāṣils*.[24]

In addition to the *fāṣil*, there was also another type of boundary called *mirin* which ran parallel with the river. It was used, particularly in Berber area, to divide up the *sallūka* land between different owners, and also for demarcating the redistributed plots in the *karrū* and the *wādīs* in Shendi area. The basic *mirin* was the deep river channel, the thalweg, which divided the land between the two river banks, and decided to which bank old and new islands belonged. A *mirin* was also drawn at the edge of the low Nile and another at the edge of the permanent river bank, dividing the *sāqiya* from the *jarf* (*sallūka*). The distance from the low river *mirin* and the upper edge *mirin* lines was called a *rīḥ* (lit. 'wind'); apparently all types of land had a *rīḥ*, moving inland from the river.

Mirin was also a term for the blocks and strips of land that were demarcated by the *mirin* and *fāṣil* lines. Thus all the *jarf sallūka* belonging to a village was known as the village *mirin*, which was subdivided into *mirin* blocks and finally into *mirin* strips, associated with certain families and individuals.[25] The breadth of a *mirin* strip was also measured in *'ūds*. The same principles with necessary adjustments applied also to the *karrū*.

Naturally the principle for asserting cultivation rights to *sallūka* land varied from one district to another. On the Atbara river, people from opposite banks used to ride towards a disputed island as the river receded after the flood, and those who reached it first, without allowing the horses to swim, would cultivate it that year.[26]

Another principle of customary prescription better known in the Shendi area (and in Dongola) for regulating access to the *sallūka* land, was the *ḥaqq al-quṣād* (lit. 'right of what is in front', i.e. right of frontage). This principle, although it required a deep-water *mirin*, differed in certain respects from the *mirin* principle, but was not inferior in securing a fair division of riverbed land. A *mirin* was never lost even if it was temporarily swept away by the Nile; it was given a name like other types of land and had its boundaries confirmed in documents. On the other hand, the *ḥaqq al-quṣād* principle could not be enforced before the *quṣād* land (the *jarf*) had reappeared after each flood. Then the potential conflicts between the owners of the *sāqiya* and the *jarf* below could easily break out, depending upon the degree of erosion (*ḥaddām*) and the extent to which ownership of the *jarf* had become separated from that of the *sāqiya*.

The principles of customary prescription and the possible variations of them indicate an attempt to adjust and regulate access to land in accordance with the socio-economic realities and cultural traditions. In this perspective it becomes apparent that the separation of the *jarf* from the *sāqiya*, the sub-division and individualisation of family land in response to external economic and social forces and the application of the Sharia, and the growing frequency of land sales, all of which were developed during the Turkiyya, had severe repercussions on the village societies.

The Turks were accustomed to measure and tax land by the *faddān* (today c.4,200 m^2), and tried to impose the same system on the riverain Sudan as well. The most common square measure in the Sudan was the *jad'a* (about 5¼ *faddān* or 64 square *'ūds*, not to be confused with the *jad'a* of length), used to measure savanna rainland. The rectangular plots on the Nile could not easily be measured by the *faddān*,

> Firstly because of the shape and location of the cultivated areas. Every hand-breadth of land fit for cultivation has its owner, although he may not cultivate all of it. Further, the cultivated plots are in the form of long strips by the river bank, six or seven strips to the *faddān*. The peasants cultivate these long strips. The high ground behind is wooded, and at various points the people cut the wood down and erect *sāqiyas*. Secondly, these people have never been able to understand measurement by *faddāns*; they know nothing but the *jad'a* [of length].

The author of this passage goes on to describe how the use of the *faddān* and the frequent land transactions led to increased disputes, 'between the inhabitants of various villages, when the cultivation season starts, on account of the disputed ownership. Sometimes the quarrel is so hot that they take up arms and attack one another until the kāshif has to come to restrain them by force.'[27]

This happened every year, we are told, under the governor-generalship of Khūrshīd and caused much extra work for the Turks. According to the author, they were therefore forced to stop using the *faddān*, and go back to the *jad'a* of length, 'which can be enforced on all without the need for searching for the actual owner of this or that property' (p. 55). In other words, it made more sense to tax whole production units than individual landowners, whose plots could not easily be measured. However, Chapter 5 will show that taxation by the *faddān* continued on naturally flooded land till the end of the Turkiyya.

The British made some efforts to understand and respect traditional land customs, but like the Turks before them they expropriated land not regularly cultivated or subject to fluctuations. Even the river-bed caught the attention of the settlement officers, particularly the phenomenon of the appearance of new land, either as islands or *jarf*. It was then that the legal weakness of the *ḥaqq al-quṣād* principle as against the *mirin* principle became apparent to the peasants. Whereas the British were reluctant to overturn the latter since it claimed to cater for land temporarily covered or removed by the Nile, they showed less scruple in declaring any new river-bed land appearing after the date of settlement as government land in areas where the *quṣād* principle predominated. Such land they distributed, as private property but most often as leaseholds, to needy peasants, favourites and shaykhs, against the loud protests of the *quṣād* holders.[28]

An institution which had profound impact upon the structure of land use and ownership and size of holdings was the Islamic system of inheritance. As long as the Jaʿaliyyīn stuck to the principle that it was only shares in the produce of the land that were inherited and divided up, and not the land itself, no harm was done, except that the shares become smaller and more numerous. However, when one started to take the Sharia seriously, or when the Sharia came to the aid of those forces which wanted the land to become fractionised and individualised to enter more smoothly the market sphere, the land itself started to become divided up among heirs. This development created problems in the traditional system of joint cultivation, and a lot of compromises were reached, whereby women might be compensated in other ways, particularly with regard to the *sāqiya* land, and brothers might choose to continue to work the land together without bothering to demarcate their individual plots. Ironically, in villages where the process of sub-division of land went unhindered into the present century, the people were forced to return to their former system of joint cultivation (*rōka* or *rawka*) as the plots had become too small for rational individual cultivation. If nothing was done under these circumstances to consolidate inherited, purchased, and bequeathed plots, an individual might end up with scattered strips of land not only in his own village, but in others as well, an increasingly frequent phenomenon in the Turkiyya.[29]

A sh̲are in land, in a slave, in animals or any other economic asset, was called *shaṭība* (pl. *shaṭā'ib*) in Dār al-Jaʿaliyyīn, *ʿaẓm* (pl. *ʿaẓām*, lit. 'bone') further north, and *khashm* (pl. *khushūm*, lit. 'mouth') in Dongola. Twelve *shaṭības* represented full ownership. However, in the Turkiyya the twelve fractions of a *sāqiya* plot could be further divided into two *qīrāṭs* each, which again were divided into twenty-four *sahms* each. Thus a *sāqiya* could easily consist of 576 and even more shares, which, if they were to be physically demarcated on the ground for an equal number of possibly different owners, would drastically hinder rational cultivation. Thus when a family holding had reached this stage of sub-division, or probably long before then, the owners reverted to the old system of *rōka* again. The British refused to register ownership of smaller holdings than 1/576 of any plot of land.[30]

The process of fragmentation was also slowed down by emigration, and by natural calamities such as disease and famine. The campaign of the Daftardar created abundant land in relation to population for many years afterwards. However, the growing unequal access to land and the spread of landlordism, meant that many peasants still found themselves short of land. Under the Funj unequal access to land resulted from sultanic favouritism and the special status of the nobility; under the Turks it was money first of all that opened up access to more land. As will be shown later, peasants came to rely more and more on loans and credit from the traders, thus entering into permanent debt-relationships, from which they could only with difficulty free themselves. When a debt-ridden peasant finally fled, as it often happened, the creditor might come to an agreement with the government about taking over the land after paying the outstanding taxes on the land and offering to maintain the water-wheel. Merchants established themselves as landlords in al-Matamma and many other places along the Nile, but it was in the rainland savanna to the south, such as the Gezira and Kordofan, that they acquired large farms cultivated by slaves.[31]

AGRICULTURAL PRODUCTION

A historical study of agricultural production must take into account the resources and technology available, i.e. the factors of production, the distribution of control over them and the social organisation of production. Some of these elements have been discussed already, but we shall now take a closer look at the production process characteristic of the *sāqiya* system and its socio-economic implications.

Land was, of course, the basic factor of production, but water, seed, irrigation machines, implements, animal and manpower were all essential. The staple crop, durra, was represented in different varieties, of which *fatarīta* and *ḥimaysī* were particularly suitable for *karrū* and *ʿaṭmūr* cultivation, as they could ripen after three to four months without additional watering after the flood or rains. Vegetables and leguminous plants, such as *bāmiyā* (okra), *ḥumuṣ* (chick pea), onions, etc. (the *fūl maṣrī* or horse bean was not yet as widespread as today), were particularly suitable to *sallūka* cultivation on islands and in the *jarf*, but no single crop was exclusively associated with a certain type of land or cultivation. Crops which needed a long irrigation and growing period or preferred the rather cooler winter climate, had to be planted on *sāqiya* and *shadūf* land. Soil fertility was kept up by regularly changing the types of plants (e.g. cereals vs. vegetables) grown on the same plot of land, and by leaving plots unused (fallow) at intervals. The *jarf* needed less preparation than the *sāqiya* land before sowing. Rectangular basins (*ḥōd*, c. 2×5m) and the canals between them were formed in the flat *sāqiya* land by the digging hoe (*fās* or *ṭuriyya*) and the earth scoop (*wāsūq*). Similar methods were used in the *karrū*, where the natural flood (*fayyaḍān*) had to be regulated. The digging stick (*sallūka*) not only broke up the soil, but also made the seed holes. The plough was not unknown, but was not very suitable to the small plots along the Nile. In the Turkiyya it was observed in use in Kordofan in the cultivation of durra and dukhn (bulrush millet).[32]

For artificial irrigation, two instruments were available, the *sāqiya* and the hand-operated lever, the *shadūf*, of which the latter was more suitable to water smaller plots and gardens. Lifting water by a *sāqiya*, constructed by wood and ropes, and with a row of pots attached to a double rope hung over the biggest vertical wheel and reaching down to the water level, was a heavy operation.[33] It was particularly demanding when the river was low; often it needed three pairs of oxen working shifts every eight hours, day and night. Slaves were set to drive the oxen and otherwise carry out the more arduous work. Thus this form of technology was both capital and labour intensive, and any problems hindering its effective operation had serious consequences for the people depending on it.

Artificial irrigation made it possible to lengthen the growing seasons of the crops standing on flooded land, taking over when the effect of the flood had ended. Or it enabled people to grow a second crop on such land in the dry season. More importantly, it made it possible to cultivate land that otherwise would have been left uncultivated for lack of flood water. However, the *sāqiya* system and the soil's capacity did not favour intensive cultivation over several years; crop rotation was widely practised, fields were allowed to lie fallow and the wheel could be moved to another field. The problems associated with cash crop cultivation in the Turkiyya, showed among other things that crop rotation and fallow had been a necessity.

Under normal conditions the slack season in the agricultural calendar was rather short. With the Nile rising in May, thus making the lift shorter, the summer (*sayfī*) season started and durra could be sown on *sāqiya* land to be harvested in October. From about July/August rainland and later flooded land (the rainy, *kharīf*, and flood, *damīra*, seasons) were sown with both durra and vegetables, to be harvested in October/November. About the same time the winter (*shitwī*) durra, wheat, and onions would be sown on *sāqiya* land, to be harvested in February/March.[34] In addition to the heavy work of clearing the ground, sowing and harvesting, including cutting and threshing, for which work parties might be organised, there was the continuous work of irrigation, weeding, and scaring the birds away. Since the crops could easily be destroyed by locusts, insects, wild animals and storms, the plots were seldom left unguarded, and additional religious protection of the fields was often sought from the local holyman (*fakī*).[35]

Under the intensive *sāqiya* system, a crucial input was labour, which may be grouped into family labour, sharecroppers, slaves, and occasional agricultural labour. By family labour is meant members of the households who owned or had shares in the *sāqiya* (wheel and/or land). Participation by them in agricultural work would probably not be extensive, if they could afford to put slaves to work instead, or if they could live on what they received *qua* land and/or wheel owners. Sharecropping arrangements and the employment of occasional labour could also help to limit the labour input of the owners and their kin. The average peasant household, however, had to shoulder a large part of the labour needed for cultivation. Various tasks, such as cutting and treshing, needed extra input of labour, which was solved informally by organising work-parties, *nafīr* or *faza'a*, in which neighbouring households participated and were treated with food and beer. The division of labour was both a result of the tradition of pooling of resources, the complex set of labour operations, the need for specialists, and the growing differentiation in the control of capital and means of production. Elsewhere the present author has argued that the *sāqiya* system in the nineteenth century had many features in common with Islamic partnerships, without necessarily having an Islamic origin.[36]

The pooling of labour and means of production came about in the following manner. In most cases there were several owners of the *sāqiya* and the land. Ownership was expressed in *shaṭība* or *ʿaẓm*, the distribution of which was the result of inheritance, bequests, and purchase. These joint owners had to come to an agreement, the *teddān* contract, before the cultivation season with the group of people known as *turābla* (sing. *turbal*), conveniently translated from the Nubian as 'sharecroppers', who provided labour, seed, *sāqiya* pots and ropes, implements, donkeys and oxen.[37] The assistance of two other specialists was also required, namely the *sāqiya* builder and repairman, the *basīr*, who was in charge of the daily maintenance of several *sāqiyas*. For this he was compensated in kind at the end of the season. The other was the *ṣamad*, who was in charge of irrigation, making the canals and *ḥōds*, sowing the seed, regulating the flow of water, and putting the slaves to work. The slave who drove the oxen could be replaced by the son or younger brother of one of the *turābla*, and called *awratti*, the usual situation in the present century after the abolition of slavery.

The use of slave labour and labour from outside the extended family did not mean that cultivation was not a household undertaking. Only those better off did not work themselves and they also kept their womenfolk out of the fields. However, slaves enabled their owners to work less on the farm and, if they so wanted, to devote more time to other activities, such as trading. It was therefore a serious blow to the *sāqiya* economy when slavery was abolished by the British.[38]

The *teddān* agreement was regulated by customary laws known to everybody, so therefore it was probably not necessary to write it down. At least no such contract has been found from the nineteenth century, to the knowledge of the present author. The rules for sharing the crop varied from one village to the next, but the following general outline from Shendi area at the beginning of the present century is probably not so anachronistic, except for the absence of agricultural slaves.[39] On flooded land (*fayyaḍān* cultivation), on islands, *jarf* and *karrū*, the land owner(s) either took a third of the harvest and paid no share in the tax or could take a larger share, perhaps a half, and paid half the tax. The *sāqiya* required a much more complicated system, depending on the relationship between the parties involved, the quality of the soil, the height of the Nile, the number of bulls, and the type of crop. Under favourable conditions, the eight bulls or oxen could irrigate up to ten *faddān* at a time (the average was three to four), which meant no less than one *faddān* a day. Taking these factors into account, the following pattern for dividing the crop was possible:

a *The land (that is its owner/-s)*; its share varied from a seventh to a twelfth.

In the case of onions and crops cultivated by *matara* (well-*sāqiya*), which were more labour-intensive, its share was comparatively lower.

b *The sāqiya*; its share was normally a ninth of the total crop.

c i *The turābla*; their share varied according to their input in addition to labour, such as bulls, seed, ropes, tools, and *sāqiya* pots, but could be about a third of the crop. The number of *turābla* was usually eight, sometimes four or twelve, and always regulated in this way to avoid problems in dividing their shares.

c ii *A boy turbal*; half the share of a grown man.

d *The ṣamad*; if he was also the *baṣīr*, he received about an eighth.

e *The baṣīr*; he received on *ardabb* of grain from each *sāqiya*.

f *The bulls*; they received a quarter.

g *The donkeys*; they received a share.

h *The owner of the jarf below*; he received a share.

i *The awratti*; he would receive something if he was hired.

When the time came to portion it out, the crop was divided into heaps (*kawm*, pl. *kaymān*) to be allotted to the shareholders according to their shares in the means of production and labour input. Thus, to illustrate the pattern described above, the following system obtained in Bajrawiyya village: If the crop was divided into forty *kawms*, the land-owner(s) received four, the *sāqiya*-owner(s) received two, the *ṣamad* five (one-eighth of which went to pay the full tax), the bulls ten, the donkeys five, the *baṣīr* one, and the rest – thirteen *kawms* – were shared among the *turābla*.

An average *sāqiya* could perhaps produce up to five *ardabbs* of durra per *faddān* and maintain from ten to twenty people.[40] The exploitation of other resources, such as *sallūka* cultivation, animal husbandry and trade, was also vital to the household economy. However, farm management and labour input were guided by subsistence requirements, including what was needed to replace implements and other worn-down assets, pay the taxes and acquire a few items in the market. When this was accomplished, the drudgery of work, the decreasing returns, and the danger of soil exhaustion or the possibility of a breakdown of *sāqiya* and bulls, convinced the peasants that to try to produce more was not worth the effort. Rather than to maximise profit, the peasants worked to minimise risks.[41]

MAKING AGRICULTURE PAY

The pre-Turkiyya agricultural economy was evidently fairly well developed within the limits set by eco-system, technology, socio-economic organisation, political conditions and cultural values. Unfortunately, there are not many contemporary observations that may help us. Around 1700 the area around Dirayra south of Shendi was renowned for its fertility.[42] Seventy years later, Bruce noted that while Kurgos island was fertile and well-populated, the environs of Shendi had been deforested and showed signs of over-exploitation.[43] Among the plants mentioned were durra, dukhn, wheat, barley, cotton, green tobacco, lemon and *nabqa* (*Zizyphus spinachristi*) and the usual varieties of vegetables and leguminous plants, except *fūl maṣrī*. Date growing was not practised, and wheat cultivation was limited south of Berber. Animals were also kept by the peasants, who arranged for some of them to be taken to the inland pastures after the rains. In the slack seasons peasants might try their luck in trade, leaving the women, slaves and other family members in charge of the farm. Burckhardt wrote, about al-Dāmir in April 1814:

> The regular distribution of the fields, and the small channels for irrigation, showed that agriculture is here more attended to than in the districts [of Berber] we had passed. . . . The cultivation of the soil is much more attended to at Damer, than in any other place from Dongola to Shendy. Artificial irrigation is carried on by numerous waterwheels, turned by cows, like those in Egypt; this custom enables the cultivators to obtain two crops every year. Damer suffered less during the last [1813] famine than any of the neighbouring countries.[44]

The agricultural reforms of Muḥammad ʿAlī in Egypt were part of a large-scale effort to build a new, consolidated state, and start a process of independent industrialisation. To achieve this goal the agricultural potential of the country had to be mobilised through government intervention, in order effectively to bring forth raw materials for the industries as well as for the world market.[45] The conquest of the Sudan must be understood in this context of internal state-building and external expansion; the (overestimated) resources of the Sudan, with some enforced modifications, were meant to give the Egyptian industry and export economy a significant push forward and strengthen the country's political and military position, with the slave troops, *vis-à-vis* both Istanbul and the West. However, conditions in the riverain Sudan were different from Egypt, as we have seen, and to transfer the Egyptian model of agricultural reforms, cash crop production and exploitation to the Sudanese peasants was to meet with difficulties. The subsistence economy of the Jaʿaliyyīn and others simply could not be adapted without preparation to include a profit-oriented sub-sector of cash crops based on a misconceived development ideology. Here lies the source of the dramatic struggle between the peasants and the Turks which dominated the Turkiyya and contributed to its downfall.

The Jaʿalī peasants who survived the massacres of the Daftardar in 1823 were in a miserable condition. Ruins, and deserted fields overgrown by shrubs dominated the scenery between Shendi and al-Dāmir. The broken *sāqiyas* served only as fuel for cooking.[46]

To bring the fields into cultivation again and at the same time reward their cooperation, Shāyqī families were settled among the Jaʿaliyyīn in Shendi and the villages upstream. At the same time the Turks started to introduce commercial plants and trees in the area, both on private farms and on land expropriated for that purpose.[47] It is possible that some changes would have taken place anyhow without compulsion, in response to the dietary demands of the foreigners for wheat, maize, sugar and citrus fruits and encouraged by closer contacts with the world market. However, such a slow development was too modest for Muḥammad ʿAlī, as it was too modest for the Western colonists in other parts of the world. Beside the alleged riches of the Sudan in slaves, gold and other minerals, which turned out to be largely illusory, three plants were chosen to form the cornerstone of the colonial economy; sugar-cane, indigo and cotton. After travelling in the area of Dongola and Shendi between 1823 and 1825, Rüppell wrote critically,

> Another idea would have given better results, namely the introduction of indigo cultivation, and to increase cotton cultivation; however, such institutions are not created for the benefit of the cultivator, but become on the contrary, as a monopoly of the government, instruments for increasing the slavery of the subjects. And as the latter have not the faintest idea about the economic value of such plants, they regard them as only despicable innovations by a despotic capricious authority.[48]

Thus Rüppell foresaw the consequences of a policy which combined compulsory cultivation of cash crops with a government monopoly system. As in Egypt, vital natural products and agricultural produce were declared government monopolies in the Sudan from about 1824 onwards; the prices of such commodities were fixed by the government and free trade prohibited. Thus, the Turks acquired export products in the Sudan at low prices and sold them at a huge profit in Cairo or Alexandria. This policy not only affected the primary producers, but also the Sudanese traders, as we shall see.

Sugar, indigo and cotton were introduced into Berber Province at a relatively early date. In 1825, Brocchi noted that the government was establishing plantations of indigo, safflower and rice at Abū Salīm village, between Faḍlāb and Zaydāb. It was apparently easy to cultivate safflower, but rice and indigo cultivation was not a success. The plantations were attended to by slaves. A number of Egyptian, Greek and Armenian workers, instructors and specialists were also sent to the Sudan to instruct the peasants and carry out difficult processing operations.[49] It was also Muḥammad ʿAlī's intention to establish a cotton-weaving factory at al-Matamma and another at Berber, and specialists were sent there for that purpose.

Cash crops were also cultivated by the peasants; in fact they were meant to produce the bulk of them. However, although it seems that some success had been achieved by 1833, the number of *sāqiyas* in Berber Province had not yet reached the pre-Turkiyya level.[50] The cultivated area was calculated at 6,000 *faddāns* and the total population at 30,000, excluding the Bishāriyyīn and other tribute-paying nomads. With part of the *sāqiya* land now devoted to cash crops, the peasants were compelled to utilise more *sallūka* and *ʿaṭmūr* land for food crops.

There was a large indigo factory at Berber which was in operation from about 1828:

> They cut it [the indigo] three times during the season, at intervals of about two months. To extract the dye, they place the stalks and leaves for eighteen hours in a cemented mud basin or cistern of water, which is then drawn off into another vessel: in this last they leave it only a few hours, stirring it well with sticks, and afterwards let it off into a cauldron, in which the final process of boiling takes place, and indigo is produced of very good quality. The Pasha receives from this manufacture nearly 14,000 okres [*uqqa* of 1.25 kg] (weight), which is sent to Cairo and sold there for fifteen dollars per okre.[51]

By 1833 the cultivation of sugar-cane and cotton was also firmly established. Sugar-cane was grown near ʿĀlīāb, but was particularly concentrated on the islands in Berber area; the peasants themselves did not process the sugar which was done at Berber in a building erected for that purpose. In 1837 this sugar factory was on the brink of collapse.[52] Traditional crafts like tanning, *dammūr* and linen weaving and dyeing were in this period particularly under some threat as new techniques were adopted, but in the long run they were adapted to the new situation. It was the traditional *dammūr* which made al-Matamma famous throughout the Turkiyya.

Indigo factories to extract the dye were established at Berber, al-Matamma, ʿĀlīāb, Thamaniyyāt, Marawī, Ḥafīr, Khandaq, Old and New Dongola. In April 1837 Pückler-Muskau was shown the factory at New Dongola by the province governor, 'It already produces indigo of three different qualities, the first one is equal to that of India. The oka [*uqqa*] of this quality costs the Government twenty-four piastres, and it is sold for eighty piastres. On the whole, 50,000 okes are annually manufactured, and no European is now employed on the works.'[53]

A year later Russegger saw a miserable indigo factory at al-Matamma. At Berber, Russegger wrote that besides the sugar factory and tannery, there was an indigo factory which produced 300 qantars of pure dye per year. The indigo factory at Marawī was established in 1829 and was still in operation in 1838. The water needed for the cement basins was lifted by a strongly-built *sāqiya*. From 6,000 qantars (270,000 kg) of dried plants (*Indigofera argenta*, *Polygonum tinctorum*, etc.), they extracted 6,000 *uqqas* (c.7,500 kg) of dye which was sold for between 20 and 100 piastres per *uqqa*. Russegger was of the opinion that a large part of the production was in fact used to dye the local cotton cloth. This could mean that the monopoly was breaking down and that transport to Egypt was becoming too inefficient and costly.[54]

After more than ten years of effort, the results were not impressive. While for cotton the best years had yet to come, sugar had obviously reached its limit and indigo showed signs of decline. For reasons to be discussed below, the profit rate decreased rapidly, and Muḥammad ʿAlī decided to end the indigo monopoly on his visit to the Sudan in 1838–9. In al-Matamma this was put into effect in October/November 1839.[55] The many petitions from the peasants as well as international pressure may also have had some effect.

A French merchant, Vaissière, now saw an opportunity to establish his own indigo business. He obtained a concession and was allowed to take over whatever he could use from the closed factories, and began to acquire land. However, the new governor-general, Aḥmad Pasha, on his own initiative forced Vaissière to give up his plans and hand over the concessions to him. This step was obviously a part of his plan to create his own private schemes. He established fruit gardens, plantations (e.g. for sesame) and factories (indigo and soap); he had date palms planted in Khartoum, and invested in *sāqiya* building; he lent money on his own account to encourage production, expropriated land (from e.g. the Shāyqiyya) and forced merchants to finance and maintain *sāqiyas*.[56]

Al-Matamma was one of the places that caught his attention. He ordered wells to be dug there and had *sāqiyas* built, 'to make an uncultivated area fruitful'.[57] At the same time he went into partnership with a local merchant, Ḥamza Mūsā, and others to cultivate indigo and produce the dye. Ḥamza was of ʿAbdallābī descent and before the Turkiyya had operated as a caravan merchant between Dār Fūr and Egypt before he moved back to the Nile to trade on Kararī, al-Matamma and Khandaq. Presumably the joint capital was invested in both land, *sāqiyas* and basins. The old basins were either repaired or new ones were built, being known locally as the *kirkhāna* (Turk. *karakhāna*, lit. 'workshop, factory'), the ruins of which can still be observed in al-Matamma today. However, the joint venture failed, as the government project had failed, and Ḥamza lost much money. Sometime after 1849 he went to the Ḥijāz where he is said to have stayed till he died in the early 1860s. (For the career of his son, see Chapter 6 below.)

This seems to have been the last effort to grow and process indigo on a commercial basis in Berber Province. Already from the latter half of the 1830s travellers remarked from time to time upon the possibility of such production. Thus Holroyd observed in 1837 that:

> The greater portion of the land between Khartúm and Berber is uncultivated, though it might be advantageously used for the production of grain, tobacco, cotton, and indigo. The inhabitants [largely the Jaʿaliyyīn] have been compelled to serve as soldiers, or have absconded into the desert, in order to avoid it, and there is great room for colonization. They are in the lowest state of degradation and oppression, and are addicted to lying to an inconceivable extent. They entertain the greatest fear of a person wearing the tarbúsh, or red cap, mistaking every one with this badge for a Turk; and whatever a traveller requires he must get done by compulsion.[58]

Holroyd attributes the bad conditions of the Shendi Reach to government conscription practices, which, of course, were a vital factor behind emigration. However, he does not see that the apparent absence of cash crop cultivation was a sign of the effect that such cultivation had had on the agricultural economy along the Nile. The cultivation of indigo tended to exhaust the soil quickly and required much and continuous watering and labour; a *sāqiya* could normally irrigate no more than three-quarters of a *faddān* of indigo plants, which produced 75 qantars (c.3,375 kg). The peasants were paid 12½ piastres per qantar, in other words 937 piastres (or 62½ dollars) per *sāqiya*. After deducting a tax of 20 dollars, the *sāqiya* owner(s) and the others dependent on it, were left with 637 piastres per year. We must assume that we are here talking about *sāqiyas* more or less entirely devoted to indigo the whole year, and that food therefore was either grown on other land or had to be bought in the market. This had two immediate effects, namely that less food was produced and the price of food went up; secondly that the absence of crop rotation, thin planting, and less fallow resulted in a systematic exhaustion of the soil and a breakdown of the *sāqiya* system. To quote an Italian chronicler, indigo production in Berber and Dongola deteriorated because,

> the peasants were obliged to sow indigo on their *sāqiya* land. As it was a plant that required a great deal of water, the cultivators tired themselves out watering it to bring it to maturity. They lost bullocks from the continual fatigue of turning the *sāqiya* and they got in arrears with the sowing of their own grain, a serious loss to them.[59]

The government, however, gained a double profit, first by taxing the *sāqiya* at a rate of 20 dollars irrespective of which crops and what area of crops were grown; secondly, by obtaining the dye at fixed low prices for sale at a large profit in Egypt. Naturally, this systematic exploitation of soil, technology, and animal motive power, and the tapping of free and slave labour for the army and the export of cattle to Egypt, could not go on for long without serious repercussions.

Cotton was already part of the subsistence economy along the Nile before the arrival of the Turks. The spinning, weaving and selling of *dammūr* were widespread activities in both villages and towns, where pieces of cloth were also used as media of exchange. The first governor of Berber, Maḥū Bey, found in the Sudan a long-staple variety of cotton, which he brought to Egypt where it was developed by Jumel. Before the 1860s, however, raw cotton was probably not exported from Berber Province to any great extent. Local manufacturing was able to absorb some cotton for cloth production. The red-striped cotton scarfs of al-Matamma were widely famous, being known simply as *al-matamma*.[60] As for the two cotton-weaving factories established at al-Matamma and Berber in the middle of the 1820s, their fate is not known.

As in the case of indigo, the peasants were reluctant to devote more time and energy to cotton lest it should affect their ability to grow food, particularly when the prices paid to them were not worth it. The government was therefore compelled from early on to establish cotton schemes or plantations on land that was more or less expropriated along the Nile, and to employ slaves as a large part of the work force. The American Civil War (1861–5), caused a higher demand for Sudanese cotton in the world market, and fresh initiatives were taken to increase its cultivation on both private and government (*mīrī*) land. An immediate side effect of this policy echoed the situation earlier under compulsory indigo cultivation, namely the fall in food production and the following rise in prices.[61]

However, a lot of cotton was apparently wrested out of the soil and the labour of the peasants. In 1871 the governor of Berber, Ḥusayn Bey Khalīfa, showed the American journalist Southworth thousands of cotton-bales at Berber, waiting for transport. It was the result of an experiment, he was told, most probably in the Ja'aliyyīn districts; 100 miles of canals had been dug, one alone being 20 miles long, and all of them for cotton cultivation. As for the labour force, Ḥusayn assured the journalist that the Sudanese loved money,

> and above all, loves to work off his taxes in lieu of paying them in hard cash. For example, if an Arab cultivates such a quantity of cotton or works on a canal for such a length of time his taxes are considered paid. As soon as the people begin to amass money emigration will pour in from Hedjaz, and the wandering nomads will cluster about the cultivated fields. But we do not intend to let the cotton fever despoil us of durrah.[62]

Ḥusayn had received orders from Khedive Ismā'īl earlier the same year to develop cotton cultivation, and not to tax the land devoted to cotton but instead to collect one-tenth of the crop as taxes. He was furthermore promised that ginning machines would be sent to him as well as merchants to buy the cotton.[63] According to the *Statistique de l'Egypte 1873*, the acreage under cotton cultivation had risen to 9,885 *faddāns* in the joint provinces of Berber and Dongola, producing annually after ginning, 12,356 qantars. Agricultural production in general relied upon the irrigation of 6,590 *sāqiyas*, 3,000 of which were in Berber, according to Shāhīn Bey, the Khedive's personal inspector. However, Ḥusayn's visions or rather those of the Khedive Ismā'īl for that matter, failed to materialise.[64]

There were several obstacles to commercial cotton production along the Nile. In addition to those connected with the traditional agricultural economy, an unwise camel nomad policy made the latter less willing to serve the government, which resulted in recurrent acute shortages of camel transport. The bales at Berber were a sign both of success in cultivation and failure in transport. In order to reduce the bulk of the raw cotton, a few steam-powered cotton ginneries were imported. Some of them never worked, others soon broke down and still others lacked wood-fuel and manpower. Labour was a critical factor at all stages of production. Falling prices and all the other problems mentioned above finally finished large-scale cotton production in the Sudan before the Condominium.[65]

THE DESOLATION OF DEVELOPMENT

The Turks showed a remarkable interest in what we would call 'economic development' in the agricultural sector and in this respect they did not differ much from the Western capitalist oriented colonists in Africa. Whether they like to be reminded of it or not, the British in fact wiped the dust off several of the development projects of the Turks in the Sudan. The relative success of the British compared with the Turks must, of course, be attributed to motorised machinery (pumps and tractors), fertilizers and pesticides, the railway and an efficient organisation. The Turks also lacked, however, a coherent policy of development which meant that measures implemented in one sector were undermined by measures in another. Suffice it here to mention how efforts to increase production among the Jaʿaliyyīn were undermined by, among other things, forced conscription to the army. In the same category comes over-taxation which will be analysed in Chapter 5.

It is very difficult to paint a clear picture of the prosperity of the Jaʿalī districts. The starting point was as bad as it could conceivably be. Local efforts to reconstitute the peasant communities and reintegrate those who chose to come back, were made difficult by the Turkish insistence on cash crop production and military conscription. This process culminated with the years of famine in 1835 to 1837, when an *ardabb* of durra rose from 6 to 200 piastres, and Khūrshīd Pasha was compelled to open the granary in Khartoum to feed the starving immigrants to the capital.[66] No wonder that Holroyd found the banks of the Nile little cultivated in 1837 (see above p. 71) and that the merchants of al-Matamma were complaining to Thibaut in July 1939 about the deserted countryside.[67]

Towards the middle of the century, the number of *sāqiyas* was still rather low in our area, and the peasants preferred to concentrate on *fayyaḍān* cultivation and animal husbandry to avoid the cash crops associated with the water wheels or perhaps also because the *sāqiya* lands were exhausted.[68] Reports from the early 1850s, however, indicate improvements in some localities. Private *sāqiyas* were again seen in operation along the Nile, drawn by oxen and attended to by slaves, but emigration and depopulation marked all the Jaʿalī districts, villages and towns alike.[69] The simple rural *quṭṭiyyas* and *tukuls* were now also frequent, together with numerous empty houses, in Shendi and al-Matamma. Thus Hamilton made the following observation in 1854:

> The banks of the Nilé between Chartum and Berber are little cultivated, the waterwheels for irrigation are rare, and the people principally subsist on the abundant crops which they can raise without labour [*sic*], by sowing after the rains. This neglect of the immense natural resources of the country is in some degree attributable to the slothful character of its black inhabitants, but still more to the exactions of the government which paralyse industry, and are gradually causing an emigration of the people southwards.[70]

A reconsideration of the economic policy was urgent, but as long as key figures profited from short-term exploitation, and those with grain stores and cash profited from the widespread shortages of food and cash, there was no real demand for reform. When Muḥammad Saʿīd Pasha visited the Sudan in 1856–7, he learnt that the number of *sāqiyas* had sunk by the thousands. On 26 January 1857 he addressed four comprehensive orders to the new provincial governors in Khartoum. They ushered in some major changes in the administrative and judicial systems; taxes were to be lowered and various incentives were proposed to attract the peasants back to their land; local shaykhs were granted more authority in economic and fiscal matters, corvées and other extra exactions were abolished to be replaced by paid labour. Peasants were guaranteed safety and security for their property, and those who wished to take up cultivation were either to be given land within already existing villages or permitted to establish new villages.[71]

However, in spite of previous experience, agricultural policy remained basically the same. The universal blessings of cash-crops were emphasised as before: 'You [the governors] will encourage the inhabitants to sow wheat, indigo, cotton and sesame. You will do all that is necessary to manufacture cotton and indigo in order to facilitate the export and let the country profit from the value; you will also encourage the inhabitants to extract sesame oil, because that is in their interest.'[72]

Apparently the Turks had not understood the real causes of the economic decline and as long as the goals of colonising the Sudan were the same, as well as the ideological orientation and administrative methods, the proposed reforms could not alter the catastrophic development. Observers in the 1860 echoed earlier visitors to the Sudan. Al-Dāmir had been reduced to nothing and the Mukabrāb section of the Jaʿaliyyīn in the vicinity had left their villages and moved to the other side of the Nile. There were few signs of commercial cultivation and the rate of emigration was growing in intensity, until it had become a major concern also for the local shaykhs.[73] The agricultural sector from time to time since the beginning of the Turkiyya had had to hand over slaves to the Turkish army. Now, by referring to the official abolition of slavery by Muḥammad Saʿīd, Mūsā Pasha Ḥamdī (1862–5) enlisted thousands of farm slaves into the army, and demanded extra levies of grain. Villages on the military route between Khartoum and Berber were particularly hard hit by the constant exactions and emigration was widespread in the villages between al-Dāmir and Shendi. Schweinfurth who, like Baker, visited the Sudan twice in this crucial period, noted that the unmarried Jaʿaliyyīn went to Khartoum to become private soldiers in the Upper Nile, while the elderly married people took their goats and sheep and withdrew inland to the savannas.[74] At the end of the 1860s, Lafargue, a resident of many years of Berber town, wrote:

> Already ten thousand families in this province being settled industrious cultivators along the Nile, have turned into nomads; at the moment of writing the departures continue; these unhappy refugees have spread everywhere, in Kassala, Qaḍārif, Qallabāt, Khartoum, Sinnār, while most of them definitely move to Abyssinia where they are given land by Shaykh Rajab of the Wad Zayd. If the system which governs the Mudīriyya at present does not change, it will be depopulated within a few months.[75]

Table 3 *The annual agricultural output in Berber and Dongola, 1971–2*

Wheat	48,288 *faddāns*	75,326 *ardabbs*
Beans	1,903	8,807
Onions	1,303	26,073
Tobacco	2,883	4,325
Barley	15,000	22,500
Oats	20,000	24,000
Lupine	1,800	2,250
Kidney beans	2,500	3,750
Maize [durra]	54,754	273,770

Lafargue had been in the Sudan for about twenty-five years, so he probably knew what he was talking about. The Turks had miscalculated the resources of the country, he continued, and preferred to exploit the people rather than to encourage them. There was a year of shortage in every three and in every five there was one of famine.[76] More than before Berber became dependent on shipments of durra from the central rainlands, a lucrative business for those who could invest in it. The provincial governorship of Ḥusayn Bey Khalīfa, 1869–73, although he expanded the acreage under cotton cultivation, was apparently also a period of growth in food production, if we are to believe the *Statistique de l'Egypt*[77] (See Table 3).

These figures must, of course, be treated with great caution. The number of *faddāns* devoted to each crop cannot be added together to give the total number of *faddāns* under cultivation, as presumably some of the crops were cultivated on the same land, one crop after the other. Still there are too many *faddāns* for the 6,590 *sāqiyas*, so we must assume that we are here also dealing with flooded land under *fayyaḍān* cultivation. This picture is further complicated by the absence of other staple vegetables in an ordinary northern Sudanese diet, and the absence of *sāqiya* land devoted to fodder (*bersīm*). Thus still more *faddāns* should have been added to the list, but such 'marginal' crops were perhaps not worth counting.

THE BREAKDOWN OF THE *SĀQIYA* SYSTEM

The development in the number of *sāqiyas* in Berber Province during the Turkiyya, as far as it is possible to know it, may serve as a concrete indicator of economic and social conditions; 2,437 *sāqiyas* were counted among the Jaʿaliyyīn before the revolt in 1822, a number which had sunk to 706 in 1828.[78] The total early figure for the province might therefore have been at least 4,000. Even after years of official encouragement and compulsion to make both peasants and traders build and maintain *sāqiyas*, no more than 3,000 *sāqiyas* (1871) were ever counted in Berber Province after 1822. In 1881 the number was probably also 3,000, but with perhaps as many as half of them abandoned.[79]

In Dongola the number of wheels was estimated at 5,250, a number which the Turks tried in vain to increase by 20 per cent.[80] In the early 1870s the number had decreased to about 3,590, if the total number of 6,590 for the combined provinces is correct. In about 1881 a total of 5,900 was recorded for Dongola, many of which were either completely ruined or just abandoned.[81] The last official estimate in 1885 gives the number as 6,541, probably with the same qualifications.[82] In both provinces the Turks used to reckon with an unrealistically high number of wheels, simply for fiscal reasons, as Chapter 5 will show, and also to conceal the real state of affairs in the villages.

Being the symbol of the riverain economy and society, it is clear that a colonial policy, which was hostile to the normal functioning of the *sāqiya* and the institutions attached to it, was shaking the very foundations of village life. This situation was not intended by the Turks, but they did not, before it was too late, try to calculate the real limits of exploitation that the peasant economy could endure, without serious damage to its viability. The *sāqiya* came under attack from different angles at the same time because of lack of coordination of development policy. A couple of additional examples of this incoherence may serve to underline this point.

Since each *sāqiya* required three to four pairs of bulls, the number of cattle for this purpose amounted to several thousands in a province. In addition cattle were needed for breeding, for milk, and for security against cattle plagues, which also occurred in the Turkiyya. For the peasants therefore the cattle represented a major capital asset as well as a *sine qua non* of the production process. Egypt's industrial and agricultural development was seriously in need of animal motive power, and Sudan was given the role as cattle exporter, a completely natural exchange, according to Pückler-Muskau, as Sudan needed cash and Egypt needed cattle.[83] However, the effects of this more or less compulsory delivery of cattle were far-reaching. Nomad cattle proved to be unfit for work in Egypt; pressure was therefore soon put on riverain cattle.[84] In the 1830s, thousands of cattle were collected and driven to Egypt, in a period when the riverain peasants were asked to get more work out of their *sāqiya* bulls to irrigate cash crops. By such a policy the Turks sabotaged their own development plans in the Sudan and wasted considerable resources on the cattle transport. In the absence of pastures, fodder stations were established along the route to Egypt, at which durra also was stacked. Thus, under the famine conditions of the latter half of the 1830s, the durra crops of vast fields were reserved for the export cattle. Starving children and women north of Dongola were observed searching for durra grains in the dung left at a feeding station by a herd of oxen on their way to Egypt.[85] Many animals died on the way and after arrival in Egypt; the whole project was a fiasco from the Egyptian point of view.[86] From the point of view of the riverain economy, it nearly led to a catastrophe, leaving only the weakest cattle to tend to the water-wheels.

Equally incoherent was the Turkish management of agricultural labour. Agricultural labour was usually provided by the peasant family, by share-croppers and occasional hired labour, and by slaves. Farm slavery existed before the Turkiyya but was widespread only in the upper echelons and the nobility. It is a common cliché among the Jaʿaliyyīn today that they never cultivated their fields themselves in the old days. The Shāyqiyya are also known to have left much of their cultivation to slaves before the conquest.[87]

During the Turkiyya, different trends emerged simultaneously, for example, the Turks wanted to increase production and knew the vital role of farm slavery in this process, and they made access to slaves easier, but on the other hand, they demanded tribute from the peasants in the form of slaves and undertook forced conscription of their slaves into the army.

Government slave raids (*ghazwa*) in the Nuba Mountains and in the south, and the general opening of the Nile after the 1840s, made slaves more available on the northern and central markets, but in the face of economic deterioration and emigration in Dār al-Jaʿaliyyīn, it is difficult to document a decisive increase in farm slavery in that area. However, the *jallāba* (itinerant traders, slave traders) from the Jaʿaliyyīn and related tribes were able to capture or buy up slaves, whom they brought north and sold in the villages before returning to the south again. 'No matter how poor a Nubian is, he possesses two to four slaves of both sexes. The comparatively well-off have any amount of them.'[88] Both al-Matamma and Shendi had slave markets in the 1830s, which also probably supplied the hinterland. At the same time a considerable slave traffic was carried out at Berber, which was 'the rendezvous of the slave-merchants from Sinnár and Khartúm, on their way to Cairo'.[89]

Most of the slaves were naturally exported; a great number went into the army (the Jihādiyya), and still more went to the rainland savannas, where lack of labour was *the* crucial factor which decided the acreage under cultivation each year. The northern immigrant merchants at al-Masalla-miyya on the Blue Nile or at al-Ubayyiḍ and Bāra in Kordofan, employed thousands of slaves in rainfed cultivation and garden irrigation. Only the availability of slaves made it possible for the immigrants to introduce their *sāqiyas* and *shadūfs* along the two Niles and in Kordofan (erected on wells).[90]

Some indications of the availability of slaves in the north may be gleaned indirectly from the availability of labour in general and from the develop-ment of slave prices. It was noted for instance that one of the reasons for the failure of commercial cotton production was the lack of labour, both in the fields and in the ginneries. When the Turks started to build the railway south through Nubia in the 1870s, slaves could not be recruited either locally or further south in Dongola, as the few that the peasants owned were considered a minimum in their economy. At about the same time, from 1875 onwards, a government effort to enlist 10,000 slaves into the army failed, first because of the needs of the peasants, secondly because the governor-general Ismāʿīl Pasha Ayyūb was not in favour of it (the decision was taken in Cairo), and thirdly because the compensation of 500 piastres, later increased to 700 or 800, was too low to tempt the owners.[91]

A comprehensive study of slave prices and their implications has yet to be undertaken. Some tentative conclusions may nevertheless be put forward. Even if we take into the account the decline in the value of the piastre in relation to the dollar and the general inflation of the period, in the period between Burckhardt's visit (1814) and the fall of the Turkiyya (1884–5), the price of slaves rose gradually in real terms. Thus, in about 1814, prices averaged from 8 to 16 dollars (104 to 108 piastres, at 13 piastres to a dollar) in Shendi; in 1837 the prices ranged from 250 to 700 piastres for males and 2,000 to 3,500 piastres for females (now 15–20 piastres to a dollar).[92] In the same year the prices at Berber were about 450–600 piastres, whereas in Khartoum male slaves cost about 70 to 500 piastres, and in Kordofan on average no less than 300. Thanks to the government *ghazwas*, which annually brought an estimated number of 10,000 to 12,000 slaves to Kordofan, and the practice of paying its soldiers in slaves who were subsequently dumped on the market, the prices of agricultural slaves were still kept within the reach of the average commoner. The many customs stations on the way to Egypt, and the prices offered there, severely limited the export profit rate so that relatively more slaves were offered for sale in the Sudan.

The end of the government *ghazwas* in the 1850s was largely compensated for by the opening of the White Nile to private slave hunting and trade. However, systematic efforts to halt this trade made fewer available in the north from the late 1860s causing prices to take a noticeable upward swing, and the percentage of those annually enslaved to become employed in agriculture in the north decreased, with the predictable effects on agricultural production.[93] In the early 1870s, an eight-year-old boy from the White Nile cost 40 dollars (800 piastres), 25-year-old men taught to work cost 150 dollars (3,000 piastres). Then, as always, Ethiopian girls were the most expensive and definitely not destined for the fields, costing between 60 and 300 dollars.[94] In an economy where the annual *sāqiya* tax of 20 dollars was considered ruinous, the slave prices quoted above must have been outside the reach of the average peasant in our area. We find now that two or more people pooled their cash in order to buy a slave, and each had a right in the labour of the slave according to his share in him/her. Similarly shares in animals were bought, sold and inherited.

The simplest conclusion we can draw from this is that there was a demand for slaves in the north, a demand that was perhaps slightly higher than the supply, and was also kept up by the slave expropriations of the government. Considering what has been said before, this demand for slaves must have been highest in the urban settings and among the upper classes (merchants, absentee landlords, peasant-traders, the local government headquarters, plantations and garrisons), and lowest among the common peasants, and virtually nil among the poor, debt-ridden and landless peasants. Thus agricultural slavery spread in the upper and middle classes, whereas the economic basis necessary for employing farm slaves was eroded for large sections of the common peasantry, for whom it became expensive and meaningless to keep several slaves even to replace migrant labour. Without a minimum of slave labour to work the land, and with all the other pressures upon him, many a common peasant decided to give up agriculture altogether.

The Turks had to give up their efforts to conscript Jaʿalī men into the army, but not before serious damage had been done to agricultural production in the area. When the Jaʿaliyyīn left their farms they much preferred a career such as that of trader. However, not everybody was able to make a full-time or part-time career in trade, and a new phenomenon of the period is the development of wage labour, which first came in as an addition to slave labour but which had started to compete with it towards the end of the Turkiyya. The workers who were hired to dig the wells at al-Matamma in 1839, were paid 1 piastre a day. Servants received 20 piastres a month and a daily wage of 5 piastres was considered high. The free wage labourers had all the time to compete with the cheaper slave labour, which could also be hired out for wages. Thus it was not until the price and hire of slaves had risen, in the late 1870s and early 1880s, that the price of free labour could really compete. In Kassala in 1882 it cost 3 dollars (60 piastres) to hire a slave for a month.[95]

This development is highly relevant to our discussion of the breakdown of the *sāqiya* system. In reality, the various sharecropping and partnership arrangements associated with this system, had also the social function of incorporating land-hungry and landless peasants and labourers into the production process, for which they were remunerated (or paid) in kind. As the number of *sāqiya* units decreased or stagnated, and ended up in relatively fewer hands, and the better-off peasants and absentee landlords and merchants were able to employ more slaves, the scope for traditional participation became narrower. This process can explain why so many people were compelled to seek other (or additional) sources of income. Another factor was the government's demand for part of the taxes to be paid in cash, which under any circumstance would have forced people to sell a part of their agricultural produce, animal stock, handicrafts or labour power.

The introduction of cash crops and a more intensive cultivation pattern to satisfy external demands, combined with all sorts of other demands (cattle, conscripts, slaves, and taxes, the latter to be examined in Chapter 5), represented a frontal attack on the traditional *sāqiya* system. Very soon soil yield sank dramatically, thus inviting shrubs, weeds and desert encroachment. The wheel and the bulls broke down under the extra pressure to lift up more water. And finally the social and economic institutions which lay at the core of the *sāqiya* system began to disintegrate. The Turks encouraged in many ways the break up of the large *sāqiya* production units and the shift from shares in output (crops) to shares in the land itself. Much more than before plots of land became associated with individual persons, who were able to sell, mortgage, and bequeath the plots or just let them be sub-divided and inherited by his children. This development of land fragmentation, unless one continued to join forces (*rōka*, undivided shares, as opposed to *maqsūma*, cultivation with divided shares) in the cultivation process, hindered a rational use of the land, particularly when parts of the family and village holdings were alienated to outsiders. The socio-cultural obstacles to the selling of land were therefore effective in many northern villages far into the present century. However, the sale of land could be an economic necessity, even if it contributed to the growing social gap between the rich and the poor in the Turkiyya.

The subsistence economy of the Jaʿaliyyīn and their neighbours rejected as an alien transplant the efforts to introduce large-scale commercial agriculture. Nevertheless severe damage was inflicted upon riverain society. Even where cash crops were introduced only on a moderate scale, there was still the burden of taxation. Hence the Sudanese saying from the period: 'Where a Turk treads, no grass will grow.'

5

Taxation

The nature and scale of the appropriation of a surplus from the producers by the ruling class changed profoundly with the installation of the new colonial regime. Again it was the primary producers, and the peasants more than the nomads, who were to carry the largest burden. The Turks demanded taxes (*ṭulba*, from *ṭalaba*, to 'ask', or *ḍarība*, pl. *ḍarā'ib*, from 'beat', 'hit', 'impose'), both in kind and in cash, and thereby enforced monetisation upon a society that knew only barter and local media of exchange, and very few metal coins outside the market centres. This policy stimulated the growth of a class of merchants and moneylenders and weakened the position of the commoners still further. In one sense, the increasing interest of the merchants in agriculture can be seen as an attempt both to overcome the commercial set-backs caused by the monopoly system in the first half of the Turkiyya and to exploit the taxation system to introduce usury capital into the agricultural economy.

More than anything else perhaps it was the question of the *ṭulba* that came to darken the relationship between the Jaʿaliyyīn and the Turks, leaving a strong imprint on presentday memories and evaluations of the Turkiyya. The revolt of the Jaʿaliyyīn in 1822 and the burning of Ismāʿīl Pasha was triggered off by what was felt to be unreasonable demands for tribute. There is a Jaʿalī proverb attributed to the Turkiyya, *ʿashara ru'ūs fi'l-turba wa-lā riyāl fi'l-ṭulba*, 'better ten heads in the grave, than a dollar in tax'.[1] If they were not actually prepared to sacrifice their heads, although that also happened, many Jaʿaliyyīn were willing to sacrifice their land to escape the tax-collectors, and that was not a minor thing.

Kremer once wrote that the secrets of the Viceroys' finances were more carefully guarded than those of their harems.[2] It is therefore difficult to arrive at precision, particularly when we are dealing with the Sudan where the relevant account books are lost. Nevertheless we will try to piece together a picture on the basis of what we know from other sources. The general trend seems to have been increasing demands and decreasing returns.

Taxation of riverain agriculture under the Funj has been described by Spaulding.[3] Various taxes, rents, dues and services were due by the peasants to the local nobility and the king as well as to the sultan. 'Custom determined the proportion of any crop that must be delivered to the sultanic treasury – half of all crops produced on the *jarf*, one-fifth of those from artificially irrigated lands, and one-tenth of what grew on the southern rainlands' (p. 87).

A notable feature of this system was that the size of the harvests was assessed by appointed officials, so that the *khurj* (land-tax) set aside for the sultan would vary from year to year. Still the *khurj* seems to have been relatively high and contrasts with the common belief among the Jaʿaliyyīn today that they did not pay taxes under the Funj.[4] This apparent paradox may be rooted in different conceptions of 'taxes', which put surplus extractions under the Funj in a different category from those under the Turks. The people had good reasons for making such a differentiation.

THE IMPOSITION OF THE *ṬULBA*: THE FIRST ROUND

The Turks brought with them a taxation system which was not merely alien to the Sudanese, but which was also largely an innovation in Egypt. Muḥammad ʿAlī's fiscal reforms represented a break with Ottoman practices in Egypt, and were meant to be a vital instrument in mobilising the necessary resources and capital for the modernisation programmes there. It is therefore not necessary to look beyond Egypt for the origins and principles of the new taxation system now imposed on the Sudan.

Between 1773 and 1833 the value of the Egyptian piastre in relation to the Spanish dollar (Charles IV) declined from 2¼ piastres to a dollar, to 3¾ in 1798, 12½ in 1822, 15½ in 1830, and 19½ in 1833.[5] Since agricultural prices were fixed by the government and consequently kept low, while the prices of consumer goods and taxes followed the currency fluctuations, the peasants grew progressively worse off. To keep ahead of inflation, the taxes rose noticeably in Egypt throughout Muḥammad ʿAlī's reign. Towards the end of the eighteenth century the peasants had paid a variety of taxes in cash and in kind to the central treasury, and to the local landlords and tax-collectors. Under the French, between 1798 and 1801, the tax on a *faddān* was 270 paras or 6¾ piastres, which had risen to between 33¾ and 36 piastres by 1807. In 1824, first-class land was taxed at 67½ piastres; in 1833 at 72 piastres. In addition came personal taxes (capitation), taxes on trades and crafts, on animals, on date trees and houses, and the extra levies to cope with urgent financial needs. This was roughly the model of taxation which the Turks imposed on the Sudanese.

In the Sudan, the work to establish a financial administration started early in the wake of the occupation, but detailed budgeting was never achieved until the last years of the Turkiyya. Muḥammad ʿAlī's idea was that not only should the Sudanese pay for their own subjugation and development, but that they should also produce a surplus for the Cairo Treasury. The chief architect of the new system was a Copt by the name of Ḥannāʾ al-Ṭawīl (called *al-mubāshir*, lit. 'the treasury assistant'), who had probably bought the position from Muḥammad ʿAlī.[6] He arrived in Shendi on 18 October

1821 on his way to Sinnār. The *kāshifs* and their assistants, the *qā'im maqāms*, were instructed about the procedure and began to count the *sāqiyas* upon which the taxes were to be based. Thereupon they visited every village to assess the taxes and supervise their collection. The number of slaves, animals and houses was also registered, as well as rainfed and flooded land.[7] Since these registers were not brought up to date every year and the local community was collectively responsible for delivering the same amount irrespective of fluctuations in production, emigration, for instance, meant heavier taxes for those who remained behind. Thus for some years the Jaʿaliyyīn paid taxes for 2,437 *sāqiyas*, whereas a count in 1827 showed that only 706 were in operation. Ḥannā' al-Ṭawīl arrived in Sinnār during Ismāʿīl's campaign in Fāzūghlī; he immediately undertook to develop in more detail the comprehensive system of taxation, together with Ismāʿīl's secretary, Muḥammad Saʿīd Efendi, and a Sudanese *arbāb* and court official, Dafʿ Allāh *w*. Aḥmad.[8]

The rates were fixed at 15 dollars on each head of slaves, 10 dollars on each head of cattle, 5 dollars on each sheep or donkey, according to the Funj Chronicle. On his return to the north the following year, Ismāʿīl Pasha found that the Efendi and the *mubāshir* had appointed clerks, carried out the assessments and issued ledgers which had already been sent to Cairo.[9] The tax on the *sāqiya* was somewhere between 12 and 23 dollars (see below).

It seems that the basic principles of taxation had the full support of Muḥammad ʿAlī and his son, but when things started to go wrong and tax-collectors were ambushed and killed and peasants started to leave their farms, Ismāʿīl was ordered to look into the problem, rumours of which had reached his father.[10] The subsequent correspondence between them admits that injustices had been committed and that the taxes were perhaps too high, but the whole affair was blamed on Ḥannā'. 'Such people are always looking after their own interests', wrote Muḥammad ʿAlī.[11] Hannā', feeling the wind of change, tried to reach the Egyptian border but orders were issued for his arrest and return to Sinnār. Shaykh Saʿd ʿAbd al-Fattāḥ *w*. Nimr al-ʿAbbādī was sent to track him down. However, once Hannā' was brought back to Sinnār, he proved indispensable.[12]

Meanwhile the peasants had their first concrete experience of Turkish taxation. The people of Shendi sold their property to meet the demands for payment in cash. In the brief absence of Ḥannā', things had changed little, except that the Turks were forced to accept partial payment in kind, the price of which was fixed to their advantage. The tax on houses was also very unpopular. In Berber Province, the houses were divided into three classes according to size, and several categories of taxes were fixed for them. The preliminary assessment in Berber was begun by Ḥannā' and completed by Saʿd ʿAbd al-Fattāḥ, but it was Maḥū Bey's responsibility to collect them. Ismāʿīl Pasha was encouraged by his father to adjust the rates according to people's means, but major changes were not contemplated and the collection continued to resemble military campaigns.[13]

The first round of collection was completed before Ismāʿīl Pasha made his fatal return to Shendi in October 1822. The demands for the fiscal year 1236 (9 October 1820 to 27 September 1821)[14] had been estimated at 135,000 dollars for the districts of Rubāṭāb, Berber and Shendi. A variety of economic assets were confiscated; money, slaves, cloths, jewellery and other valuables, but despite Turkish thoroughness, it amounted in the end to no more than 50,000 dollars. Maḥū Bey, therefore, thought of renouncing part of the taxes to encourage the peasants to continue cultivation. 'My son [replied Muḥammad ʿAlī] governors must act neither with excess nor negligence. Keep to this rule in all your doings; adopt the most appropriate measures in order to exact the tax and punish the trouble-makers.'[15]

There was obviously no room for leniency, although Maḥū Bey had demonstrated that it could have a positive effect. The ruthless way in which the first collections and confiscations had been carried out promised little better for the future.[16] Before Ismāʿīl returned to Shendi the Jaʿaliyyīn had already paid more than they thought reasonable and were not prepared either economically or psychologically for Ismāʿīl's further demands. The revolt of the Jaʿaliyyīn was therefore triggered off by a policy of outright extortion, based upon a profound misconception of the revenue capacity of the Nile Valley as well as of the limits of Sudanese tolerance.

AFTER THE REBELLION

1823 witnessed a series of repressive campaigns along the Nile, north and south of Shendi. The human and economic losses were large and Shendi never fully recovered the prosperity it had enjoyed a few years before. No significant changes in administrative goals and methods were carried out; the taxes were gradually increased to cover the expenses and to enable the transfers of tribute to Cairo.

The sources of revenue ranged from direct taxes to dues, customs and concessions.[17] However, the present chapter concentrates mainly on agricultural revenues in Berber Province, first because of their importance to the provincial treasury and secondly because of the effect they had on the farming communities along the Nile. The *sāqiya* became the cornerstone of the tax system.

The Turks had very unclear ideas about the level of productivity in the Nile Valley south of Aswān and the insignificant role of money in the economy. Shendi market, where money did play a role, was not representative of the riverain economy in general. To simplify the collection of taxes in cash, a large-scale introduction of Egyptian coins was required, either as payment for exports or as salaries for employees and soldiers. However, this occurred only occasionally and was not the result of any clear and consistent monetary policy. Money was transferred from time to time to pay the soldiers, but more often than not the latter were left waiting for their pay and had to accept slaves in lieu of money. *Ḥikimdārs* such as Aḥmad Pasha could even reverse the flow of cash by transferring to Cairo large sums of dollars and gold collected from the Sudanese.[18]

Muḥammad ʿAlī, however, must take most of the blame for the financial difficulties, which he aggravated by extreme pressure on his officials in the Sudan. He reproached Khūrshīd Pasha for not sending him more cash, to which Khūrshīd replied, 'If my [*sic*] Sinnarians cultivated ten times more than they actually do, they will have nothing but cereals and animals to give you, and no money at all.'[19] Nevertheless Muḥammad ʿAlī was relentless in his demands and wrote to Khūrshīd, 'I do not understand how each time that I ask you for tribute, you object on the grounds of the poverty of the subjects, whom I have given you to govern; *they have two Niles whereas I have only one*; make these lazy ones work like I do in Egypt, and they will become rich.'[20]

The estimates of total annual revenues must be regarded as highly unreliable, at least before the 1870s; Khūrshīd Pasha collected an estimated 25,000 *kīs* (purses of 500 piastres) from the whole of the Sudan, probably excluding profits from slave raids. Under his successor Aḥmad Pasha (1838–43), the annual figure rose to 33,000 purses, plus 7,000 purses from the slave raids. At the same time the annual estimated revenues from Berber Province reached 5,900 or 6,000 purses (2,950,000 to 3,000,000 piastres) which was nearly twice what Maḥū Bey set out to collect in 1822 (1,587,000 piastres) and four times the sum he actually managed to collect (725,000 piastres).[21]

Rüppell and Brocchi were among the first European observers after the revolt to outline the system of taxation and they confirm the rates quoted from the *Funj Chronicle* above. Brocchi travelling in 1825–6 says that the annual tax on each slave was 15 dollars (about 194 piastres at that time), as was the tax on cattle and camels, while the *sāqiya* paid 12 dollars.[22] If Brocchi's *tallari* and Rüppell's *Speciesthaler* were roughly equal in value, then the latter's *sāqiya* rate was even higher. Rainland and flooded riverain land paid according to the *jadʿa* (c.5¼ *faddān*) at a rate of 21 piastres per *faddān* under Khūrshīd and 31½ under Aḥmad Pasha. While the taxes on *sāqiyas*, slaves and camels often equalled their market value, taxes on cattle could actually exceed it.[23]

The high rates can only be explained by the fact that there was no direct tax proportionate to production or earnings; it was easier and more convenient to tax fixed property and assets. Those who gained their livelihood from trade paid 5 dollars a year, in addition to the general house tax and the capitation tax of about 32 piastres, similar to the Egyptian system.[24] Except in the case of traders and craftsmen, and various groups of workers, who paid a tax on their estimated incomes, taxes were generally based on the assumed economic benefits which their assets were supposed to provide their owner, or the assumed wealth of those who could afford to possess certain assets. However, these principles enabled the Turks to manipulate the rates to their advantage.[25] The high slave taxes may have been one-time levies rather than a permanent measure, since they are not referred to in later sources. They were thus similar to the extra tax in the form of slaves imposed in Dongola in 1821–4, whereby every five *sāqiyas* had to hand over a slave to the government. If there were no slaves, 20 dollars were demanded instead.[26] It is difficult to see how landlords and merchants, not to speak of the average peasant, could expand the employment of agricultural slaves under such conditions. Taxes on slaves or in the form of slaves continued less systematically throughout the whole Turkiyya, but necessarily at lower rates.

Rüppell who travelled in the area between 1823 and 1825 thought that the new administration would not last long both because of its severity and because the costs outweighed its revenues. When the Turks set out to measure the land and count the wheels, they came to the conclusion that the ratio of land as well as of man to wheel was too high from a fiscal point of view. The number of *sāqiyas* from Wādī Ḥalfā to beyond Dār Shāyqiyya, or roughly within Dongola Province, was estimated at 5,250, which supported an average of eighteen people each. The Turks decided that the area to each *sāqiya* should be cut down and the excess land should provide for about a thousand more *sāqiyas*. In order to redistribute the labour force, a maximum of four adult men were allowed to work and depend on each wheel.[27] Henceforth, taxes were assessed according to these norms, regardless of whether more *sāqiyas* were built or not.[28]

Except for the two northern districts of Dongola Province, each *sāqiya* paid 15 dollars (195 piastres) annually, partly in cash and partly in grain calculated at a 'very low price', for example four *ardabbs* at 7½ dollars. Finally, each *sāqiya* had to deliver an unspecified quantity of butter, sheep, tobacco, onions, cotton, charcoal, hens, leather sacks and fodder. In total the *sāqiya* paid about 23 dollars (or 209 piastres) a year.[29] Assuming that the *sāqiya* yielded only one harvest annually, which was not always the case, as we have seen, Rüppell calculated the net surplus of *sāqiya* and *sallūka* cultivation and possible other incomes of a household at 1,014 piastres. Ten years later, Hoskins calculated the net surplus of a *sāqiya* devoted to indigo at about 2 piastres a day, which excluded *sallūka* and extra-farm incomes. In 1881 the net return, before taxes, of a food-producing *sāqiya* had sunk to below an average of 1 piastre a day, which must have been far below the level of viability.[30]

By 1825–6 the price of certain commodities such as cattle and durra had increased markedly compared with 1821. Consequently, while in 1823–4 the tax on a *sāqiya* equalled the price of three average cows, two years later one and a half to two cows sufficed.[31] Usually the Turks calculated the total taxes in cash, and the value of the fraction paid in kind was calculated below the market price, so that relatively more in kind had to be handed over to make up the tax in monetary terms. When the Turks were selling from their granaries, they reversed the principle, and might force merchants to accept grain above the market price.[32] It can be estimated that from a quarter to three-quarters of the tax was collected in cash depending on local circumstances. The rest had to be set aside from the harvest, and even if it was not collected at once right after the harvest, the peasants were not able to sell this produce when the prices were favourable so as to gain from the difference of the market price and the government price, and let the Turks have cash instead. It was more likely that in critical periods, the peasants consumed the grain thus set aside for the tax-collectors and had to borrow from the grain stores of the traders. It seems therefore safe to say that whether the taxes were paid in cash or in kind, the peasants lost in either case.

The people knew they were being manipulated and cheated whenever they paid in kind. It was, however, worse to be forced to sell valuable property, means of production, or the produce of the land when the prices were low, in order to pay the taxes in cash. When Maḥū Bey was transferred to Khartoum in 1825, he promised not to impose taxes in cash for three years. However, to obtain cash in another way, he raided the camel nomads of al-Qaḍārif and sent 3,000 camels to Sinnār, Wad Madanī and Khartoum, and ordered the *kāshifs* to force the people to buy them for 9 dollars each.[33]

The question of monetisation will be discussed in Chapter 6, but several features of this process are relevant here. Desperate small revolts by peasants are constantly reported throughout the Turkiyya, these being protests against taxation, both the method of collection, amount, and the proportion demanded in cash. A petition of 1298/1881, on the eve of the Mahdist revolt, concerned with production of *dammūr* to facilitate the payment of taxes in Dār al-Shāyqiyya, is an example of this continuing conflict. The petitioners complained that on the one hand the government demanded a large part of the taxes in cash (such as the *sallūka*, date and slave tax) whereas on the other hand, the people were prevented from producing a special kind of *tōb* which could earn them the cash needed.[34] Thus peasants and others resorted to the merchants to obtain grain advances and borrow money, offering repayment under the most unfavourable terms, in the form of grain at the next harvest. It was therefore the taxation system more than anything else, which encouraged rural borrowing and indebtedness (the famous *shayl* system) and enabled the new merchant class to channel part of their commercial capital out of commodity circulation and into the agricultural sector as usury capital and investment capital.

TAX COLLECTING

The principles and methods of taxation took form in the 1820s; they became permanent and feared institutions under ʿAlī Khūrshīd Pasha. When the expected revenues from trade and commercial agriculture failed, the administration had to rely more and more on the *ṭulba* to fill the treasury. A system was developed for recording collected revenues, but it was far more difficult to make reliable budgets for the revenues and expenses of the coming fiscal year. Thus the word 'deficit', so often encountered in the sources, may mean different things; apart from the negative difference between estimated revenues and estimated expenses, in which case it had only a theoretical significance, it more often meant the negative difference between realised and estimated revenues. However, real 'deficit' obtained only when the expenses of a year were found to be larger than the incomes. All these meanings of 'deficit' seem to occur indiscriminately in the sources, which makes the reconstruction of the fiscal and financial history of any given province even more difficult, in view of the fact that the account books have disappeared.

The collection of taxes was usually a military operation, led largely by the Shāyqiyya irregulars (*bāshībūzuqs*, from Turk. *bazūq*, lit. 'crack-brained'). A former soldier says the following:

> the members of the regimental band were frequently called out for duty in patrols against the local inhabitants. The way in which the government collected taxes was to send out soldiers who went from house to house with the tax-gatherers. The soldier who accompanied the tax-gatherer was entitled to take, in addition, 1 per cent of the tax for himself. This was a very profitable business for the soldiers who drew no pay during tax collection but lived on their share of the takings.[35]

Beatings and other forms of maltreatment were inflicted upon those who did not pay. The clerks, book-keepers, accountants and weighers were at all levels key personnel. As their expertise in keeping accounts was not shared by their superiors, they could easily purloin part of the taxes for their own benefit and were therefore regarded with suspicion by both the Turks and the tax-payers alike. The other key figures were the *kāshifs*, assisted by their *qā'im maqāms* and soldiers. Their Sudanese counterparts were the shaykhs and the commoners, and the growing intermediate class of merchants and money lenders. These were the main actors in the drama of tax-collecting.

Instructions about the assessment and collection of taxes were transmitted down the hierarchy of officials. It was well known that each subordinate official and soldier collected more than ordered for his own pocket. The village shaykh was also involved. Peasants who paid in instalments might receive receipts showing a sum lower than they had actually handed over. Similarly, the peasants were cheated because the officials 'kept two sets of measures and two of weights: a large set for receiving and a short set for issuing. And so the peasant is brazenly robbed without being able to complain, for fear of the stick, a very persuasive instrument among the Turks.'[36] The chronicler goes on to tell the story about the *kāshif* who cheated those who paid in gold-dust by emptying it onto some angora fur for examination before he had it weighed. It was all the extraordinary, 'illegal' exactions which really made the taxation system unbearable for the people.[37]

The tribute that was sent occasionally to Cairo did not impress Muḥammad ʿAlī or his successors; extra contributions were constantly demanded. Thus Aḥmad Pasha was asked to send 10,000 ounces of gold, which triggered off a large-scale campaign to collect gold. The precious metal was officially bought at 350 piastres per ounce, while the market value rose to 700 piastres; 30,000 ounces were collected, says the chronicler.[38]

Under this type of bureaucracy, as long as revenues were satisfactory, there was little daily control over subordinates until popular complaints and agitations and accusations from rivals and enemies endangered stability. Stealing from the Treasury was considered far more serious than squeezing the peasantry, and when such cases were discovered, as on several occasions in Berber Province, it was easier to get rid of undesired officials than to try to change the system. When no other culprits could be found, there was always the Coptic book-keeper who could easily be blamed for irregularities. This happened in Shendi and al-Matamma where the chief accountants were hanged by Aḥmad Pasha during his tour in the north in 1839 to audit the books. In Shendi, the inspectors found that 1/24th of the durra in the granary had been removed and replaced by an equal amount of dirt.[39]

THE *SĀQIYA* TAX

Along the Nile the *sāqiya*, and to a lesser extent the *shadūf*, were the basic units of taxation. Taxes were also estimated by the square measures of the *jadʿa* and the *faddān* on flooded and rainfed land. In the Shendi area, the rainfed *ʿaṭmūr* was vital for the supply of durra in good years, and the taxation of this production was deeply resented when imposed in poor years.

It was only slowly realised that the *sāqiya* depended on a variety of factors, the most important of which were the condition of the soil, the level of the water, the availability of seed, labour, and bulls. However, little is known of a possible classification of *sāqiya* before the 1850s, when the *sāqiya* were classified into three categories. Evidence suggests that in the early Turkiyya the average tax on a wheel was about 200 to 300 piastres.[40] The rates varied within Berber Province, however, from one district to the next, and to the nominal taxes were added extra levies imposed on the peasants. The proportion to be delivered in kind was obviously fixed for one season at a time.[41] It is therefore extremely difficult, if not impossible, to give any reliable figures for the total amount paid by a *sāqiya* in any one year. Not even the Turks managed, or bothered, to keep detailed track of collected revenues over a year. A large unknown amount never reached the treasury, and even the real number of working wheels was unknown to the Turks most of the time.

There was a gradual rise in the rates from between 200 to 300 piastres in the 1820s to between 400 to 600 piastres in the 1850s. As in Egypt, this development was partly in response to diminishing returns from agricultural taxation.[42] Hamilton reports a tax increase in the first half of the 1850s, but goes on to say that the revenues were still shrinking and failed to match expenses; only 36,000 purses entered the treasury annually. This he compares with the situation in the early 1840s when, he says, 14,000 ounces of gold had been sent to Cairo annually, probably referring to the extraordinary contributions levied by Aḥmad Pasha.

Hamilton's estimates of the *sāqiya* taxation must be exaggerated. Referring to Dongola, he says that the number of *sāqiya* had sunk by 1854 from 5,000 to less than 2,000; as one example, the number on Arqū Island had sunk from 800 to less than 10. The official tax was 404 piastres plus one slave a year; the latter's market value was about 1,200 piastres while the government valued the slave at 600. Thus the nominal tax was 1,004 piastres and the actual tax 1,604. This sum, if correct, seems rather like the expropriations of the 1820s, when we consider all the other impositions on the peasants and the gross amount a *sāqiya* unit could possibly produce over a year. However, it indicates a serious trend which is confirmed by others. Thus Taylor says that a *sāqiya* just north of al-Dabba was nominally taxed at 300 piastres, but paid in reality 475, and, strangely enough, in the poorer areas of Sukkūt and Maḥas the real tax was 600 piastres. Many peasants had left for Egypt, Kordofan and other places, and those who stayed behind became more dependent upon dates as their staple food.[43] The Turkish administration was clearly heading towards an economic breakdown, and the time had come for an honest review of the situation.

REFORMS AND SET-BACKS, 1857–69

Even friends and apologists of the Turks as well as Muḥammad Saʿīd himself admitted the grave abuses committed by his administration before his visit, 1856–7. They were, however, confident, after some feigned or real hesitation, that the malpractices could be eradicated.[44] The main tax reforms were expressed in his edicts promulgated in Khartoum in January 1857 and may be listed as follows:

1 Taxes were to be regulated according to the size of the village population, which meant reduced contributions from villages where there had been considerable emigration.
2 Free movement, that is emigration, was to be allowed and no longer regarded as flight or desertion.
3 The tax rates were to be decided in cooperation with local shaykhs, according to the following reduced figures:
   a) The rate of a *sāqiya* in Berber Province was reduced from 250 piastres (nominal tax) to 200 piastres;
   b) Island lands (*jazā'ir*) were to pay 25 piastres per *faddān*;
   c) Flooded river bank land (*jarf*) to pay 20.
4 The *mudīr* was to be advised by a council of notables; they were to come together in the slack season to negotiate the taxes to be levied on a

monthly basis, the largest part of which was to be collected after the main harvest.

5 The irregulars (*bāshībūzuq*) were to be kept away from the collection of taxes; local shaykhs were to be responsible, receiving as payment the tax from one *sāqiya* in every twenty-five and similarly from one *faddān* in every twenty-five *faddān* of flooded or rainfed land.

6 The shaykhs were to count the *sāqiyas* and measure the land and lists were to be sent to the province headquarters.

7 Taxes were to be paid by the one who sowed the seed.

8 The new tax rate was to begin from the year 1272 AH (beginning 13 September 1856) on *sāqiya*, flooded and rainfed land.

9 Nomads who also cultivated were not to pay more than one tax, the one of their fields.[45]

Promising, not to say idealistic, as these reforms may look, economic conditions along the Nile continued to deteriorate. These paragraphs are therefore more revealing as to what was considered to be the main problems in the taxation system, than what was actually achieved in terms of improvements. In fact, the reforms involved a greater dependence upon agricultural revenues than before, while the removal of the capitation tax and reduction in animal taxes favoured nomads and other non-cultivators (traders and craftsmen). Critical observers, therefore, attributed the continuing decline in agricultural production and the rising prices precisely to these reforms. The irregular soldiery were employed to collect the taxes as before.[46]

The continuing financial problems were also blamed on the independent and separate status of the Sudanese provinces; they were brought together again under Mūsā Pasha Ḥamdī (1862–5). However, the latter's policy was apparently more harmful; Heuglin reported that:

> He [Mūsā Pasha] intends to introduce great reforms in the organisation of government, especially of finance and of the army, and the governor-general has already imposed a good many new taxes. Formerly only peasants and Arabians [nomads] were taxed directly here in the Sudan, and the taxes were collected by their own *sheikh*, on whom no proper check could be kept and who pocketed as much as he pleased. This system is now being changed by the appointment of paid tax collectors, and a revision of the assessments themselves has been set on foot; everyone liable to be taxed receives a form showing how he is rated, and this is also used as a receipt. Now merchants and manufacturers, all officials, servants, sailors, etc. are to be taxed ... [at 12 per cent].[47]

This was perhaps not such an innovation as Heuglin imagined, considering the situation before 1857, but it is clear that the rates were raised markedly, and tax-paying became a duty for a larger section of the population. One aim was to tax the White Nile traffic more thoroughly, not only the boatmen, but particularly the big merchants, one of whom was John Petherick who consequently gave up trading on the White Nile.

Furthermore, thousands of agricultural slaves were recruited into the army, largely to be stationed in Kassala where a serious revolt erupted shortly afterwards. It is said that Mūsā Pasha managed to triple the taxes; the capitation tax rose from 33 to 100 piastres and the tribute from the nomads was quadrupled.[48]

Thus *sāqiyas* continued to fall out of production; in 1864 empty villages and uncultivated fields dominated the area between Shendi and Kabūshiyya. Lower production, bad harvests, cattle disease and confiscations meant that less food came to the markets. Food shortages and higher prices were observed in Berber in May–August 1864. The spread of cotton cultivation in the same period also affected food production. According to the shaykhs of Berber, so many peasants were leaving their cultivation 'for the rosy prospects of the White Nile trade that the province was experiencing a serious dearth of men to till the soil who were consequently depriving the treasury of taxes'.[49] However, instead of improving conditions in Berber, the governor-general decided to limit the White Nile traffic by, among other measures, imposing a tax (the so-called *wīrkū*) on each member of a ship's crew.

The enlarged army was a heavy burden upon revenues, in turn requiring more soldiers to collect the taxes; the vicious circle meant not only ruined villages near garrison towns like Shendi and along the military road north to Berber, but also unpaid and unruly soldiers, leading to a minor uprising in Berber. The estimated military expenses for the year 1281/1864–5 amounted to at least 73,346 purses, out of a total budget of some 85,310 purses. At the same time the revenues were estimated at about 46,500, forcing Mūsā Pasha to ask Cairo for 30,000 purses to pay his troops. Before him the annual revenues had been 20,000 purses, according to Lafargue, which if correct, shows that Mūsā Pasha managed to raise the revenues by more than 125 per cent.[50] Still the increased revenues did not cover the expenses and the deepening crisis reached its first peak with the severe famine of 1864–5.

The Khedive Ismāʿīl (1863–79) reacted to the abuses of Mūsā Pasha and appointed Jaʿfar Pasha Ṣādiq to clean up the mess. He was required to establish a regular budget and if cash was needed as a temporary relief from Cairo, he was encouraged to ask for it. This resulted in the transfer of 26,000 purses in 1865. The Ministry of Finance in Cairo estimated that the Sudan owed some 163,000 purses which it hoped was not completely lost. To relieve the pressure, however, Cairo agreed to cover a part of the military expenditure.[51]

In November 1865, Jaʿfar Pasha inspected Berber Province on his way to Khartoum and appointed ʿUmar Bey as *mudīr*. The high Nile promised better times, but in the meantime, at the Khedive's initiative, durra was distributed in Berber, Kassala and Khartoum. It was under these gloomy conditions that a last group of Nimrāb refugees returned from Ethiopia to Shendi.[52]

The Khedive was not, however, satisfied with the progress made and decided to replace Jaʿfar with a more energetic official who had impressed him when he was governor of Tāka, Jaʿfar Maẓhar Pasha. The Khedive Ismāʿīl encouraged him to learn from Mūsā Pasha's mistakes and act accordingly. The subsequent cuts in expenditure were in fact large enough to enable Jaʿfar Maẓhar to send a contribution of 15,000 purses to Cairo in 1867, in order to make a good impression. As if that was not enough, he promised to increase the annual contribution to 50,000 purses, according to Thibaut, which he tried to achieve by the dreaded method of increasing the taxes again by somewhere between one and two-thirds from the year 1283/1866–7. Thus Berber was taxed at 11,000 purses for the year 1285/1868–9, in addition to the usual illegal demands.[53]

Complaints soon reached the Khedive; for example, Muḥammad Darwīsh, *muʿāwin* or assistant of the governor of Berber, made allegations of venality, theft and embezzlement against his superior, the *mudīr* ʿAlī Bey ʿUwayḍa. An investigation was undertaken in Jaʿfar Maẓhar's absence, but when the latter passed through Berber from Egypt in 1868 he managed to cover up the scandal and Muḥammad Darwīsh was forced to withdraw his accusations. A few months later Jaʿfar Maẓhar admitted to Cairo that his investigations had in fact revealed some negligence on the part of the *mudīr* in collecting taxes, but the accusations of fraud brought against him by certain shaykhs and merchants were without foundation. Consequently, ʿAlī Bey was stripped of his property and replaced by Aḥmad Rāmī Efendi in 1867.[54]

Berber Province was, in the late 1860s, the scene of economic deterioration and extortion on an unprecedented scale. The circulation of money almost came to a halt, as did exports and imports, and the rate of emigration reached a new peak. At the end of 1285/1868–9, 4,000 purses remained to be collected and there was no hope that the 11,000 purses for the next year would ever be found.[55]

Both Baker, Schweinfurth and others noted signs of economic recession throughout Dār al-Jaʿaliyyīn, particularly between Shendi and al-Dāmir, but it was apparently only Schweinfurth who could not explain the causes of emigration.[56] Jaʿfar Maẓhar had been appointed governor-general to improve economic conditions and lessen the burden of taxation; what he achieved was a drastic increase in the taxes, just like his predecessors. The increasing tax pressure seems to have been motivated, not by the cost of administering a province like Berber, which was not particularly expensive, but by the huge costs of keeping a standing army and by Cairo's demands for tribute.

THE GOVERNORSHIP OF ḤUSAYN BEY KHALĪFA AL-ʿABBĀDĪ

Ḥusayn's name has been associated with cotton production, but he was active also in the promotion of agriculture in general, the building and registering of *sāqiyas*, and the revision of the taxation system in his province. Ḥusayn belonged to the chiefly family of the ʿAbābda who, as agents of the government, controlled the caravan route from Berber to Kuruskū. In 1869, Ḥusayn replaced Aḥmad Rāmī and was appointed the first Sudanese *mudīr* of Berber, on the understanding that a solution to the agricultural crisis was to be his main task. In other words, how to stop emigration and persuade those who had left to return and take up cultivation again.[57]

In 1871 the *ḥikimdāriyya* was again abolished in the Sudan. In the north, Berber was united with Dongola with Ḥusayn Bey (later Pasha) as *mudīr ʿumūm* over the combined provinces and Muḥammad Efendī Ḥijil as *ma'mūr* over Berber. In the centre and the south, Ismāʿīl Ayyūb Pasha became governor over the combined provinces of Khartoum, Sinnār, Kordofan and Fashoda, while the Eastern Sudan, including Kassala and Massawa and at its largest in 1873, came under the Swiss Johann A. W. Munzinger Pasha.[58]

By 1870 the tax arrears in Berber had reached 8,000 purses; the *sāqiya* tax had risen from 275 piastres in 1279/1862–3 to 534 piastres, *jazzā'ir* land from 25 to 64 piastres a *faddān*, and *jarf* from 20 to 53. The tribute from the nomads had risen from 403,487 piastres (c.807 purses) to 672,478 piastres (c.1,345 purses). Ḥusayn reported to Cairo that the taxes were estimated and collected at the level of the *khuṭṭ* (sub-district) which together with the lack of survey instruments to measure the land, made an equal distribution of the burden difficult to implement. To overcome the more obvious injustices, he suggested certain reforms which were endorsed by the Khedive. The *mudīr* of Upper Egypt was ordered to send the survey tools necessary to revise the cadastral survey. Meanwhile Ḥusayn was advised not to tax the cotton fields but instead to collect a tenth of the crop.[59]

Largely as a consequence of the new cadastral survey of 1870–1 an additional deficit of between 2,200 and 2,346 purses appeared in the revenues of the financial year of 1287 AH (beginning 11 September 1870) compared to the previous year.[60] This underlines the earlier over-estimates as well as the fact that uncultivated land and unused *sāqiyas* had been regularly taxed in the years preceding the new survey. The lower revenues were more realistic, considering the frequency of emigration, and Ḥusayn wrote to Cairo and asked that henceforth the taxes should be based on the revised survey. The letter was apparently not answered and the closing of the accounts of Berber was delayed. In a dispatch from the Privy Council (*majlis khuṣūṣī*) dated 1 July 1873 to Ḥusayn, he was ordered to impose the taxes in accordance with the assessment of 1286 AH (1869–70), that is the year before the revision, pending a decree on the subject. However, Ḥusayn had already collected the taxes according to the new survey, with the result that the accounts for the years 1288, 1289 and 1290 remained suspended.[61]

Ḥusayn's letters throw light on the problem of establishing a 'fair' tax on the *sāqiya*; the land irrigated by a *sāqiya* varied greatly in size and annual output. As one solution, the *mudīrs* now decided to fix the average land served by an island *sāqiya* at eight *faddān* and for a *sāqiya* on the riverbank at ten *faddān*; tax on additional land up to five *faddān* was paid by the owner(s), and the tax on any land beyond fifteen *faddān* was to be paid by the community as a whole.[62] This system, in so far as it was enforced, was a positive reversal of the policy in Dongola in the 1820s, in that more land was now allowed per *sāqiya* unit. However, it was probably also just another way of making the remaining population pay the taxes for vacated land.

When Ḥusayn took office in 1869, he recorded that 400 *sāqiyas* had gone out of use, and to reverse the trend, he fixed the tax on island *sāqiyas* at 500 piastres, and bank *sāqiyas* at 350; this apparently resulted in 300 wheels being repaired and 159 new ones built. He further proposed to write off some 902 purses, being the arrears for the financial year 1290/1873–4, in the belief that the loss would, after a period of three years, be recovered through increased population.

At this crucial point, Berber suffered from a suspension of durra imports from the south, as cash payments were now required. This led to strained relations with the authorities in the rainfed districts who were also in disagreement over the question of who had the right to tax the migrant Jaʿaliyyīn who had settled on the Blue Nile and southwards towards the Ethiopian border.[63]

Ḥusayn also tried to deal with the question of expenditures. Salaries took about one-tenth of the estimated revenues in Berber in 1866, rising to about a quarter in 1882.[64] Other expenditures were rations and transport; thus the camel transport across the deserts to Sawākin or to Egypt was deducted from the Berber treasury. Compared with Dongola, Berber was clearly at a disadvantage. However, Khartoum Province was even worse off because of its extra military and administrative expenditures, particularly in periods as now when the provinces were independent of each other and therefore not obliged to aid Khartoum directly. This was probably one reason why Ayyūb Pasha, as governor of Khartoum and the provinces further south, managed to convince the Khedive of the financial advantages of re-establishing the *ḥikimdāriyya* in 1873. The situation was so parlous that Ayyūb had once been obliged to borrow money from a leading merchant house, al-ʿAqqād.[65]

The time had again come for a serious reconsideration of the whole tax system and the causes of the diminishing returns. It was found that the shaykhs were deeply in debt to the merchants; the former were accused of large-scale embezzlement as they covered the interests on their loans by pressing more money out of the peasantry. Ayyūb endorsed the policy of building more *sāqiyas* and devoting more land to cotton, which could then be used to pay the taxes. The *mudīrs* were empowered to expropriate unused land and transfer it to people who would cultivate it. In a report to the Privy Council, Ayyūb criticised the tax reforms of Muḥammad Saʿīd, because from the beginning the government had taxed according to means (*sic*), whereas Saʿīd established taxation on the land measured in *faddān* (which we know was not entirely accurate). The result was, according to Ayyūb, that the people left the registered land near the river to take up cultivation in the rainfed areas, which since it changed every year, could not so easily be measured and assessed. In this way the government lost 33,600 purses in taxation. Mūsā Pasha had, however, partly restored the earlier system, including the capitation tax.[66]

Naturally the peasants left the lands that required the heaviest work and capital input and paid the highest taxes, to take up a more insecure but less taxed cultivation away from the Nile. Or they shifted entirely over to animal husbandry which was also relatively less taxed and at least more out of the reach of the Turks. Finally thousands left the primary sectors altogether to start as traders, servants, or as mercenaries and slave hunters on the White Nile. As long as the Turks did not see, or did not want to see, these elementary implications of their own policies, they remained ignorant of the causes of the miserable finances and the widespread poverty in the northern provinces. It was easier to blame corrupt officials rather than the system.

When Giegler stayed in Berber in the summer of 1873, he found Ḥusayn Bey in charge of an inquiry against several high officials, including the former *mudīr* Aḥmad Rāmī Bey, on suspicion of corruption.[67] This led to much political agitation and counter-accusations against Ḥusayn, who was accused of all kinds of abuses.[68] Finally, after Ḥusayn put his leading opponents in prison, the Khedive gave in and asked Ḥusayn to report to Cairo and a commission was set up in February 1874 to investigate all the charges against Ḥusayn, Aḥmad Rāmī anḍ Alī Bey ʿUwayḍa. The latter was thought to have been involved in the disappearance of a shipment of tribute from Khartoum. The commission was also to establish the causes of the arrears of 4,200 purses in Berber.

Meanwhile Ḥusayn made it clear that those who complained loudest were those who owed the most to the treasury. Account books had been falsified, he protested, in order to ruin his efforts to promote development.[69] A final effort by six village shaykhs of Berber, who presented a petition to the Khedive complaining about the way the taxes were imposed by ʿAlī Bey Sharīf in Ḥusayn's absence and lauding the conditions under Ḥusayn, produced no effect. On the other hand, Aḥmad Rāmī and ʿAlī Bey were found innocent by the commission.

THE DEEPENING ECONOMIC CRISIS, 1874–84

In Khartoum, Ayyūb Pasha was now governor-general of the whole of the Sudan, except for Munzinger's eastern province, and he set about cutting expenses in order to balance the budgets. Sometimes salaries were lowered or suspended and high-ranking officials were replaced by subordinates. As usual the army swallowed the biggest share, and this was a period of expansion into Dār Fūr in the west, into the southern Sudan, and south along the Red Sea Coast.

The salaries of the Berber ulama were suppressed in December 1873; they were offered land in compensation. The ulama (Muslim scholars) protested, however, that they were busy in the mosques and since the land offered them could not immediately be irrigated, it could not provide them with a living. Riḥān Aghā, former deputy governor of Berber, was the object of similar economising in the following year, 1874–5. He suffered from a serious illness which obliged him to have a medical examination every six months. Pending his recovery, he was put on half salary (1,000 piastres a month), but Ayyūb decided to provide him with land instead. He protested and Cairo reversed the decision.[70]

The cadastral survey of 1870–1 resulted in an annual deficit or loss in the land revenue of 2,346 purses compared with that which had been collected the preceding year. This discrepancy was never corrected since a final decision from Cairo seems never to have come. Although Ayyūb had used the deficit in the proceedings against Ḥusayn Bey, he was realistic enough to propose that the survey should be final and that the loss in taxes should be covered by an increase in the taxes on movable property, animals, and persons.

The next governor-general, Charles Gordon, 1877–9, started out as a reformer in many fields, but he inherited an overriding interest in the abolition of the slave trade from the time when he was governor of Equatoria, 1874–6, and found less time for the fiscal problems. His main objective was to get the northern traders out of the south but without attacking the causes of why so many of them had gone south in the first place. He appointed a young Austrian officer, Rudolf von Slatin, as financial inspector to examine the issue of taxation in the northern and central provinces. After his appointment in February 1879, Slatin made a tour up the Blue Nile. He reported that the government did not regard the taxes as unreasonably high and therefore the complaints and social unrest were difficult to account for, as usual. However, he found that:

> the distribution of taxes was unjust, and resulted in the bulk of taxation falling on the poorer landed proprietors, whilst those who were better off had no difficulty in bribing the tax-gatherers, for a comparatively small sum, to secure exemption. Thus enormous quantities of land and property entirely escaped taxation, whilst the poorer classes were mercilessly ground down, in order to make up the heavy deficit which was the result of this most nefarious system.
>
> I further pointed out that much of the present discontent was due to the oppressive and tyrannical methods of the tax-gatherers, who were for the most part soldiers, Bashi-Bozuks, and Shaigias.[71]

As he could do nothing to change the system, Slatin sent in his report together with his resignation. Gordon Pasha himself resigned towards the end of the year, after appointing Slatin as governor of Dār Fūr. The problem of taxation was therefore passed on to the next governor-general, Muḥammad Ra'ūf Pasha (1880–2).

After a preliminary investigation in Dongola and Berber and having been met with complaints and misery everywhere, Ra'ūf submitted a report to Cairo. The crux of the problem was excessive estimates and over-taxation, which Ra'ūf considered had begun in 1872 under Mumtāz Pasha, the famous promoter of cotton production in the Eastern Sudan in the 1860s, and governor of the combined central provinces of Khartoum, Sinnār (with Fāzūghlī), Fashoda (White Nile) and Kordofan, 1871–2.[72] He proposed to cut the taxes by a quarter. The tax on the *sāqiya* had risen from 500 piastres to 640, which was considered too high. The response from Cairo was negative; he was advised to appoint tax-assessment officers who knew their districts well and in the future to present more reliable budgets.

In the following year (April 1881), another report on the question of taxation appeared, probably also on Muḥammad Ra'ūf's initiative. Attached to it were the proceedings of a committee of Dongola notables. The report and the proceedings were unanimous in describing the deplorable situation in Dongola and Berber.[73] A substantial reduction in the taxes seemed the only solution, while eroded *jarf* land and the numerous abandoned *sāqiyas* should be removed from the assessment lists. Referring to the proceedings of the Dongola notables, Stewart noted that they gave,

> a melancholy account . . . of the ruin this excessive taxation brought on the country. Many were reduced to destitution, others had to emigrate, and so much land went out of cultivation that in 1881, in the province of Berber, there were 1,442 abandoned sakiyés, and in Dongola 613.[74]

The commission of notables gave further details.

> they had begun by carefully calculating the earnings and cost of working of two sakiyés irrigating fair average land, and that, after deducting all expenses, including the maintenance of the cultivators, they had found that the net returns, exclusive of taxes, were for one sakiyé 391 piastres, and for the other 201 piastres . . . They then state how the cultivator, in order to meet the tax, is compelled either to depend on other sources, to sell his cattle, or to borrow.[75]

To this last statement we may add Stewart's own observation (p. 14) two years later, that 'notably . . . in the Province of Dongola . . . it is notorious that the people would be quite unable to pay the tax if they were not assisted by other members of the family who are employed in other trades'. This he says even after admitting that the taxes were reduced after the 1881 report. He gathered from this report that the tax increase on a first class *sāqiya* from 1856–7 to 1881 had been around 200 per cent (from 200 to 500 plus 107 piastres on each *sāqiya* to cover arrears, salaries, etc.). To turn this general upward trend, the 1881 report had put forward the following main proposals:

1 To reduce the *sāqiya* tax from 500 piastres to 400, with the exception of some 130 *sāqiyas* which should be charged only 350 piastres, and some at the cataracts which should only pay 250 piastres.

Table 4 *Tax rates in 1883*

A The *sāqiya* in Dongola Province.		
1 class *sāqiya*	500 piastres	
2	400	
3	350	
4	300	(at the cataracts)
B The *sāqiya* in Berber Province.		
1 class *sāqiya*	450 piastres	
2	400	30 paras
3	350	
4	281	10 paras
C The *matara* (well-*sāqiya*).		
1 class *sāqiya*	350 piastres	
2	250	
3	175	
D The *shadūf*.		
1 class *shadūf*	350 piastres	
2	250	
E Island and riverbed land (*jazā'ir*).		
1 class, per *faddān*	60 piastres	10 paras
2	60	
3	52	20 paras
F *Jarf*.		
1 class, per *faddān*	45 piastres	
2	26	10 paras
3	22	20 paras
G. *Karrū*. (In Berber Province only; including perhaps also rainfed ʿ*aṭmūr* land.)		
1 class, per *faddān*	56 piastres	20 paras
2	40	3 paras
3	28	10 paras
4	28	5 paras
5	15	
H Date palms.		
Per palm tree	2 piastres	

2 Each *shadūf* was to be taxed at 100 piastres.
3 Each *matara* (well-*sāqiya*) to pay 300 piastres.
4 Land on islands (*jazā'ir*) to pay 40 piastres per *faddān*.
5 *Jarf* land to pay 35 piastres per *faddān*.
6 Land no longer irrigated should not be taxed.

7 To remit the taxes due on abandoned *sāqiyas* since 1877, with a view of encouraging the return of the owners.
8 Upon the payment of a tax of 350 piastres, to allow the site of an abandoned *sāqiya* to be reoccupied.
9 To appoint honest and capable land surveyors.
10 To discontinue the levying of taxes on lands and dates carried away by the flood.
11 To reduce the tax on *karrū* land by 25 piastres per *faddān*.

It is uncertain to what extent all these proposals were accepted by the authorities, but Stewart was of the opinion that some improvements had been made under Muḥammad Ra'ūf. The rates found in operation in the two northern provinces of Dongola and Berber in 1883 indicate some restraints, but not any clear reversal, in the growth of the taxes. Classification rested on soil qualities, but *sāqiyas* irrigating more than eight *faddāns* were charged proportionately more.[76]

In response to popular demand, certain smaller taxes on ferry-boats, beer and so on had been abolished, and to cover the loss, the government added some 1.14 per cent to the rates in Table 4 in the case of Berber Province.

The figures here quoted indicate that flooded and rainfed lands were on the average taxed at the same rate as *sāqiya* land in terms of acreage, that is a good *sāqiya* could be charged 50 to 60 piastres per *faddān*, if it irrigated the allotted eight *faddān*. In reality, it would irrigate on the average only half that area, and the actual tax was therefore some 100 to 120 piastres per *faddān*. The *sāqiya*'s ability to produce two harvests in a year decreased dramatically during the Turkiyya, and when we consider that the *sāqiya* system was both capital and labour-intensive, we may safely conclude that the *sāqiya*-tax was relatively much higher. Even the scanty evidence available clearly shows that after the household(s) depending on a *sāqiya* had set aside what was needed for reproduction, there was not enough left to pay the taxes. To carry on, peasants were compelled to alienate part of their capital (e.g. animals), to reduce consumption to a minimum, to engage in part-time trade or wage labour, to borrow or to rely on remittances from family members engaged in other activities in the diaspora. The loss in manpower through emigration was outweighed by having fewer mouths to feed and the crucial capital infusion from other sectors, particularly trade, which kept many villages from dying completely out. However, these were only temporary solutions for many, and when the pressure from creditors and the government became too great, it was always the *sāqiya* cultivation that was given up first. This development is also reflected in Stewart's budget for 1882, in which the taxes collected from some 3,000 *sāqiyas* in Berber Province are less than 50 per cent of the total land taxes. Emigration was not the only alternative, particularly for the older established sections of the population, who might prefer to build on the animals left and embark on animal husbandry, or to concentrate on flooded and rainfed cultivation, often in combination with the keeping of animals.

The system of agricultural taxation analysed in this chapter was intimately connected with the government's general plans to turn a subsistence economy into a profit-oriented market economy, from which the government could extract a surplus, indirectly through taxation, and directly through labour service and the expropriation of cash crops. The growth in taxes clearly surpassed inflation and can best be understood against the background of the failure of the cash crops to constitute the basic revenue producing sector. When the expected crops were not delivered, the peasants found that taxes on their food production were to compensate for this loss in revenue, irrespective of the fact that cash crop production in the mean time had given the agricultural economy a lethal blow.

The question then remains: was there any financial or other reasons why the Turks were willing to risk undermining their own rule in order to implement this ruinous taxation system? The administration of the Sudan was not particularly bureaucratic and overstaffed – in 1866 there were only some 200 salaried officials in Berber – but the large garrisons, the military campaigns, the widespread corruption and the tribute to Cairo, easily turned a budgetary surplus into a deficit for the Sudan as a whole. Thus, in Berber the final accounts for 1881 reveal that £E 40,683.55 33 para (8136.7 purses) were collected, and after expenditures of £E 14,410.98 29 para (2888.2 purses), a surplus of £E 26,272.57 4 para (5,254.5 purses) were recorded. The following year £E 42,529.85 18 para were collected, of which £E 23,915.79 27 para were recorded as surplus after expenses. The average annual revenue in Berber Province was around £E 43,000 in the nine years between 1870 and 1879. It was always below *estimated* revenues, but probably above expenditures, the figures for which have not been recovered as yet.[77] Giegler's financial notes from 1878, probably referring to the fiscal year of 1877 (the fiscal year followed the Christian calendar after 1875), confirm to the pattern in which the taxes collected in Berber Province were below estimated or 'lawful' taxes, but still the revenues far outweighed expenditures. The same pattern obtained in Dongola, Kordofan, Sinnār, Sawākin and Massawa, and Tākā (Kassala).[78] To this we may add the sums that were exacted but never recorded, thus making the total amount collected much higher still than what seems reasonable when comparing them with the provincial expenditures.

It is therefore tempting to conclude that the systematic policy of exploitation could not be justified on the grounds of an expensive administration alone. The Jaʿalī tax-payers in the north were also expected to contribute financially to military expansion in the east, south and west, to the Cairo Treasury, to industrial experiments, to the development of communications, such as the river steamers, the post and telegraph service, and finally the beginning of a railway from Egypt to Khartoum. The overruling principle of short-term profit which guided the government militated against any efforts to use the revenues for long-term investments and development for the benefit of the rural communities. The taxation system and all the additional irregular expropriations were channels for a one-way flow of resources out of the peasant economy, and represented surplus appropriation in its purest and most violent form.

'Kill the Turks and cease to pay taxes!', was a war cry that many people could immediately identify with under the Mahdist Revolution, and Shuqayr regarded the tax system as one of the causes of the revolution. Holt admits that it was a source of permanent grievance, 'but it was frequently evaded by the flight of the victims from their homes to remoter districts where the authority of the government was less felt'.[79] In this perspective, however, the tax system still played a crucial role in the Mahdist Revolution, as it swelled the ranks of unruly northern slave hunters and traders in the south. It was largely the Jaʿaliyyīn and the Danāgla in the south who, forced northwards by Gordon after 1877, carried the flag of the Mahdiyya to al-Ubayyiḍ, Khartoum, Shendi and Berber. Their subdued peasant brothers who had remained in the north, naturally responded more slowly to the call of the Mahdī. On his return to the Sudan in early 1884, Gordon announced substantial tax reductions and the remittance of all arrears in an effort to turn the tide, but it was too late.

The somewhat lengthy expositions of the agricultural economy of the Jaʿaliyyīn, land use systems, commercial crops and the fiscal policy of the Turks, have been necessary both intrinsically and to provide a basis for the following examination of trade and emigration. It has been shown that some of the characteristics of the *sāqiya* system and the peasant economy in general militated against the unrealistic hopes of the government to extract huge profits from the agricultural sector. Although a sophisticated instrument of irrigation, the *sāqiya* was not *ipso facto* an 'easier' or more remunerative form of cultivation. On the contrary, as Boserup has argued, technological improvements of this type often mean less output per man-hour. Thus the centuries-old, and capital and labour-intensive instrument may best be understood in light of population pressure and limited flooded land. In Egypt, for example, large-scale building of *sāqiyas* was first undertaken by Muḥammad ʿAlī, and then largely for commercial agriculture which required perennial irrigation. Until then the huge naturally flooded basins along the Nile had provided the bulk of agricultural produce.[80]

6

The transformation of commerce

THE TURKIYYA FRAMEWORK

As Lejean wrote in a report in 1862, the imposition of the Turkish colonial regime radically disrupted and changed traditional commerce.[1] It was widely held, not only in the Ottoman Empire, that trade was vital to economic development and prosperity, but the fact that commerce between unequal partners has a tendency to turn into exploitation was given less consideration. The Sudanese traders, confronted with the new situation, sought to reformulate their strategies in order to cope with the new restrictions as well as to take advantage of the new opportunities.

With so much emphasis on commercial exploitation it was only natural that merchants of all categories, both local and foreign, came to play a significant, if not always heroic role in the spread of the colonial economy. However, in areas where huge profits were expected, the government tried as long as they could to keep the independent traders out, and for this and several other reasons, the relationship between the Turks and the traders fluctuated.[2] The Turkish Sudan attracted foreign traders and speculators of every type, some of whom made fortunes. Among the Sudanese traders, Jaʿaliyyīn and others, some learned the new rules of the game quickly and became successful, particularly in the diaspora, whereas the majority remained or became petty traders.

An economic system may be defined substantively as the production, circulation and consumption of commodities. The bulk of the commodities in circulation were foodstuffs, natural products and manufactured commodities of local, regional and foreign origin. More people came in touch with the market, both along the Nile and in the peripheral areas, some as professional middlemen, but the majority as sellers or customers or both. However, the principles of market exchange could not have spread so far and taken such firm roots without the trading expertise and networks of the Jaʿaliyyīn, the Danāgla and others from the north.

A fundamental feature of Jaʿalī society was a diversified occupational structure without a complex social differentiation. Economic strategies involved a combination of pursuits, either simultaneously or over time. Brothers might coordinate their activities so that one or more cultivated their common land, while others traded. Also today a man's career may shift between farming, trading, public service, and a craft, which naturally requires knowledge and expertise in each field.

The variety of individual and collective economic interests sprang out of the social, economic and political opportunities and constraints along the Nile. The limited resources available as well as their socially and politically defined distribution made it sensible to be familiar with and rely on several economic options. Seen in retrospect, this flexibility of Jaʿalī society became crucial during the Turkiyya, enabling them to adjust and survive, either within the Turkish dominion or on its frontiers. As we have seen, the Jaʿalī peasants were not favoured by the Turks. Despite this, or perhaps because of this, many Jaʿaliyyīn sought to establish themselves as entrepreneurs in order to get out of the depressing conditions in riverain agriculture. This process coincided with and contributed to the opening up of the White Nile in the 1840s and the Baḥr al-Gahzāl in the 1850s, when thousands of northerners turned slave hunters and slave traders (*jallāba*) and joined the Klondyke-like rush for slaves and ivory.

At the same time as more traders entered the commercial sector, the new government introduced a trade monopoly which severely restricted free pricing and exchange of commodities. Trading in monopoly commodities required government concessions. This system was against both local and foreign commercial interests, and the term *jallāba* lost much of its former connotation of caravan traders and became more associated with petty trading and the slave trade. Thus the *jallāba* who operated in long-distance trade and apparently welcomed the invasion, soon found themselves worse off than before.[3] Admittedly the Turkiyya united a vast area to the benefit of the traders, not least in regard to security and better communications, such as a regular river traffic, and later also a postal and telegraph service. But the old local lords exacting taxes, bribes and presents along the Nile, were now replaced by a row of customs stations which cost the traders as much.

The ʿAbābda had traditionally controlled the desert route between Berber and Egypt, and the Turks confirmed this monopoly in the Khalīfa shaykhly family in exchange for future cooperation. During the Turkiyya, ʿAbābda camel drivers and guides were engaged further south, for instance between Omdurman and al-Ubayyiḍ, and they became the backbone in the operation of the postal service, from as far west as Dār Fūr and south as Fāzūghlī.[4] The Turks were similarly dependent upon the Bishāriyyīn for the route from Berber to Sawākin, and on the Kabābīsh for the Kordofan–Dongola route.

Both foreign and local traders were united against the monopoly system and the prohibition of private trade on the White Nile in the 1840s, but the subsequent gradual disappearance of government restrictions benefited the foreign merchants more directly than the Sudanese in the first round. The former possessed the necessary capital for investment in commodities, partnerships, boats, sailors and private servants and soldiers, whereas many of the latter functioned also as agents, partners, servants and soldiers in the service of the foreigners. In this way, operating on the frontier of Turkish control, the northerners gained capital and slaves, commercial and military expertise, which later turned out to be a dangerous combination for the government. In his efforts to control and tax the trade on the White Nile, Mūsā Pasha Ḥamdī (1862–5), inaugurated the gradual disappearance of foreign merchant firms on the White Nile. The 1860s and 1870s saw therefore a great influx of independent northern traders and adventurers, partly by river and partly by land, into the areas of the Upper White Nile and the Baḥr al-Ghazāl. There the new empires of Muḥammad Khayr al-Arqāwī, a Dongolāwī, and al-Zubayr Raḥma Manṣūr, a Jaʿalī, rapidly surpassed the areas controlled by the remaining foreign merchants such as Ghaṭṭās, al-ʿAqqād and Küchük ʿAlī.[5] Thus northern Sudanese traders opened up vast new territories for the Egyptian government, which later came in and replaced the merchant princes.

This happened at a time when, in response to international pressure, the first serious anti-slavery measures were imposed in the Sudan. During the Turkiyya, slavery had become more widespread and economically important in the Sudan, particularly in the rainfed areas, and numerous prominent merchants as well as the average *jallāba* had their whole fortunes attached to the slave trade. A serious conflict was therefore building up between the authorities and the *jallāba* and slave owners. European governors, such as Baker, Gordon and Gessi were appointed to the south in order to attack the problem at its roots. The conflict reached its first violent peak with Gessi's war against, and killing of, Sulaymān, son of al-Zubayr, in southern Dār Fūr, and Gordon's alliance with the Baqqāra cattle nomads against the *jallāba* in southern Kordofan, who were literally stripped of their belongings and sent north. The resignation of Gordon in 1879 gave the *jallāba* and the big slave-owners renewed hope, and the manifestation of the Mahdī in 1881 was enthusiastically received by them.[6]

The Turkiyya saw the growth of new towns and markets and the decline of others. Commercial developments and urbanisation went hand in hand. Market activities were supervised by the authorities, who appointed market officials and head merchants, to facilitate taxation and the implementation of the Ottoman commercial law (the *humāyūnī*).[7] The towns with bureaucratic military establishments and the non-producing classes who maintained large families, harems and servants, represented an important consumer market for foodstuffs, natural products and manufactures from the surrounding countryside. Declining rural population and agricultural production, such as in Dār al-Jaʿaliyyīn, had an adverse effect on the commercial life of Jaʿalī towns. The latter also found their situation aggravated by being outflanked by the growth of Khartoum and other towns, by the river traffic between Khartoum and Berber, and by the new caravan routes.

MONETISATION AND COMMERCIALISATION

One immediate result of the Turkish presence along the Nile was the introduction of Egyptian and Turkish currencies. Traditionally, barter had been the main mode of transaction, however, foreign coins like the Spanish dollar, were not completely unknown.

From the first days of the occupation the Turks fixed the exchange rates of their currencies in relation to the Sudanese media of exchange and forced a reluctant population to accept them. However, whereas the people accepted Spanish dollars, Venetian and Dutch gold sequins, and to some extent 'Stambuli' gold coins, the other Turkish and Egyptian coins were refused since the people thought they were false.[8] Gold (in ounces) had been in use before in larger transactions, and the vendors had more confidence in gold and silver coins if their value could be ascertained; gold coins could even be heated for checking before they were accepted.[9]

Although the Spanish dollar had occasionally been cut into pieces to serve as small change, local media as well as barter completely dominated small-scale buying and selling. Theoretically, the piastres and paras could have had a positive function, but their continuous debasement and the official currency manipulations, made the northern Sudanese reluctant to accept them. Waddington and Hanbury report an episode where an old woman was beaten to death for refusing to accept Egyptian piastres.[10]

However, soon both Egyptian and Turkish piastres were in circulation, the latter being slightly more popular, a tendency that was reversed from the end of the 1830s, when Muḥammad ʿAlī forbade the Turkish piastre in Egypt.[11] The Egyptian *taʿarīfa* (official rate) piastre was rapidly debased from about 15 to an Austrian Maria Theresia dollar in 1820, to 20 in 1834 when its exchange value was officially attached to the Spanish dollar.[12] The Turkish *majīdī* dollar (*riyāl*) and the Egyptian dollar of 20 piastres, also confusingly called *majīdī* in the Sudan, retained a slightly lower value than their European counterparts.

The smallest denomination was the *niṣf fiḍḍa* or para of which 40 were equal to a piastre; it appeared in silver coins of 20 paras, namely the half-piastre also called *taʿarīfa*, and of 5 paras called *khamsa fiḍḍa*. In the latter half of the 1830s a gold coin of 9 piastres, called *khayrī* or *khayriyya*, was introduced. Russegger noted its circulation in Shendi. A plot of land in al-Matamma was bought for *khayrī* coins in 1849.[13] It was received with reluctance and its market value was generally equal to 7 or 8 piastres. In an effort to improve its circulation, its value was fixed at 8 and then 8½ piastres in July 1838, but the people continued to resist it which resulted in further beatings and imprisonment.[14] However, the new Egyptian silvered copper piastre, which was introduced about the same time, was much better received in Shendi. Another feature of Shendi market was the disappearance of the Spanish dollar and its replacement by the Maria Theresia dollar.[15] The Austrian dollar became widespread from Shendi and the

Table 5 *Some currencies, their local names and approximate official exchange rate.*

Currency	Local names	Metal	Official	Origin
Para	*niṣf fiḍḍa*	silver	1 para	Egyptian
Piastre	*qirsh taʿarīfa*	silver/copper	40 para	Egyptian and Turkish
	qirsh akhdar ('green')			
	qirsh ṣāgh			
Khayriyya	*khayriyya*	gold	9 piastres	Egyptian
Riyāl (dollar)	*riyāl majīdī*	silver	20 piastres	Egyptian and Turkish
Pound	*jinayh*	gold	100 piastres	Egyptian
Charles IV dollar	*riyāl abū ʿamūd* ('column')	silver	20 piastres	Spanish
	riyāl abū madfaʿ ('cannon')			
	riyāl abū arbaʿ ('four')			
Maria Theresia dollar of 1780	*riyāl abū nuqta* ('drop')	silver	20 piastres	Austrian
	riyāl abū ṭayr ('bird')			
	riyāl abū niʿāma ('ostrich feather')			
	riyāl qūshlī ('bird' – Turk.)			
Pound sterling	*jinahy afrankī*	gold	97½ piastres	British
Napoléon/Louis d'or	*jinayh bīntū* or *bintū* cr *sawā*	gold	77 piastres and 6 paras	French
Franc		silver	4 piastres	French

southeast. The Khedive Ismāʿīl had to order large shipments from Austria of this coin with the year 1780 stamped on it. West of Khartoum the Spanish dollar retained its popularity. In the 1870s the Egyptian gold pound (*jinayh*) of 100 piastres, modelled on the British guinea, gained some standing in Sudanese trade, particularly in transactions with Egypt. The pound contained 21 carat gold and weighed 8.5 gr., while the Turkish *majīdī* silver dollar weighed 24.055 gr. and contained 83 per cent silver.[16]

Local monetary preferences varied greatly, something which hindered business and opened the way for speculation,

> Moreover in the different provinces different dollars were circulating and an Arab [who brought gum] would accept no other dollars than those circulating in his own province. And so the news was often published in the town [Khartoum] for example, 3000 Maria Theresa dollars were wanted at 20, 30 or 50 pfennigs higher value than the legal value. If anyone had such an amount in such currency he could save a tidy sum of money by the exchange in other currency alone.[17]

In the market, exchange rates were thus subject to discussion, as with all the other prices, which required some skill and persistence on the part of the customer, not least because the seller would not indicate his price before the customer happened to hit on it. If the latter had only coins of higher denominations, like dollars, he was also likely to loose because of the widespread lack of small change.[18]

Disregarding all these fluctuations and regional differences, it has been found that the American, European and Ottoman silver dollars were officially valued at 20 piastres after 1834, unofficially at rates from 16 to 19 piastres. The British pound sterling equalled about 97½ piastres; the French Napoléon or Louis d'or equalled 77 piastres and 6 paras, while the French franc was equal to about 4 piastres, i.e. there were 5 francs to a dollar (see Table 5).

The table says nothing about the process of monetisation and the obstacles it encountered. Outside the central areas the use of money was still not widespread at the end of the Turkiyya. The main agents of monetisation were the merchants and the government. The government demanded taxes and dues in cash, which stimulated exchanges against cash or borrowing of cash. However, the government also drained the market of cash by the transfers of tribute to Cairo. ʿAlī Khūrshīd was one of the few who understood this problem and he occasionally managed to get dollars transferred to the Sudan to pay the soldiers. It is reported that he also guaranteed, in the absence of money, all promissory notes issued by the government, so that each note would be accepted by the treasury at its face value in payment for taxes and dues. 'By this arrangement most of the commerce in this country was conducted by credit operations and there were small traders who made great fortunes.'[19]

The government system was therefore not favourable to the recycling of money collected. When anything was needed from the people, goods or services, it was taken rather than paid for. The Coptic clerks, who oversaw the treasuries, were also forbidden to recycle government money illegally through speculation in the market.

However, government officials were able to use part of their salaries to buy shares in trading operations or for more direct speculative purposes, just like any other Sudanese or foreigner with ready cash, and this set some money in circulation, although at inflated prices. The lending of money was a lucrative business, with interest rates of 4 to 5 per cent and up to 15 per cent per month. Marno noted how huge profits in cash were taken out of the country. Franz Binder became rich as a moneylender and Giegler Pasha admits that he augmented his salary by lending to gum merchants, who were often without cash when shipments arrived.[20]

Although exports of gum and other commodities brought some money into circulation, observers continued to comment upon its scarcity.[21] This was connected with the Sudan's balance of trade, which in some years, such as around the 1850s, made merchants come with cash to buy export commodities quickly, and in other years, such as around 1875, made merchants bring commodities to sell for cash, which they then, instead of waiting to buy export commodities such as gum, transferred back to Egypt to buy more commodities for the Sudanese market. This latter situation, which drained the Sudan of cash, may reflect both a trade imbalance and the absence of banks to help regulate the availability and circulation of money.[22]

The merchants themselves, who in many ways profited from speculation, complained about the scarcity of money and the currency fluctuations, blaming the problems on the government. Mūsā Pasha thought that the complaints were lodged at the wrong place, since in his opinion as a result of the payment for merchandise from Egypt, there ensued a scarcity of cash which enabled the merchants to make profits of 50 per cent or more.[23] It was known that money tended to be hoarded among government officials and in the treasury (the officials had to plan for their future retirement back in Egypt), but gradually it was the big merchants and speculators who gained control over the flow of money in the Sudan. This may be illustrated by an incident in Khartoum where the merchant al-ʿAqqād was the only one able to cash a draft for the Austrian explorer Ernst Marno. The *ḥikimdār* himself was obliged to ask this merchant for financial assistance.[24]

The persistence of barter and local media of exchange, particularly outside the main market towns and on the frontiers, shows that money did not find easy access to the spheres of basic transactions. The south was first opened up by the aid of *dammūr*, salt and beads. In the northern Sudan, however, being much longer exposed to external economic influences, we find that the surviving documents, recording inheritance, maintenance, bequests, dowries and sales, increasingly calculated the relevant assets and goods in monetary terms. In a response to a claim for maintenance by a woman against her absent husband, the *qāḍī* of Shendi Sharia court lists in monetary terms the monthly necessities allowed to her as maintenance, according to the actual prices in Shendi at that time, 1866 (see Table 6). Even more interesting, a clause is added providing for an increase in the allowance in response to price inflation.[25]

Monetisation was uneven in its impact, with regard both to geographical and social dimensions, but at least in Shendi, al-Matamma and other market towns along the Nile, dealings and calculations in monetary terms had become a fact of life before the end of the Turkiyya, even though the actual cash was severely limited. The extent of monetisation can best be seen from the need for money in the early days of the Mahdiyya and the establishment of one of the first indigenous African mints in order to prevent commercial breakdown.

With monetisation and the spread of the market forces, even larger sectors of social and personal relations became commercialised. We may talk about the commoditisation of elementary necessities such as food, of factors of production such as land and labour, and of the reciprocal exchanges of labour, beer and gifts among neighbours and relatives. Some of these features were present to some degree under the Funj, but then the cultural and institutional framework did not favour their development. Under the Turks, labour services, family obligations, and marriage alliances were increasingly estimated in cash. Wealth in cash began to count for more than age, religious learning and family background. Noble and chiefly families, deprived of their traditional rent and slow to learn the new game, might easily break down under the pressure of debts owed to the *nouveaux riches*. Creditor/debtor relationships penetrated all social layers and communities, appearing even within families, as the struggle for daily bread became more bitter. The merchants' habit of accepting repayments on earlier advances to the peasants in cheap grain, and of buying up grain to be stored away, now also with grain from their own farms, waiting for the prices to go up, added to the social tension, impoverishment and disintegration of the northern communities. From being almost exclusively a part of the domestic economy, grain was now dragged by the middlemen (and the government) into the market sphere and thus out of the control of the producers. During the frequent periods of food shortage, the average town dweller and the peasant alike became more dependent on the market (i.e. the grain-hoarding merchants) for their daily supply of food. The disruptive role of the commoditisation of grain can therefore not be overestimated.

The Ottoman Turks, experienced in governing foreign lands with various degrees of monetisation, were confronted in the Sudan with a traditional subsistence economy, in which money played an insignificant role. The need to introduce money to facilitate surplus extraction and trade was recognised from the beginning, but the practice of currency manipulations, the hoarding of money and the shipments of private fortunes to Egypt, undermined the government's own efforts, and paved the way for speculation and grave price fluctuations.

Table 6 *Maintenance assigned to Fāṭima, daughter of* fakī *Muḥammad ʿAwaḍ al-Sīd in 1866 by the* qāḍī *Muḥammad Aḥmad Jalāl al-Dīn.*

	Price per unit (piastres)	*Annual expenses (piastres)*
To Fāṭima:		
Grain, 1 *wayba* per month (40 litres i.e. 2/9 of an *ardabb* or 8 *midds*)	20 per *murabba*ʿ (i.e. per 4 *midd*[a])	480
Meat, 4 *uqqa*[b] per month	1.5 per *uqqa*	72
Mutton, 1 *uqqa* per week	2 per *uqqa*	101[c]
Salt		96
Dihn (butter oil)		240
Perfume		120
Hairdresser	6 every 4 months	18
Clothing	18 for shawl, 24 for *tōb*	42
Shoes	25 per pair	25
Total		1,194
To her daughter, Amina:		
Durra grain, 1 *murabba*ʿ per month	20 per *murabba*ʿ	240
Indian muslim, 3 *dhirā*ʿ, every 6 months.	1 piastre 10 para per *dhirā*ʿ	7½
Meat, from her mother's assignment		
Total		247½
To her slave woman:		
Grain, 6 *midd* per month	30 per 6 *midd*	360
Meat, 1½ *uqqa* per month	1½ per *uqqa*	27
Salt, 1 *dawka*[d] per month	2 per *dawka*	24
Farda baladi, local *tōb*, every six months	10 per *farda*	20
Total		431

Notes: [a] 1 *midd* in Berber Province may be estimated at about 5 litres. [b] *uqqa* or *wuqqa*, equals 1.248 kg. [c] 50½ weeks in a Muslim year. [d] *Dawka*, an unidentified unit of measurement.
Source: NRO, Misc. 1/13/119.

The increasing cost of living in the northern Sudan was not the result of too many coins in circulation, as the opposite was actually the case, nor the result of the old Ottoman practice of debasing the coinage to lower government expenses. In fact, the limited circulation of money was probably instrumental in keeping inflation at a relatively low level under the prevailing circumstances. The relative official value of the various currencies showed a remarkable stability after 1834, and also in relation to the

Table 7 *Wages and prices in the early 1870s (piastres)*

Wages per month:	
Doctor	1,500
Engineer	1,500
Clerk	1,200
Mechanic	1,500
Captain of steamer	800
Captain of bark	150
Sailor	60
Cook	40
Doorkeeper	60
Kavass (police man)	300
Tailor	300
Carpenter	1,000
Joiner	1,000
Shoemaker	600
Tin-maker	300
Agricultural worker	50
Commercial servant	100
House servant	80
Prices:	
Slave boy	1,600
Slave girl	1,800
Ethiopian horse, average	900
Arab horse, average	2,000
Camel	240
Dromedary	800
Donkey	100
Donkey to ride	800
Sheep	20
Cow	100
House	10,000
Two acres of land	20
Tusk, average	2,000
First quality gum, 100 pounds	200
Second quality gum, 100 pounds	50

Source: Figures based on Southworth (1875), 170.

local strips of *dammūr*, for example, the rate of two *tōbs* for a dollar is recorded over several decades. Only the iron money of Kordofan suffered severe devaluation, from some 150 to 800 iron pieces to a dollar, until it went completely out of use.[26]

The major reason for the increase in prices must be found in the disruption of food production and the commoditisation of grain. If the peasants had only the whims of the climate and the river to wrestle with, their production might have been higher and more even, and the food markets in al-Matamma and Shendi would not have looked so miserable. The effect of the decline in agricultural production on prices, particularly that of durra, comes out very clearly in Brocchi, to give only one example, who stated that the prices rose sixteen-fold between approximately 1820 and 1825.[27] Seasonal variations in prices reflect the natural changes in the availability of grain between harvests. Years of crop failures also caused prices to rise temporarily, to the benefit of merchants and the government granaries. In 1835–6, a bowl (2 litres) of durra cost about 15 piastres, whereas under more normal circumstances a few years later an *ardabb* (180 litres) of durra cost about 15–20 piastres.[28] By 1876 the price of durra in Qadārif, a rich grain-producing area, was 50 piastres, which then was considered cheap as the prices rose steeply that year.[29] A document from a merchant gives the price of 240 piastres per *ardabb* at al-Matamma at the beginning of the Mahdiyya.[30]

The steady rise in durra prices, perhaps several hundred per cent, is often concealed by the recurrent extreme peaks. The pattern is therefore easier to follow in the case of other necessities of life, like animals and their products. The price of sheep grew from 5 to 9 piastres to nearly 20, with the highest price always in the central markets. Similarly, the price of a cow also increased about 100 per cent, from around 4 to 6 to about 8 to 10 dollars.[31] Tables 6 and 7 list some prices and wages relevant to the 1860s and 1870s, which will illustrate these points.

THE JAʿALĪ TOWNS IN A REGIONAL PERSPECTIVE

The Turkiyya with its military, administrative and commercial requirements initiated a process of urbanisation which in some cases built on older foundations and in others on new ones. Born, in an article on urbanisation with special emphasis on al-Ubayyiḍ, stresses the location of military camps as the major factor in this process, referring to the growth of Khartoum, Wad Madanī and Kassala.[32] However, the presence of a garrison did not itself initiate urbanisation when other factors were lacking, as the case of Shendi clearly shows. The factors which caused the decline and growth of towns like Shendi and al-Matamma were firmly linked to the broader political and economic framework of the Turkiyya.

Such towns were on the one hand dependent on the economy of the producers and consumers of the surrounding countryside and on the other hand on the regular visits by regional and international caravans. Being thus structurally situated between the village and regional levels, they reacted to changes on both levels in various ways.

The destruction of Shendi and part of al-Matamma in 1823 was a severe blow to the Jaʿalī economy and society. Henceforth, the Jaʿaliyyīn were far more prominent in town-building outside their homeland. In fact, much of the urbanisation in Khartoum and further south and west would have been impossible without the thousands of Jaʿaliyyīn and Danāgla migrants. From contemporary observations, it is clear that Shendi never regained its former prosperity; al-Dāmir also suffered from stagnation and the same can be said about al-Matamma, although the district administration there and some caravan traffic breathed some life into the town. Berber, on the other hand, prospered more than before, first because it was the province headquarters, and secondly because it was an end station for both the river traffic and the caravans from Egypt and the Red Sea.

Al-Matamma and Shendi continued to attract merchants from other areas, the Ḥaḍāriba were still to be seen there, as were the Danāgla, and the Shāyqiyya formed a dominent element in Shendi till the end of the century.[33] The size of the urban population was lower in the whole period than before the occupation; the quality of the houses deteriorated, many were abandoned for good, and the flat-roofed mud houses were replaced by the simpler *quṭṭiyyas* or *tukuls*. This indicates the absence of a substantial merchant class, particularly in Shendi, and the miserable state of the markets just confirms this impression. Both towns are now also sometimes referred to as big villages in contemporary sources. Population figures are naturally not very reliable, but the sources indicate a population for Shendi of around 3,000 to 4,000 people, and somewhat more for al-Matamma in the 1840s. Apparently the development thereafter was one of further decline.

Some trade continued with the Red Sea, Dongola, Kordofan and Egypt. Animals, animal products, coffee, tobacco, spices, henna, cloth, cutlery and slaves were bought and sold. Russegger commented upon the local production of leather goods, whips, mats, gold and silver work in Shendi.[34] Hoskins observed that merchants from Shendi and Sinnār furnished Berber with soap, rice, Mocha coffee, mirrors, glass beads, shells, cotton articles, tobacco, pipes, crockery, cooking dishes, etc., as they passed through to and from Egypt.[35] In addition came grain, vegetables and salt; the craft industries provided the peasants with *sāqiya* pots, ropes and wheels, implements, shoes, cotton and linen cloth, and basketry. Al-Matamma relied mostly on its cotton cloth exports and more merchants were found there than in Shendi, but the appearance of the town did not indicate much prosperity. By the mid-century, Taylor gives a very gloomy picture of the sister-towns, concluding that 'El Metemma and Shendy are probably the most immoral towns in all Central Africa.'[36]

For the rest of the Turkiyya Shendi, and to a minor extent also al-Matamma, suffered a gradual loss in population, which also shows that the migrants from the countryside did not go to the local towns, but moved further away. In 1885 the population of al-Matamma was 3,000, which decreased to 2,500 at the end of the Mahdiyya. At the latter point of time, Shendi housed only 500 people, mainly Shāyqiyya, and al-Dāmir 700, all Ja'aliyyīn.[37]

The growth of other commercial centres and caravan routes attracted people and trade away from Shendi and al-Matamma. The role of Khartoum was crucial in this process; growing from a small village, it had in about 1860 around 30,000 to 40,000 inhabitants, of whom the majority came from the north. It became a natural point of departure for the White Nile expeditions, and consequently a place where equipment, rations, and exchange goods were bought, and boats, crew, soldiers and agents were hired.[38] To the west, al-Ubayyiḍ became a vital export market for gum, ivory, slaves, feathers and hides to Egypt by the way of Dongola. Further west, in Dār Fūr, independent till 1874, the commercial centre of Kobbei remained a transit point of some importance, linking areas further south and west to the Nile Valley and Egypt. Many riverain *jallāba* moved there during the Turkiyya, and after 1874 people of Jaʿalī stock came to dominate commercial life there.[39] On the Blue Nile the growth of al-Masallamiyya was outstanding, attracting trade away from Wad Madanī and Sinnār. Further south and east, markets grew up that traded in Ethiopian goods and local grain and cotton, such as Karkōj, al-Qaḍārif, also known as *sūq* Shaykh Abū Sinn, Qallabāt, sometimes also called al-Matamma after the town on the Nile, and Kassala which traded mainly with the Red Sea Coast. The Jaʿaliyyīn constituted a substantial part of the population of these towns.[40]

This new urban pattern was closely connected with Turkish export policy. The towns on the Blue Nile and southern Butāna exported locally produced grain and cotton.[41] The main arteries of trade within this network tended to skirt around both Shendi and al-Matamma. Caravans from Khartoum to the Red Sea followed the Blue Nile and passed via Abū Ḥarāz to Qaḍārif and Kassala to the coast, or they crossed the Buṭāna to Qōz Rajab on the Atbara and then to Sawākin, or they took off from the Nile at Berber, to which commodities were first shipped from Khartoum on the river. Trade between Egypt and Khartoum was conducted either on boats between Khartoum and Berber and then on camel-back across the desert, or caravans might cross the Bayūḍa from just north to Kararī to Dongola. Fewer caravans now took the old land route along the Nile through Dār al-Jaʿaliyyīn, or used al-Matamma and Shendi as desert harbours as under the Funj, and the river traffic between Berber and Khartoum had little or no stimulating effect on the two towns.

Large western caravans made directly for Khartoum or north to Dongola, if they carried goods destined for Egypt. There was also a direct route between Dār Fūr and Dongola. Al-Matamma and Shendi were thus left with the smaller caravans from Kordofan and Dongola on the one hand and from Berber and the Red Sea on the other. The opening of the White Nile only strengthened Khartoum and the western trade centres and routes.

Obviously the picture was not entirely one of gloom; the role of Shendi and to a greater extent al-Matamma as administrative and military centres brought about some economic activity. Transactions between nomads and peasants continued; crafts and manufactures activated both men and women, the cotton yarn and *dammūr* found customers all over the Sudan, palm-leaf mats were exported as far as Egypt, whips, ropes, saddles and leather bags were produced for the caravans as well as for local use. In certain places the salt industry flourished again and Khartoum became the main importer along with the Ethiopian borderlands. Thus Dār al-Jaʿaliyyīn exported certain attractive commodities, both raw and manufactured, in exchange for smaller commodities such as utensils, essence and spices, perfumes and kohl, mirrors, dates, wax, honey, Indian cottons, coffee, sugar, durra and slaves.

The postal service and the telegraph had no profound effect on the local economy, but at least they did connect the sister-towns more closely with an international network, and a document from 1882 suggests that these services were used to transmit information about the Sudanese market situation to commercial partners in Egypt.[42] When the time came to plan the railway, it was argued that Shendi and al-Matamma would be suitable as the final station after crossing the Bayūḍa, probably due more to their geographical position than to their economic importance.[43]

OLD AND NEW TYPES OF TRADERS

The stereotype figure most frequently associated with Sudanese trade is the *jallābī* (cl. Ar. *jallāb*, pl. *jallāba*) who is usually defined as an 'itinerant petty trader'. The root *j.l.b.* has the meaning of bringing or importing goods. However, prior to the Turkiyya, the term *jallābī* meant 'caravan trader' both in Egypt, Sinnār and Dār Fūr. Walz has discovered contracts in Egypt from the latter half of the sixteenth century, in which merchants entered into partnership or *commenda* with travelling *jallāba* who frequented the roads between Egypt and the Sudan. Walz's definition of the *jallāba* as 'merchants who transported goods between Egypt and the interior, either on their own account or on that of an associate', holds true also in a Sudanese context.[44]

A seventeenth-century reference to the *jallāba* arriving in Egypt described them as dark skinned, indicating a Nubian or Sudanese origin.[45] Later contemporary references to them leave no doubt as to the participation of 'Nubian' *jallāba* trading in Upper Egypt and Cairo. The products they brought were slaves, ivory, rhino-horn, feathers, civet and gold.[46]

In the nineteenth century the characteristic features of the *jallāba* underwent some crucial changes in response to the new economic and political environment. The *jallāba* were mainly recruited from the Jaʿaliyyīn, the Danāgla and other riverain groups. In the diaspora and market places visited by them, as far west as Lake Chad, the term *jallāba* became synonymous with people or 'strangers' from the Nile, variously also called *baḥḥāra* (river people), *awlād al-baḥr* (sons of the river), *awlād al-balad* (village or town dwellers). Also today, as among the Ḥassāniyya on the White Nile, bordering upon Kordofan, *jallābī* means 'stranger' (from the north). Merchants who conducted caravans and operated over wider areas, often in the service of the Funj or Fūr sultans and preferably with Egypt as part of their network, were always referred to as *jallāba*. A *jallābī* who advanced in experience and status might become royal caravan leader with the title of *khabīr* (pl. *khubarā'*). It seems that before the Turkiyya, being a *jallābī* referred more to the geographical scale of operations than to the commodities carried. In other words, the term had not yet become synonymous with 'slave trader' and 'petty trader'. Today in the west and south, *jallābī* means riverain merchant or shopkeeper.[47] Generally speaking, in the Turkiyya the people so described by others ceased to use the term *jallāba* when referring to themselves.

The government monopoly system forced the *jallāba* out of various prestigious forms of long-distance trade and into the non-monopoly slave trade and short-distance petty trading. The economic power and social standing of the *jallāba* diminished accordingly and increasing competition both among themselves and with the foreign traders when the monopoly was ended, made it impossible for the majority to rise above the level of small scale trading.[48] As the government *ghazwas* (slave hunting expeditions) came to a halt around 1850 and private trading and slave hunting on the White Nile gained widespread popularity, many *jallāba* soon moved from junior partners to leading slave traders. Big and small traders, *fakīs* and adventurers, impoverished northern peasants, hunters and former soldiers, flocked to the south, bringing beads, cotton, salt and other items to barter for slaves and ivory, or bringing firearms with which to spread terror and enslavement to ever larger areas.

From the 1850s onward a new upper and less mobile stratum of Sudanese merchants started to crystallise, distancing themselves from both the status and the name of *jallaba*, and all the other categories of average middlemen. They associated with the Turks, obtained capital through partnerships and agencies with foreign merchants, organised and financed long-distance trade ventures through partners and agents and preferred to be addressed as *tujjār* (sing. *tājir*, merchant) or as *khawājāt*, which was even more prestigious.[49] Even those big merchants whose whole business consisted of slave hunting and trading, such as the Ja'alī merchant prince and later pasha, al-Zubayr, would have been grossly offended if they were called *jallāba*.[50] This tendency among the big merchants to dissociate themselves from the label of *jallāba* in the central areas of the Sudan where their set-backs had been most devastating, was not so noticeable among the Egyptians and Nubians who conducted caravan traffic between Egypt and the Sudan.[51]

The degradation of the *jallāba* was also closely connected with changes within the lower echelons of the merchant class. Following the campaigns of the Daftardar, the market and roads of Sinnār, Kordofan and Dār Fūr swarmed with dispossessed Ja'aliyyīn, traders and peasants alike. This meant a dramatic increase in the number of traders in relation to commodities and customers, a situation which in addition was made much worse by the trade restriction of the monopoly system. The *jallāba* represented the upper echelons of this heterogeneous body of traders, but distinctions were often difficult to make; mobility and the possession of a single slave or more for sale was usually the distinctive criterion.[52]

Slaves were largely obtained by regular visits to the south. Travelling in the south around 1870, Schweinfurth distinguished between the following three categories of *jallāba* who were in the slave trade either as agents or independent traders in the Baḥr al-Ghazāl:

(a) The small traders with a donkey or an ox, who arrived in January and return by March and April.

(b) The agents and companions of bigger merchants in Kordofan and Dār Fūr, who have settled in the *zarības* (fenced stations) and who may also operate as *fakīs*.

(c) The sedentary slave traders with their own soldiers, territories and stations further west, who make regular excursions into the interior.[53]

Pallme and many others give colourful descriptions of market places and traders, but few actually bother to distinguish between categories. Marketing was described above as a natural part of primary production, either by the producers themselves or by middlemen. Women were often seen offering foodstuffs for sale. Similar products tended to be exposed for sale in the same section of the market, but there were also traders who moved around in the market place carrying their commodities, such as textiles, trying to raise the bids. The *jallāba*, when about to leave for Egypt, competed to buy up slaves and thus caused the prices to rise. On their return, they offered various items of foreign origin, which they would lay out for sale themselves or hire a broker (*simsār*, pl. *samasra* or *dallāl*, pl. *dalālīn*) to take care of the tedious work of finding the highest bidder, as has been described by Pallme.[54] The market place exhibited both a remarkable degree of specialisation in the case of larger or more expensive commodities, but on the other hand a whole variety of small articles could be exposed for sale by a single trader. The petty traders seem to have bought and sold the same set of articles over long periods of time.[55]

The traders who operated on a small scale, both in terms of goods and number of markets visited, and who formed the majority of the itinerant traders, were called *sabāba* (sing. *sabābī*), *tashshāsha* (sing. *tashshāshī*), or more often *mutasabbibīn* (sing. *mutasabbib*). The latter were referred to as *musabbabīn* in the sources, a term which is not recognised today and is therefore probably a corruption of *mutasabbibīn* which means retailers. They were almost exclusively Jaʿaliyyīn and seen everywhere, with their donkeys and small selection of commodities. Poncet calculated that in Khartoum around 1860 there were around 4–5,000 *mutasabbibīn*, nearly all Jaʿaliyyīn. They bought merchandise on six or twelve months' credit, such as red and blue-bordered *fardas*, cheap jewellery (agates), empty bottles, sandalwood and odiferous oils from the Ḥijāz, which they sold in the Upper Blue Nile and Kordofan, passing from one village to another. They returned after a period of up to a year.[56] These traders should not be confused with the *jallāba*, although Marno says that the *jallāba* were both pedlars and slave-traders.[57]

In the more prosperous villages, the first stationary retailers appeared in this period, among whom were also found women. They brought farm produce to the nearest town or chief marketplace, to exchange for various necessities for the rural areas or they returned with commodities obtained from a wholesale merchant on credit. In the early Condominium every village might have two or three retailers of this type.[58] Some of the more entrepreneurial among them imitated and cooperated with town-based merchants to take advantage of the fluctuating prices and seasonal availability of grain, and capitalise on the urgent demand for grain and seed among peasants before the next season. Speculation of this kind was more the domain of merchants in the big villages and towns, but the small village retailer was one helpful link in tying the subsistence and market economies together.

Among the traders and middlemen not associated with the *tujjār* and the *jallāba*, we may therefore distinguish five types:

(a) *simsār*, a broker who operated within the market and who negotiated buying and selling on behalf of others.
(b) *dallāl*, a crier or auctioneer, stationary or moving about in the market place, trying to obtain higher bids for his slaves or retail commodities (for example, clothes) which he offered for sale on behalf of a merchant.[59]
(c) *sabbābī*, a small trader or village retailer, who brought farm produce to the market town in return for commodities retailed among the villagers.
(d) *tashshāshī*, itinerant small trader, today often associated with spices.
(e) *mutasabbib*, small itinerant retailer carrying a variety of commodities, obtained on credit, between towns and villages.

RECRUITMENT AND NETWORKS

Recruitment to the profession of trading, from the simplest peddling to the large-scale operations, took place through family connections; the necessary skills and initial capital and credit were obtained from the older generation of fathers, uncles, grandfathers and patrons. It is, of course, difficult to generalise, and what follows is mostly concerned with traders who operated above a certain economic level and geographical scale. All beginners, whether or not they were sons of peasants, traders, *fakīs* or craftsmen, would have to work for a period as servants and agents of a patron; in fact, among the established trading families, to work as a travelling agent was often a necessary training stage before entering into business on one's own.[60] Among the Jaʿaliyyīn and other northern groups, every family or lineage had some connections with part-time or full-time trade, which would make the preliminary steps beyond village retailing and small scale marketing for a young apprentice relatively easy. In the

Turkiyya, it was possible to move to Khartoum and become clients of fellow Jaʿaliyyīn or of the foreign merchants, and use the period of service to accumulate some capital, and learn the basic techniques of trade, before one obtained one's first assortment of goods on credit.

Small-scale trading was seasonally defined and operated in the grey zone between production, marketing and trade. The complex occupational pattern meant that the same persons might engage in cultivation, crafts, marketing and trade at different parts of the year. Most people marketed or bartered part of their own production in the market in exchange for money or other goods, and they would not be called traders under any circumstances. However, both cultivators and craftsmen can be said to act as part-time traders when they used the slack season to bring their own and neighbours' locally produced dates, tobacco, salt, cotton cloth, basketry, etc. to other areas to profit from the price differences. Progress from the categories of peasants, craftsmen and manufacturers to that of full-time trader went through stages, depending on skills, luck, family ties and personal inclination. The desire to have a family member engaged in trade was motivated by the objective need to supplement diminishing household income and to earn cash with which to pay the taxes. Extra income was also needed at certain critical moments to repay family debts, to regain mortgaged land, and to put together a proper dowry in preparation of a marriage contract, which was all the time becoming more expensive.

For a small trader or travelling agent with long-term trading ambitions, a decisive stage was reached when one was able to obtain a few slaves to sell further north.[61] Those with a peasant background who saw their capital increase in this way were less likely to revert to active farming themselves, unless indirectly through investments in wheels, land and agricultural slaves in the diaspora. Back home in the north, the family farms were attended to by women, children, slaves and the old people, and supported by remittances. A migrant trader might invite his wife to settle in the diaspora, or he might marry again and establish new families in the main market towns he frequented.

The large-scale shift from agriculture to trade and other professions among the Jaʿaliyyīn in the Turkiyya altered the pattern of recruitment in that numerous Jaʿaliyyīn, evicted from their land, made their first experiences in trade without the traditional structural support and period of apprenticeship. In the same way as baskets and mats enabled women to engage in local trade, so did salt and cotton cloth enable a man to start off in trade.[62] *Dammūr* from al-Matamma was famous throughout the Sudan and always yielded some profit to the one who took it south and west. Cotton strips continued to function as media of exchange, usually at the rate of two *tōbs* to a dollar. Thus the Jaʿaliyyīn could to some extent make their own currency as before. However, circumstances were not favourable for all to obtain a stake in commerce. Many flocked to Khartoum to earn a living; various services were needed there, including that of driving caravan camels. Big merchants there of both foreign and local origin provided many Jaʿaliyyīn with commodities on credit, which was a popular career possibility. In this way imporated goods were brought out and exchanged for Sudanese products suitable for export.[63] From the 1840s the demand for sailors and private and government soldiers for the White Nile increased, and the wages earned in this way, though small, in addition to the possibility of bartering on one's own, enabled many to gain enough capital to invest in the Nile expeditions, to form partnerships or to start off independently in petty trade.[64] A part of this process was observed by Marno, who said that only a few dollars were necessary to obtain a donkey and then some tobacco to pound and mix with *naṭrūn* to sell as a form of snuff. Other commodities were dates, peanuts (*fūl* Dār Fūrī), perfumes, kohl, *dilka*, *dammūr* and wood. Without reflecting much on the deeper causes of depopulated villages, Marno was of the opinion that the desire to trade had caused the land to remain uncultivated or in some cases left to be worked by slaves.[65] In Cairo, the Northern Sudanese (Nubians) were also known to form partnerships and invest a part of their capital earned in household service in the Sudan-bound trade, and sometimes to engage personally as *jallāba* in the caravans.[66]

Trading was far more organised and much less individualistic than foreign observers were able to see on the surface. The traders were bound together as patron–clients, as partners and agents, as debtors and creditors, and as members of the same religious brotherhoods and tribes. When a family business grew out of the local level, members would move to strategic market centres in the diaspora to form strong networks in order to handle themselves the flow of investments, letters of credit and commodities over longer distances, collect information on price fluctuations, and particularly to be present in frontier areas where the exchange of import and export articles was most profitable. This was the era of the 'family incorporated' as Jay Spaulding rightly says.[67] The family network was supplemented by tribal networks with basically the same functions; people from the same locality and tribal group used to live together in their own quarters in the diaspora, and business cooperation was more likely to happen within than across ethnic boundaries. The Jaʿaliyyīn and the Danāgla were reputed arch-rivals in this respect both before and under the Turkiyya. Thus ethnicity had both commercial, social and political functions in the diaspora networks.

The foreign merchants and firms, with their headquarters mainly in Khartoum, were major competitors with the Sudanese traders. However, strong as they may have been in terms of capital, the foreigners could not really beat the Sudanese at home. Lejean assures us that any European firm that arrived at Masallamiyya or Qallabāt with perhaps 100,000 francs, would find themselves driven out of business by the trading networks of the Danāgla and the Ḥaḍāriba, the richest of whom possessed no more than 1,500 dollars. In his opinion, lack of credit and credit institutions led to the formation of such ethnic networks, but it is also true to say that the extension of credit was made easier through them.[68]

The most prominent ethnic networks around 1860 were the Danāgla, the Ḥaḍāriba and the Jaʿaliyyīn. The Ḥaḍāriba were not numerous, but active and influential as in Shendi before the Turkiyya, with their origin at Sawākin they established branches and agencies at Masallamiyya (the most important), in Khartoum, Kassala, al-Matamma, Berber, and Jidda across the Red Sea (from the latter place they traded with India). The Danāgla were most active in Khartoum and Kobbei, in Dār Fūr). From the latter place they conducted caravans to Asyūṭ in Egypt, as did also the Jaʿaliyyīn. In Khartoum the Danāgla were closely associated with Egyptian commercial houses, like those of ʿAbd al-Ḥamīd, ʿAlī Abū ʿAmūrī and al-ʿAqqād. In al-Ubayyiḍ, the house of the Dongolāwī Sughayarūn was famous for its wealth and influence. He possessed hundreds of slaves and was head of the merchants there in 1858, and acted as the host of Munzinger in 1862.[69] The Danāgla traded mostly in ivory, arms, beads, dates and cotton cloth. Whereas many of them joined or followed the Europeans on the White Nile, some preferred to operate within Khartoum market, mainly as brokers in ivory from the White Nile. They were also engaged in the slave trade; others went up the Blue Nile and traded in grain from Masallamiyya, gum from Karkōj, gold from Fāzūghlī, sesame from the area of Sinnār, Galla slaves from Qallabāt and Fadassī. Their operations in this area were facilitated by the numerous Danāgla settlements there.[70] However, feeling the competition from foreigners and the exactions of the government, many found the sultanate of Dār Fūr more tempting, trading from there to Wadai, Kordofan and Egypt.

Generally speaking the Jaʿaliyyīn followed the same pattern, except for the brokerage business in Khartoum, and observers did not always distinguish between the northern traders, whom they often called Danāgla without distinction. However, for various reasons Jaʿalī traders operated at a lower level than their Danāgla counterparts till around 1860. Contrary to the Jaʿaliyyīn the lower echelons among the Danāgla migrants did not trade, but became servants, sailors, soldiers, boat builders and small farmers. It is difficult to say which group had the largest number of migrants, but it seems clear that the percentage of traders among the migrants was higher among the Jaʿaliyyīn. The trading networks of the latter covered a much larger geographical area, from Massawa on the Red Sea to far into the areas of Lake Chad and Central Africa.[71]

From around 1860 some Jaʿalī diaspora careers made the Jaʿaliyyīn surpass their rivals in many respects. Thus a Jaʿalī merchant, Ilyās (Pasha) Umm Birayr, who had reached some prominence in al-Ubayyiḍ already in the 1850s, was appointed governor of Kordofan by Gordon in 1878 for a short time. His appointment secured the employment of many Jaʿaliyyīn in the administration of the province, and ironically they managed to outdo the Shāyqiyya as ruthless tax-collectors.[72] Further south and west, and largely beyond government controlled territory, another Ja'alī, al-Zubayr (Pasha) Raḥma Manṣūr, carved out a slave hunting and trading empire on the Baḥr al-Ghazāl, with his fellow lieutenants and slave troops. After being appointed governor of the new province, to confirm a *fait accompli*, he set out to add even more territory to the Turkish Sudan and conquered Dār Fūr in 1874. The government hurried in to reap the fruits of conquest and evict the powerful and ambitious merchant prince al-Zubayr from the leadership of the province.

In conclusion then, ethnicity played a vital role on many levels, from making recruitment and advancement easier, to providing credit and security in the diaspora, and finally to keeping up ties and the area of origin. The Turks found it convenient to deal with merchants of any town through the appointed chief merchant and below him through the chief merchants of each ethnic group represented there.[73] There were definitely great differences in wealth among Ja'alī traders, but the ethnic (and religious) networks secured that the less fortunate would find support, employment and credit among fellow migrants of the same tribe and sometimes also of the same brotherhood. We may therefore add ethnicity to an old cliché and say that trade, ethnicity and religion went hand in hand.

THE CAREER OF 'ABD ALLĀH BEY ḤAMZA

From the 1850s onward a merchant by the name of 'Abd Allāh Ḥamza flourished in al-Matamma. His long and eventful life (c.1824–1937) has not yet been recorded, but an outline relevant to the Turkiyya will here be given, based upon documents left by him and information provided by his son, Sulaymān.[74] 'Abd Allāh was the son of Ḥamza, who was mentioned above as an investor in indigo production in al-Matamma. In many ways 'Abd Allāh, and to some extent his father, typify the new features of the merchant class. If we distinguish between (a) travelling merchants who took commodities from one place to another to profit from geographical price differences, and (b) the stationary holders of stock who profited from seasonal price variations, and (c) the stationary organising merchants, who financed and organised trade through partners and agents,[75] 'Abd Allāh's grandfathers would come in the first category and he himself and his father would come closest to the second and third. 'Abd Allāh's career and the unique documents he left offer an extraordinary insight into most of the themes discussed in this chapter. The fact that he was not a Ja'alī but an 'Abdallābī, and that al-Matamma was first a sort of diaspora in the family network, does not detract from this reality.

Sometime in the eighteenth century 'Abd Allāh's great-great-grandfather, 'Abd al-Mūlā from Khandaq established himself as *khabīr* in Kobbei in Dār Fūr, a position he transferred to his sons Abbakr and Shādhūl. Their main trade route was the *darb al-arba'īn* to Egypt, but they kept close connections with Khandaq, an important riverain port for much of the Dār

Fūr and Kordofan trade before the Turkiyya. A grandson of Shādhūl, Muḥammad Ṣāliḥ, became one of Muḥammad ʿUthmān al-Mīrghanī's first *khalīfas*, and guided the religious figure and founder of the Khatmiyya brotherhood from Dongola to Bāra in Kordofan in 1816 on his first visit to the Sudan.[76] Mūsā, a son of Abbakr, traded as a *jallābī* between Kobbei and Egypt, and two sons of his, Abbakr and Ḥamza took up the same profession. Sometime in the early part of the nineteenth century, Ḥamza moved to Khandaq because of the disruption of the *darb al-arbaʿīn* trade. The presence of the refugee Mamluks in Dongola from 1811 did not make commerce much easier there and Ḥamza moved on to al-Matamma where he built a proper rectangular mud house with a *ḥōsh* wall. At that time al-Matamma (like Shendi) was emerging as a vital commercial centre and therefore attractive to merchants with interests in long-distance trade. Ḥamza's network stretched from Dār Fūr to Egypt and south to Kararī, where he had a second wife, ʿAjba bt. al-Shaykh Nāṣir, daughter of the last king of the ʿAbdallāb.

His brother Abbakr, although it is said that he came to take up residence in al-Dāmir, continued to keep up close relations with Dār Fūr and at the time of the Turkish conquest he brought a letter from the sultan of Dār Fūr to Moḥammad ʿAlī.[77] Ḥamza happened to be in Egypt during the conquest and the subsequent revolt of the Jaʿaliyyīn. Abbakr is said to have sided with *makk* Nimr, but in the early 1830s he was living in Khandaq, where he invited Cadalvène and Breuvery to his wedding celebrations. When Cuny visited Khandaq in early 1858, the famous Abbakr was dead, but the memories of his riches and large-scale trading with Dār Fūr were still vivid.[78] His son al-Nūr traded in Kordofan.

During Ḥamza's absence in Egypt, his wife in al-Matamma gave birth to Aḥmad, ʿAbd Allāh's elder brother. Returning from Egypt, Ḥamza found al-Matamma ruined by the Daftardar, and he therefore took his family and settled at Dabbat al-ʿAbdallāb near Kadarū, where ʿAbd Allāh was subsequently born in about 1824–5.

When security was restored, Ḥamza returned to al-Matamma and engaged in trade. We have already mentioned his investments in indigo production in around 1840, and there are clear indications that he also invested in land and thereby laid the foundations to the family's landed estates. A contract shows that he bought land in al-Matamma in 1849.[79]

It is interesting to note how ʿAbd Allāh and his brothers divided up and at the same time always coordinated their commercial enterprises. They had inherited a family name of wide reputation and creditworthiness, an international commercial network with affiliations to the government-friendly Khatmiyya brotherhood, and the necessary skills and 'know-how'. These assets were worth far more than mere capital.

Al-Matamma, an administrative centre which regained some, if not all, of its earlier commercial standing in the Turkiyya at the expense of Shendi, remained the key centre in the network of the sons of Ḥamza. Khandaq was another important entrepōt, Khartoum became another point, while al-Ubayyiḍ and Kobbei continued to be the chief source of merchandise forwarded by them to Egypt, such as gum, ivory and feathers. The following outline will give an idea of the movements of the brothers, their associations and range of economic activities. The relevant brothers here are Ḥasan, Muḥammad Aḥmad, ʿAbbās, Aḥmad and Khayr.

ʿAbd Allāh's son, Sulaymān, says that his father started as a trader, without trying any other occupation first and that he settled in Khandaq. There his main job was to forward merchandise from his brothers to Egypt. The brothers also helped each other by extending credits and loans and by repaying loans to a third party and making payments for commodities on behalf of each other. The extra-family third party were Sudanese, Turkish and Egyptian business associates, partners, etc., who, once mutual trust was established, tend to occur more than once, over several years and in different capacities in the documents.

The earliest document concerned with ʿAbd Allāh so far recovered from the collection was written in 1856–7, being a certificate of repayment of a debt of 400 piastres owed by ʿAbd Allāh.[80] The documents from the 1860s are largely concerned with similar matters, the discharging of debts or promising repayment of debts. However, the roles are reversed so that in all cases except one it is ʿAbd Allāh who is the creditor. The amounts due to him varied from 350 piastres to 18,670 piastes, to be repaid within a specified time, ranging from five to seven months. Of course, no interest rate is mentioned, but then neither is the initial loan or credit, so that the recorded sums to be repaid probably incorporate a hidden interest.

The predominance of credit and promissory notes in ʿAbd Allāh's favour in this period indicates that he had become a substantial merchant and moneylender. At an early stage he cultivated a good relationship with the government, to their mutual benefit. He might enter into *commenda* (sleeping partnership) contracts with Turkish officials, as he once did with the son of the governor of Berber, in which the latter provided capital (1,000 dollars) and ʿAbd Allāh the trading expertise, which resulted in a net profit of 1,130 dollars.[81] On other occasions he lent money to the Turks, and in his capacity as big merchant he was also obliged to provide them with certain commodities and give them presents.[82]

At least three of the brothers lived in Khandaq at various stages in their careers. Thus towards the end of the Turkiyya, ʿAbd Allāh seems often to have been in Khandaq, and the epithet al-Khandaqāwī appears frequently. A letter from the Mahdī (June 1885) to ʿAbd Allāh, Ḥasan and a nephew Imām Muḥammad Aḥmad was sent to Khandaq.[83] In a letter from the Jaʿalī leader ʿAbd Allāh w. Saʿd in 1874–5, ʿAbd Allāh now living in al-Matamma, is referred to as *ʿumdat tujjār bilād al-sūdān*, which may be translated as 'head of the merchants of the Sudan', but it is uncertain whether he really occupied such a position or if this was only an expression of politeness. In a letter from the same author in 1878 he is referred to as the 'head of the merchants of al-Matamma', *'umdat tujjār al-Matamma.*[84] Ḥasan and Muḥammad Aḥmad used Khandaq more or less as their permanent base. Another brother, Khayr, was a merchant in Khartoum, while still another, al-Ṭāhir and a nephew, Aḥmad w. al-Bashīr Ḥamza, represented the family in Dār Fūr.

Successful merchants put more efforts into organising business operations and tended more often to leave the caravan transportation of their commodities in charge of others. However, for various reasons the conditions of the Sudano-Egyptian trade made the big merchants accompany their commodities themselves at certain periods.[85] Thus 'Abd Allāh appears sometimes in Kordofan, in Khandaq or in Egypt.

Any Sudanese merchant or association of merchants with international pretensions would seek to establish contacts with foreign merchants, either in Egypt or in Khartoum. The Egyptian link was well-established in this family before the occupation, and passed on to the sons of Ḥamza. Their Egyptian partner was no minor figure, namely 'Abd al-Ghanī al-Ṭayyib al-Tāzī, a Moroccan merchant in Cairo, who on one occasion obtained permission from the Khedive Ismā'īl to trade with Dār Fūr.[86] In around 1869–70, 'Abd Allāh and 'Abbās were conducting business with him, and it does not seem to be a recently established relationship. A few years later the role is taken over by his son Sulaymān 'Abd al-Ghanī and now Ḥasan also enters into the network, living at Khandaq.

It is clear that the documents do not give a full picture of the partnerships and other transactions between 'Abd Allāh and 'Abd al-Ghanī and Sulaymān. The letters between them often refer to previous business operations. But they introduce a new dimension into our understanding of the organisation of long-distance trade between Egypt and the Sudan.

From the latter half of the 1860s, gum arabic became the most important export article from the Sudan, a development which 'Abd Allāh was ready to take advantage of. Several documents confirm his involvement in gum, and although he included commodities like feathers, it seems that gum was his staple export commodity and probably that of his brothers as well. Among the imports we find textiles. In addition to family matters, the documents show that much business was transacted between the brothers, acting as each other's representatives in forwarding commodities and bills of exchange. Credits and loans were also elements in their relationships, but so far no evidence indicates that formal commercial partnerships were contracted between them.

A factor which cemented the corporateness of the family was their many landed estates, to which they must have added substantially and which were administered partly jointly and partly individually. From the eighteenth-century estates were acquired in Khandaq and Kobbei, to which were later added estates in Kordofan, al-Matamma and finally in Egypt. Investment in land was seen as a means of security as well as a source of revenue. 'Abd Allāh was also involved in grain trade and we may assume that his two boats at al-Matamma and six in Dongola were used for the transport of grain and other commodities.

Apparently ʿAbd Allāh was not in a hurry to answer the letter from the Mahdī in June 1885, in which he was forgiven for his alliance with the Turks and asked to come and join the Mahdī. Anyway, the Mahdī died shortly afterwards before ʿAbd Allāh could have managed to reach him in Omdurman, and at the end of the year (1885) ʿAbd Allāh had chosen exile in Egypt. His properties in the Sudan were confiscated by the Mahdists, and hoping he would get compensation from the government, he made four claims listing his losses, and wrote a letter about his property to the commander-in-chief of the Egyptian army. In al-Matamma he claimed to have lost a house, furniture, carpets, livestock, grain, two boats, and jewellery to the value of 20,400 dollars. In Dongola, he lost, together with Imām Muḥammad Aḥmad, houses, goods, cattle, furniture, carpets, and six boats to the value of 37,925 dollars. In Kordofan he lost 15,000 dollars in cash, and gum, feathers and other commodities, its total 116,250 dollars. In Dār Fūr, together with al-Ṭāhir Ḥamza and Aḥmad al-Bashīr Ḥamza, he lost a house, livestock and goods to the value of 12,000 dollars.[87] He hired a lawyer and promised him a quarter of the sum, if he managed to regain it.[88] The result of the case remains to be investigated. The claims were referred to here to show the immense riches ʿAbd Allāh had acquired as a merchant at the key points in his trading network. In addition came the value of the landed estates which were kept out of the claims, either because compensation for them was unlikely, or because landed property would be regained at an eventual reoccupation.

ʿAbd Allāh had started to invest in land also in al-Rammādī in Upper Egypt in the 1870s, and that is where he stayed while in exile. His commercial connections with Egypt and his leanings towards the Khatmiyya brotherhood, would make it difficult to continue to trade on the basis of the network outlined above under a government hostile to Egypt. From the rise of the Mahdī in 1881 to the fall of Khartoum in January 1885, documentary evidence shows that ʿAbd Allāh continued to ship gum to Egypt as if nothing was happening.[89] In 1885–6 the Khedive Muḥammad Tawfīq conferred upon him the title of Bey.[90]

Bābikr Bedri was a prisoner of war in Darāw in Upper Egypt under the Mahdiyya, and there he received letters from ʿAbd Allāh Bey inviting him to come to see him in al-Rammādī. Bedri has devoted some paragraphs to him in his autobiography and this is the only known contemporary description. ʿAbd Allāh's documents from this period confirm Bedri's impressions, namely that the former was deeply involved in trade, agriculture and horse-raising. ʿAbd Allāh cross-examined Babikr about the prices in Darāw. His extensive fields made him a substantial grain merchant and enabled him to provide the prisoners of war with free rations of durra each month. He maintained a large household, which is confirmed by his son Sulaymān, and is described as very rich, possessing many horses, and enjoying a cosmopolitan way of life.[91]

After the reconquest of the Sudan in 1898, ʿAbd Allāh started to wind up his affairs in Rammādī and sold off a part of his land there to free capital for new ventures in the Sudan. The last *faddāns* reverted to his heirs in due time, but in the 1950s the land was expropriated by the new regime of Gamāl ʿAbd al-Nāṣir (Nasser). My informant Sulaymān went to al-Rammādī at that time to reclaim the land but was thrown into jail and had to return empty-handed.[92]

Back in al-Matamma in around 1902, ʿAbd Allāh Bey started a series of land purchases, particularly from women, which lasted over several years. How and to what extent he regained his earlier landed possessions, is not yet clear. He was the first in the area to import a British steam-powered irrigation pump, a *wābūr*, which was shipped to the Sudan with the aid of the exiled al-Zubayr Pasha.[93] This was a major step forward in enhancing the family's agricultural incomes, and an inspiration for other merchants and big landowners to give up the old *sāqiya* and invest in pump schemes. The *wābūr* may still be seen on the bank of the Nile at al-Matamma, in the shadow of a huge diesel pump belonging to the family today.

Being only a few years older and born in the same area, ʿAbd Allāh knew al-Zubayr, the famous Jaʿalī slave trader and conqueror of Dār Fūr, before their exile in Egypt. However, it does not seem that they had any commercial dealings with each other during the Turkiyya. ʿAbd Allāh was in Kordofan at the time of al-Zubayr's occupation of Dār Fūr (1874), but did not follow the many, like Ilyās Bey Umm Birayr, who accompanied the government army to take hold of the new province. Their areas of interest differed widely both in terms of commodities and geography. Whereas al-Zubayr made his fortune in the Baḥr al-Ghazāl, mainly in slaves and ivory, which he forwarded to Dār Fūr, Kordofan and Khartoum, ʿAbd Allāh's network of markets and associations covered the Northern Sudan and Egypt, often directed and organised from al-Matamma, and excluding slaves almost completely. The different business patterns and careers of these two men who came from the same socio-economic environment may perhaps be attributed to their backgrounds. ʿAbd Allāh grew up in a merchant family and found a firmly established framework to build on. Al-Zubayr, a son of a minor chief, followed the footsteps of some older relatives and joined the White Nile traders, first as an agent and later as an independent trader.

It is noteworthy that a successful commercial career in the Sudan in the nineteenth century did not have to depend on or derive from slave trading, as is usually assumed. In fact the numerous *jallāba* who went south and west and dealt in small-scale slave trading, rarely made more than a modest profit, because the risks, losses and customs dues were so great. Independent success in the south required private armies to subdue hostile populations and fight off competition from rival 'companies' and *zarība* owners. ʿAbd Allāh operated in more stable and less dangerous regions, chosing to conduct business within the Turkish domains rather than on the outer frontier. After all, the family estates to which he wanted to add more were located there, and there were also his debtors and creditors. These two career patterns required different forms of organisation to facilitate long-distance operations, but both of them utilised similar systems of networks and associations, and both of them facilitated the expansion of the Western market into the Sudan.

It was in the sector of commerce that the largest capital accumulation was generated in the Turkiyya. Some of his capital was naturally channelled out of the country, for the benefit of the world market and/or the Egyptian treasury, for private investments abroad, and much was squandered on luxury and conspicuous consumption. However, a substantial part of the surplus was reinvested in trade, in commercial agriculture and farm slavery, in loans, rural credit and currency speculations.

CONTRACTS AND PARTNERSHIPS IN TRADE

The nineteenth-century Northern Sudan produced a substantial body of private legal documents, most of which are lost for ever. Recent discoveries, however, indicate that there are still documents privately held along the Nile. Islamic law emphasises the usefulness – if not the duty – to record transactions and agreements, 'for fear of forgetfulness', as some documents phrase it. The science of writing documents, *ʿilm al-shurūṭ*, appeared early in Islamic jurisprudence. In the Sudan it was generally the *fakī* who acted as the notary. It must be noted, however, that signed and witnessed documents were not legal proofs in themselves, unless witnesses to the transaction or to the signatures could stand up and confirm them whenever necessary.[94]

What kind of private transactions were recorded? Beginning with the family, *ṣadāq* documents figure prominently, being marriage contracts which list the assets to be transferred as dowry from husband to wife, normally by two instalments. Most of the stipulations of the *ṣadāq* contract did not become operative before divorce or death, when the wife had the right to receive the remaining dowry. If she herself had asked for divorce, as might happen, she had no claim on the remaining dowry.[95] *Ṣadaqas* or testamentary bequests (alms) and *waṣiyya* or deeds of inheritance are also expressions of legal rules governing family relations with regard to the transfer of property. As a corporate unit the extended family possessed and administered a body of property that was transferred in portions and over time from the elder to the younger generation.

A different category of documents are bills of sale, mortgages, certificates of indebtedness, promissory notes, quittances, land surveys, claims to property, records of disputes, and so on.[96] These documents emanated both from the peasant and the merchant classes, and in many cases reflected the widening gap of social inequality in the nineteenth century. We meet peasants of moderate means who pooled their capital to buy shares in vital productive factors, creditors and debtors, and smallholders selling land to the big farmers and/or merchants. The merchant class produced yet another group of documents which emanated from the institutions of long-distance trade, commercial cooperation and partnership, i.e., letters of credit and partnership contracts. Long-distance trade did not only depend on institutions for transferring commodities but equally important were legal instruments which transferred capital, payments and credit over long distances. Two instruments were available for such purposes, the *ḥawāla*, which was an assignment which provided a mandate either to collect or to pay, to fulfil an obligation already existing (also termed 'delegation of credit'). The *suftāja* or letter of credit (cheque) was a form of money-loan to B in order that he may pay it to A in another place, or rather a loan of money to avoid the risk of transporting coins to distant places. They gained the same importance as similar institutions had in Europe in the Middle Ages, for example the Italian *tratta* without which long-distance trade would not have been able to function. The travel literature as well as the documents give examples of such money transactions by way of letters of assignments and credit.[97] The following discussion will be confined to the partnership contracts.

In spite of the differences between the legal schools, Islamic Law distinguishes between four broad categories of contractual partnerships, *ʿaqd sharika* or *sharika al-ʿaqd* (*societas*), and put the sleeping partnership or partnership of profit (known in Arabic as *qirāḍ*, *muḍāraba* or *muqārada*, and in Italian as *commenda*) in a category of its own.[98]

Contractual partnerships or 'societas':

1 The unlimited commercial partnership (*mufāwaḍa*) with full power and liability for each partner and which involves the whole property of both partners. (In its broadest definition it is only acceptable to Ḥanafī jurists.)
2 The limited liability and investment partnership (*ʿinān*). It may be general or specific with regard to the trade engaged in and the number of operations, but whereas it implied mutual agency, it did not stipulate mutual surety.
3 The partnership of crafts, most often designated as *sharikat al-sanāʾiʿ wa'l-taqabbul*, in which the partners' skilled labour in some manufacture is the input capital, for the joint pursuit of a craft or related crafts.
4 The credit cooperative, *sharikat al-wujūh*, in which the partners bought commodities on joint credit, in order to share the profit after the resale.

The sleeping partnership or 'commenda':

1 The *commenda* combines capital or commodities from one of the partners with the input of trading skills, labour, travelling and time from the other, and the latter is not responsible for the possible loss of the capital, and the profit is to be shared on an equal basis, 50–50.

In the papers left by ʿAbd Allāh Bey Ḥamza there are examples of both contractual partnerships in the *ʿinān* variety and of *commendas*. In the medieval East and West the *commenda* was the most important instrument for the financing of commercial ventures, particularly suitable to the requirements of long-distance trade. Its significance for long-distance trade has been documented by Goitein in his analysis of the medieval Geniza documents, by Walz in his study of Egyptian/Sudanese trade in the eighteenth century, and by Postan in his book on medieval trade and finance in Europe.[99] It 'combined the advantages of a loan with those of a partnership; and while containing elements characteristic of both, it cannot be strictly classified in either category.'[100] It was particularly the freedom of the travelling agent, the *tractor*, in the use of the capital provided by the *commendator* in the pursuit of profit, and the freedom from any liability in the event of the partial or complete loss of the capital, that tempted him to engage in such ventures. The *commenda* brought capital and labour together in such a way that capital bore the losses, but in the case of profit, capital received only 50 per cent of the profit, the other 50 per cent going to labour. The *commenda* is termed *muḍāraba* in Ḥanafī law, *qirāḍ* and *muqārada* in Mālikī and Shāfiʿī law.[101] Investors in a *commenda* were either merchants or other people with ready investment capital. The agent was normally a merchant who sought more capital, or as in the case of industrial *commendas* (defined illegal by the Mālikists), it could be an artisan. The *commenda* varied therefore from a simple contract of service to a more elaborate contract of investment and finance.

Islamic legal tradition in the Sudan was dominated by the Mālikī school. The Ottoman Turks followed the Ḥanafī school. There was probably no conflict here; the Sudanese continued to regulate affairs among themselves according to Mālikī and customary law, but when dealing with the local Turks or with people in Egypt, Ḥanafī law was adhered to. Thus in the *commenda* contract between ʿAbd Allāh Bey Ḥamza and a Turk in Berber the Ḥanafī term *muḍāraba* is used, but in a similar contract between two Sudanese, the Mālikī term *qirāḍ* is used.[102] A striking difference between these two schools is that Mālikī law prohibits the use of goods and merchandise as investment in a *commenda*, which in theory prevents a merchant from shipping his merchandise with an agent to another market under the rules governing a *commenda*. To overcome this difficulty, and still adhere to Mālikī law, the merchant sold his merchandise to a third party, gave the money to an agent as a legal investment in a *commenda*, whereupon the latter repurchased the merchandise and set off. The practicalities of long-distance trade would count for more than theoretical rules.[103]

In the case of contractual partnerships, Mālikī law restricts the scope of the *mufāwaḍa* and the *ʿinān* to the joint capital of the partners. Each partner confers upon his colleague full authority to dispose of their joint capital in any acceptable manner which will benefit their partnership. The Mālikī *ʿinān* partnership is the narrowest in scope, confined to a single commodity or a single transaction and the mutual mandate is also restricted. Furthermore emphasis is put on proportionality or balance between the input of the two partners, which can be in cash, goods or work. As for the cash, it has to be in gold or silver coins, and it has to be present at the contracting of the partnership in order to be physically mixed, one sum with the other. There are also examples of such partnerships in the collection of ʿAbd Allāh Bey. Work partnerships, combining labour and cash between persons of the same profession, are allowed, but not credit partnerships.[104]

In the following analysis socio-economic data and context will be considered, leaving aside diplomatic structure and legal formulations. Partnership institutions were not confined to trade and crafts, but lay at the core of the organisation of agricultural production as well.[105] The jointly owned means of production can be seen as proprietary partnerships (*sharikat al-milk*), forming the basis of the partnerships in production. Partnerships in production came about in two ways, first when the share-owners worked and produced together, secondly, when external specialists were invited to put in skills, labour, animals, implements and seed. Partnerships in agriculture were not Islamic in origin, but grew out of centuries of socio-economic adaptations. They were not committed to writing and have left few traces of earlier formal rules. In Islamic culture the widespread use of partnerships in almost any economic enterprise that required more than one man, was a way to avoid the somewhat repugnant direct paid employment, although some of the work partnerships and industrial *commendas* came very close to it. It was also a way to avoid borrowing money for commercial investments. When the Nubians became Arabised Muslims, they did not find these cultural attitudes and legal rationalisations completely alien to their own way of thinking about economic cooperation. After all, wage employment is a recent (nineteenth century) phenomenon in the Sudan and it was more natural for them to stick to partnerships than it was in the far more developed and monetised central areas of the Middle East.

The idea of partnership and its application to various economic sectors was therefore not alien to the riverain societies when commercial connections abroad acquainted the Sudanese traders with Islamic commercial law and the legal instruments (*commendas* and contractual partnerships) available to them. Walz has shown how Sudanese *jallāba* long before the Turkiyya obtained capital and merchandise from big merchants in Egypt under both the *commenda* and the commercial partnership forms of cooperation.[106] Interestingly enough, Egyptian and Sudanese commercial terminology does not always make a clear distinction between these two main types of contracts, using in both cases the term *ʿaqd sharika* or *sharikat al-ʿaqd*.

THREE CONTRACTS FROM THE ARCHIVE OF ʿABD ALLĀH BEY ḤAMZA

The following is a commentary on three commercial contracts. The translations can be found in the Appendix.

1 Berg: NI 363. 15/91 (13 Shawwāl 1299/28 August 1882)
The two parties were together in Egypt at the time of the writing of the contract. ʿAbd Allāh was to act as the travelling agent (*tractor*) for Sulaymān and was to go to Kordofan, where he was staying at that time, and where he was to take over the capital of the joint venture, namely 10,000 *tōbs* consigned to Ilyās Pasha, the one-time governor of the province, and deposited there with him. With this initial capital he was to acquire Sudanese commodities in consultation with Sulaymān, and send them to Egypt, where the latter would sell them and share the profit with ʿAbd Allāh. The *tōbs* represented a capital of 5,000 dollars, which was a fortune in those days, and which indicates the economic dimension of this business venture.

This is clearly a *commenda* contract, although that is not explicitly stated, and although there are some features that seem incompatible with a correct *commenda*. First the capital is not present at the time of concluding the contract, and secondly the trading restrictions imposed on the *tractor*. The *commenda* stipulations are first of all: (1) the joining of capital with travelling and trading (2) the risk of losing the capital is completely on the *commendator*, and finally (3) the profit is to be shared equally 50–50. The introductory reference to the founder of the Ḥanafī school indicates that the contract is set up in accordance with the rules of this school. Although it might have happened frequently, it is not often stated openly in commercial contracts, as in the present case, that each partner receives a copy. The third contract below, however, seems to indicate that it was written in only one copy and this was to be kept by the *commendator*.

The contract confirms that ʿAbd Allāh used to trade on Kordofan and that he was heading for Kordofan after his present visit to Egypt. It is also interesting to note that the contract was signed a year after the Mahdī had declared himself and just one month before his forces laid siege to the capital of Kordofan, al-Ubayyiḍ, and half a year before al-Ubayyiḍ fell to the Mahdists and Ilyās Pasha went over to them. It is therefore not certain that ʿAbd Allāh really managed to fulfil his obligations and carry out the transactions laid out in the contract.

2 Berg. NI 383. 15/111 (15 Shawwāl 1299/30 August 1882)
The present contract is an *ʿaqd sharika*, a contractual partnership, and therefore different from the one above. It belongs to the *mufāwaḍa/ʿinān* group of commercial partnerships, in the West known as *societas*. The two partners put in an equal amount of capital in precious coins which were mixed in front of them to become one capital. The stipulations regarding the sharing of the eventual profit or loss as well as the duration of the partnership follow Islamic law.

These two contracts show that both types of joint venture were utilised to promote long-distance trade. In the first case, the travelling partner put in travelling, time and labour, for which he received 50 per cent of the profit, and any loss would be on the investor. In the second case, Sulaymān and ʿAbd Allāh were equal partners; although ʿAbd Allāh went to the Sudan with the jointly owned commodities, he was not Sulaymān's travelling agent as in the previous contract, his input was cash and not work; for his work and expenses he would be paid, and for his cash input he would receive half the profit after the capital had been returned.

3 Berg. NI 347. 15/75 (27 Shaʿbān 1307/18 April 1890)
In spite of the use of the vague term *sharika* (partnership), this contract which is also written in Egypt, must be treated as a *commenda*, and it exemplifies a situation where ʿAbd Allāh is the investor (*commendator*). The capital invested was in pounds sterling. It was both taken and received, two separate and necessary actions in the transfer of a loan and the standard formula for a contract of sale. This and the examples above also show that whenever two business partners engaged in several ventures at the same time, they kept them separate in different contracts. A brother of ʿAbd Allāh, Ḥasan appears here as a witness.

The present chapter has analysed some basic features of the profound changes that took place in the commercial sector with the imposition of a colonial regime. Most of the changes were seen from the perspective of Shendi and al-Matamma. The analysis also focused on the trading networks linked to the area, from an individual and family level to the larger ethnic trading networks. Their interaction with the rulers and the foreign traders, after the difficult years of the monopoly, was found to be a factor which facilitated the flow of commodities into the hands of the foreigners. There was both competition and mutual dependency between the foreign firms and the Sudanese networks, but the latter were extremely helpful in spreading imported coins and commodities and in bringing local commodities to the export centres. The colonisation of the south would have been impossible without them.

The emerging Sudanese merchant class became a key factor in the process of monetisation and the spread of rural indebtedness. This happened in two ways, first by turning foodstuffs into commodities and thereby depriving the food producers of the customary management of their most basic necessities; secondly, by providing the peasants with cash (as loans or in exchange for foodstuffs) so that the Turks could collect a part of the taxes in money. This was one of the reasons why the merchants, whether they came from a village background or not, gained substantial interests in agriculture, landed estates and farm slavery. In other cases the merchants helped the Turks by taking over confiscated tribute in kind (e.g. grain and cattle) in exchange for cash. The conclusion to be drawn from this is that extra-commercial or semi-commercial activities of the merchants, i.e., outside pure buying and selling, and the infusion of merchant capital into the agricultural sector, had profound socio-economic repercussions.

Long-distance trade across the Sahara is usually analysed in quantitative terms and from an external point of view. The archive left by a merchant in al-Matamma provides new insight into the internal organisation of trade. The collection also indicates how local merchant capital could be built up in the period, resting on three legs, first on the old family networks, secondly on a good relationship with the Turks, and thirdly on the connection with foreign merchant capital.

As has been suggested above, commerce was undoubtedly the sector where the greatest capital accumulation took place. Most of this capital was the result of outright exploitation of the producers and the natural resources of the country. The regional and international system of unequal exchange, the dependence on merchant-creditors, and official price manipulations, made the Sudanese producers economically powerless, both when they were selling and buying, and when paying their taxes. Private commercial exploitation went hand in hand with government exploitation, and in the northern Sudan, both the government and the merchant class undermined their own continued prosperity by extracting too much from the debt-ridden peasants and driving them to flee from their farms.

7

Conclusion: dispersion and return

EMIGRATION

A characteristic feature of Sudanese society today is the widespread settlements of northerners throughout the towns and villages of the central and southern savannas. This diaspora has pushed the frontiers of Islam further into Africa and continues to do so also today. 'One comes across Danāgla in every town in the Sudan', wrote a diarist in 1839.[1] From before the Turkiyya the Danāgla were among the most numerous and prosperous immigrants to Kordofan, closely followed by the Ja'aliyyīn and outnumbered by them in many areas during the Turkiyya. In Kordofan, the migrants were in a somewhat freer situation, but they might still be subjected to arbitrary treatment by the Turks and be forced to move further west or south. Müller observed an episode there in 1848 in which a peasant set fire to his house in protest after being subject to maltreatment and extortion by six soldiers; he claimed that the Turks had slaughtered his hens, stolen his sheep, driven his camels away, made a soldier out of his son, and raped his womenfolk. 'Now you will take nothing more from me. I will go to Dār Fūr!'[2]

The sources do not indicate when this process of migration started, probably because there has always been mobility between the Nile and the savannas, and not always *from* the Nile. The Arabs who intermarried with the Nubians to form the Ja'aliyyīn Group may have moved into the Nile Valley from Kordofan where the founding father, Ibāhīm Ja'al, is said to have been buried. A few tribes in the area stretching from the Nile Confluence into Kordofan, such as the Jamū'iyya and the Jawāmi'a, regard themselves as belonging to the Ja'aliyyīn Group, but they are probably not emigrants from the Main Nile.

The savanna and the sahel is largely open country across which it was easy to move. Centralised political units dominated the Nile Valley and discouraged the out-migration of peasants upon whom the polities rested. However, population pressure, periods of political disintegration, wars and insecurity, made some people leave their villages before the Turkiyya also, but never on a comparable scale. They sought the protection of the shaykhs of the savannas and the sultan of Dār Fūr, and asked for permission to trade and cultivate within their *dārs*.

Once emigrants had settled in the diaspora, they started to attract fellow tribesmen and relatives from the Nile and some would be encouraged to move further afield. The local ruling classes took advantage of the services offered by the learned strangers, who could both read and write and cure sick people, in addition to importing luxuries for them. Thus in many cases religious and legal expertise were as valuable assets as commercial wealth, being rewarded by landed estates, tax exemptions and other privileges by local rulers.[3] Some migrants even married into the royal families, a step that in some cases led ambitious Jaʿaliyyīn to found their own kingdoms and dynasties.[4]

The Turkiyya united a vast territory which, combined with severe exploitation of the riverain peasants, opened up for waves of emigration from the Main Nile. The gradual southward spread of the *sāqiya* and the flat-roofed mud houses south and west of the Confluence, is a clear indication of what was taking place. The emigrants represented a serious loss of revenue to the governors of the north, and for the same reason they were welcomed in the central and southern districts by the Turkish governors there. In the second phase of colonial expansion, 1840–75, the northern migrants contributed their expertise, labour, networks and capital, and in most cases they were ahead of the Turks and cleared the road for them.

Commercial capital played an important role in imperialist expansion in the eighteenth and nineteenth centuries. Under Muḥammad ʿAlī and his successors, Egypt was drawn into the periphery of the expanding Western market. At the same time and partly in response to the same development, Egypt embarked upon a secondary imperialist expansion in Africa, supported by both local and Western capital. Despite some international irritation over the monopoly system, which Egypt was forced to abandon in around 1840, Western interests supported Egypt's expansion since it automatically created what may be called a secondary periphery for the Western market. The subsequent expansion into southern and western Sudan came about in a joint effort by European, Levantine, Turkish, Egyptian and northern Sudanese merchant capital, together with government forces and Christian missionaries. This created a tertiary periphery, subjected to both European, Egyptian and northern Sudanese interests, and laid the foundation for the special status of the south which became institutionalised later under the British and which is the main reason for the current civil war, 1955–72, and 1983 onwards.

THE CAUSES OF EMIGRATION

In describing the causes and effects of migration in Africa, Hartmann wrote that the Jaʿaliyyīn suffered from real 'travelmania', *Reisemanie*. A genuine Jaʿalī could easily find an excuse to satisfy his lust for travelling. He could be found all over East Africa. If he ran out of money *en route* he could survive as middleman, missionary, doctor or writer of charms and marriage contracts. When in serious need he could even become a soldier.[5] Munzinger had a similar impression of the Jaʿaliyyīn, saying that they went wherever they expected to obtain profit.[6] This un-nuanced stereotype does not distinguish between sons of peasants and sons of merchants, who would have different motives for leaving their villages, and it is misleading with regard to the causes of emigration. However, Hartmann and Munzinger say something about the magnitude of the emigration of the Jaʿaliyyīn around 1860, which is confirmed by many others. Although many perhaps hoped to return one day with enough capital to get married, build *sāqiyas* and enlarge the family farm and so on, others invited their family to come after them or they established new families in the diaspora. These pockets of northerners transmitted their culture, language and religion to the host population. Hence the significance of the Jaʿaliyyīn diaspora in Africa.

Under the Funj as well as under the Turks and the Mahdists, wars, raids and famines were the most obvious causes of emigration from the north. The Shāyqiyya have been blamed for terrorising many Danāgla and Jaʿaliyyīn into fleeing to Kordofan and Dār Fūr in the eighteenth century.[7] The punitive campaigns of the Daftardar uprooted thousands of Jaʿaliyyīn who took refuge across the Ethiopian border.[8]

Apart from these acute causes of emigration, which are so numerous in the sources, other economic, ecological, social, cultural and political factors caused a steady emigration from the north (see p. 75). It is tempting to use the modern term of 'structural violence' to define some of the less visible causes of emigration, so often referred to in the sources as laziness and an urge to travel. We have found that land scarcity in relation to population was not acute in the Turkiyya. However, when people started to divide up their holdings in earnest in response to the Sharia and the market forces, and land also became a commodity, the unequal distribution of land and the difficulty of access to vacant land for poor peasants, forced many debt-ridden families out of a village even if there was plenty of land. Furthermore, emigration tended to affect *every* family rather than *whole* families, as it was the men who left first. This led to a serious drain on the labour force, only partially alleviated by slave labour and *teddān* arrangements, and to a general inability to exploit vacant land.

From his childhood, a boy would learn that some of his relatives lived outside the *dār*, and he would learn that to travel abroad for shorter or longer periods was a normal part of a Jaʿalī career. The growing frequency of emigration is expressed in a Jaʿalī saying: 'The north gives birth, the south gives manhood.' A girl back home might be told that one day a cousin from the diaspora would come home to marry her, as was often the case.

Irrespective of period, the causes of emigration may be divided into two interrelated categories, the 'pull' factors and the 'push' factors.[9]

The 'pull' factors. The positive picture of life and opportunities in the diaspora, particularly in the sector of trade, which was undoubtedly a motivating force in general. The breakdown of what may have remained of the old political and socio-cultural sanctions against migration made it easier also to leave when life became too difficult, even if the Turks erected new barriers against what they saw as defection. The individual perception of the misery and lack of opportunities back home was reinforced by success stories from the diaspora.

Success in the diaspora was usually achieved in trade, and to some degree in religious activities. The geographical spread of the diaspora was congruous with the trade routes and networks. The availability of land was also a structuring factor, as the northern agricultural settlements in the Khayrān in Kordofan and along the Blue and White Niles clearly show. Religious men were also tempted to try their luck in the diaspora, where the chances of gaining a living by offering their services would be much greater than at home. A document from al-Matamma shows how the members of a religious family spread to various districts throughout the Sudan in this period.[10] Students as well as teachers travelled and stayed for long periods in various places; 'shaykh-seeking' is an ancient Islamic practice. Renowned *fakīs* and religious shaykhs attracted students and would-be members of the religious brotherhoods they represented.

The 'push' factors. The most obvious causes of emigration ranged from natural calamities to political insecurity and war. In the Turkiyya the regular harassments by the unruly soldiers were naturally enough to make people leave, but the role of structural factors has been emphasised previously (p. 76–81), and the incompatibility between a market directed agricultural and fiscal policy and the local subsistence economy. Cash crops were found to have exhausted the soil, the animal motive power, and the wheel, and limited the space and time left for food production. The cutting of trees to clear land for government schemes, to build boats and to get fuel for the steam-powered river boats was another serious attack on the eco-system.

Contemporary observers and finally also the rulers themselves saw, albeit reluctantly, a clear connection between high taxes, the methods of collection and emigration. The amount to be collected each year did not fluctuate with or correspond to the annual farm output, and with decreasing returns, the weight of taxes grew proportionately. The demand for taxes in cash caused special difficulties, as it forced the peasants to sell grain at very low prices and to borrow from local merchants. Outstanding taxes and debts were therefore a main 'push' factor.

A common denominator in the complex set of 'push' factors seems to have been what may be termed 'incomplete reproduction'. This means in plain words that riverain societies became unable to replace or reproduce from one year to the next such crucial necessities as labour, soil fertility, tools, seed, water and animals. Not only did the Turkiyya seriously interfere with what the peasants could put aside from the harvest for future social and economic investments, including seed for the next season, but the natural and necessary maintenance of the means of production in general was hampered and in many cases destroyed.[11]

ABSENTEE HUSBANDS AND FATHERS

Jaʿalī women and children were not completely unaccustomed to the absence of their fathers, brothers and husbands before the Turkiyya. It gave the wives a freer position in society but also more responsibility for the children and the family farm. Wives of the professional long-distance traders and camel drivers would see their husbands even less often. The loss of farm labour and supervision which this caused, was compensated for by slave labour, *teddān* and *amāna* contracts and seasonal work-parties. In the Turkiyya, large-scale emigration put unprecedented pressure on the peasant family and particularly on the women. 'Grass-widows' became frequent both along the Nile and in Kordofan, and destitute town women might resort to prostitution in order to survive. Under normal circumstances a husband would perhaps appoint a guardian (Ar. *wakīl*) for his wife and children before he left, but many factors could hinder him from returning at the promised time or from sending remittances home.[12]

A husband who had no farm back home to maintain his wife was obliged to maintain her in other ways. The case of the defaulting husband from Shendi is probably not unique, but we do not know how often destitute 'grass-widows' came to the local Sharia court to seek help, as in this case. In 1866 a woman by the name of Fāṭima bt. *al-fakī* Muḥammad ʿAwaḍ al-Sīd appeared before the *qāḍī* of Shendi, Muhammad Ahmad Jalāl al-Dīn, and lodged a complaint against her husband who had left her to trade in Dār Fūr and Dār Fartīt, 'outside the Ottoman dominion', without providing maintenance for her, her daughter and female slave. Since she had no other income, the court granted her maintenance by specifying what she could buy in the market on her husband's credit (see Table 6). However, her husband failed to return, and three years later she again appeared before the same *qāḍī*, this time suing for a divorce, which the court, considering her difficult economic situation, granted her according to Mālikī law.[13]

For the children of absent fathers life could be tragic, particularly when the mother was dead. The traumas caused by absent fathers have passed into Jaʿalī folklore. A recurrent theme is that the guardian of the children makes them do heavy work and denies them proper care. One story is about two children whose father 'used to travel with the merchants, who took a caravan of camels to Egypt to sell them there. The camels' owners used to give him commission. Then he used to come [back] and wait for the next caravan.' After the mother died, he left his children with his brother as *amāna*, sacred trust. The latter, however, instigated by his wife, exploited the children and when the father finally came back, he gave up travelling with the caravans.[14] In another story the uncle and guardian of the children kills the nephew for eating some grain. The young girl, however, managed to escape and searched every passing caravan till her father finally came one day. Learning of his son's fate, he went after his brother and killed him.[15]

It is therefore not surprising to note that wives might be tempted to accompany their husbands into the diaspora and even take part in the caravan traffic. Normally the *jallāba* brought concubines on their travels to cook for them, but their legally married wives might be invited as well.[16]

FOUR EMIGRANTS

The travellers who visited Berber Province in the 1860s noted deserted villages and depopulation. The local shaykhs were alarmed at the high rate of emigration by young men and whole families. As a concrete example from this period we may mention the case of Babikr Bedri. He was from the Rubāṭāb tribe of the Jaʿaliyyīn Group and was born near Atbara River in 1861.

> And I [Babikr] remember that towards the end of the year 1283 (spring 1867) my father left home, and there was a famine (it was general in the Sudan), and my half-brother Saʿīd used to bring gum-arabic in his *tōb*, for my mother to mix with the millet flour [durra]. I remember, too, my uncle Muḥammad ʿAlī Ḥamad al-Sīd taking us to Rufāʿa [on the Blue Nile], . . . and we lived there in Rufāʿa till I got married. [My father had first gone] with a party of six other men to Khartoum and beyond, in search of a living. [After a while] my father came to Rufāʿa, where we were. . . . That same year my father went to Karkūj [south of Sinnār] and came back with plenty of money.[17]

Babikr attended a *fakī's* Quaran school, *khalwa*, and became later a staunch follower of the Mahdi, because of which he ended up as a prisoner in Upper Egypt where he met ʿAbd Allāh Bey Ḥamza. During the Condominium he was a pioneer in the development of girls' education and was never to return to the north. The opportunities were greater in the diaspora.

A famous figure in the trade on Dār Fūr and Wadai was a Dongolāwī by the name of *al-ḥājj* Aḥmad Tangatanga. Nachtigal travelled with him from Wadai to Dār Fūr in 1874. He was born in Dongola and had studied at al-Azhar in Cairo before he went to Dār Fūr where he stayed for some time at the court. He then moved to al-Ubayyiḍ and founded a family there. His trading activities took him to Wadai, where he settled at al-Tīniyyāt, on the road between Dār Fūr and Wadai, where he traded in Egyptian commodities. However, his hospitality to numerous passing *jallāba* ruined him and at the invitation of the Wadai sultan, he went to settle at Abeshr, the capital, to act as the sultan's adviser.[18]

Perhaps the most famous and important of the Jaʿalī migrant traders was al-Zubayr Raḥma Manṣūr, the conqueror of Dār Fūr, whom we have mentioned earlier (p. 124). He was born north of Khartoum in 1830 and was sent to school in Khartoum where he studied the Quran and Mālikī law. At about sixteen years of age he joined a trading expedition up the White Nile, and after working for some time as an assistant of the Egyptian trader ʿAlī Abū ʿAmūrī, he decided to go independent. He recruited a large slave army and appointed Jaʿaliyyīn, such as ʿAbd al-Raḥmān w. al-Nujūmī, as his generals and lieutenants. Having established himself in the Baḥr al-Ghazāl, he came into conflict with Dār Fūr, whereupon he launched an attack upon the sultanate and conquered it in 1874.[19]

It seems appropriate to end this short gallery of emigrants by sketching the early career of a Dongolāwī who was to unite the different anti-government forces across ethnic and social boundaries and bring about the fall of the Turkiyya. His name was Muḥammad Aḥmad b. ʿAbd Allāh and he was born in Dongola in about 1844.[20] His father was a boat-builder, a common occupation among the Danāgla, and claimed to descend from the Prophet. As the supply of timber shrank in the north, the family moved to Kararī, near present-day Omdurman, where the father died. Muḥammad Aḥmad did not take up boat-building as did his brothers, but devoted himself to religious studies. He studied under various shaykhs and became himself a shaykh of the Sammāniyya brotherhood. When his brothers moved to Abā Island in the White Nile where timber was more plentiful, he accompanied them and soon students started to gather around him.

In around 1880 he visited al-Ubayyiḍ where there was much agitation between the pro and anti-government factions, particularly among the Jaʿaliyyīn. From being an ally of the Turks, Ilyās Pasha after his dismissal as governor in 1879 became the leader of a large group of anti-government Jaʿaliyyīn in Kordofan together with ʿAbd al-Raḥmān Bān al-Naqā.[21] His opponent was another Jaʿalī merchant, Aḥmad Bey Dafʿ Allāh who supported the new Turkish governor, Muḥammad Saʿīd Pasha. Muḥammad Aḥmad's contacts with the opposition groups in Kordofan initiated a formidable alliance between religious and commercial interests. Gordon's anti-*jallāba* policy a short time before had sent numerous destitute and remorseful northerners back north to Kordofan. Many waited for the expected Mahdī, *al-mahdī al-muntaẓar*, to deliver them from the hands of the infidel Turks and Christians. It came therefore as a relief rather than as a surprise when the pious and ascetic Muḥammed Aḥmad announced in spring 1881 that he was the expected Mahdī. For a second time he contacted the Jaʿalī opposition in Kordofan and they swore allegiance to him.

THE RETURN: HARVESTING THE WHIRLWIND

In contrast to most of the people back home, the *jallāba* of the diaspora had at least the opportunity to win wealth, self-confidence and power. Some took up farming also in the diaspora, or gained a living as *fakīs*, teachers and notaries, many remained petty traders known as *mutasabbibīn*, but in combination with those who made conspicuous commercial, religious and political careers, they became a considerable force. The military experience gained in the Baḥr al-Ghazāl and Dār Fūr was to become crucial in the coming confrontation with the Turks.

As a first step against the slave trade, Gordon forbade the formation of private armies, but a remnant of al-Zubayr's forces under the leadership of his son, Sulaymān, and outside the reach of the government, continued their slave raids in the Baḥr al-Ghazāl. Sulaymān therefore could not be controlled easily, and one might as well appoint him Turkish governor (1877) of the province, as his now exiled father also had been. A rival of Sulaymān, the Dongolāwī Idrīs w. Abtār, subsequently challenged his authority and after a revolt, Gordon switched his support to Idrīs, who then became governor. Serious unrest now spread among the Jaʿaliyyīn in Kordofan, Dār Fūr and the Baḥr al-Ghazāl, and Romolo Gessi, an Italian, was sent to crush Sulaymān, who was killed in July 1879.[22]

The government appeared to be winning over the free-booting *jallāba*, but a group of al-Zubayr's former lieutenants under the leadership of Rābiḥ Faḍl Allāh, with their remaining slave army, decided to seek their fortune in the west, where they toppled chiefs and kings all the way to Lake Chad. After conquering the kingdom of Borno, in present-day north-eastern Nigeria, Rābiḥ set himself up as the new ruler when the French colonisers were just around the corner. In the ensuing battle in 1899 at what was later to become Fort Lamy (Ndjaména) he was killed.[23] This terminated the momentum of a unique outburst of Jaʿalī emigration towards the west.

An effective measure against the *jallāba* was to instruct the tribal shaykhs of southern Dār Fūr and Kordofan to expel to the government posts any *jallābī* found in their territories. This order from Gordon was apparently received with enthusiasm. 'The traders were hunted down and plundered of all they had and the news of their treatment aroused consternation, not only in the west but amongst their kinsmen in the valley of the Nile. In this harrying of the *jallāba* the Jaʿaliyyīn were perhaps the principal sufferers.'[24]

The return of the *jallāba* to Kordofan and further north naturally intensified political agitation and unrest throughout the country. It was no coincidence that Muḥammad Aḥmad, after declaring himself the Mahdī, and being attacked by Turkish troops at Abā Island, moved to Jabal Qadīr in Kordofan, where he felt more secure among his natural allies and followers, the *jallāba*. As a religious leader he was able to unite people irrespective of tribal affiliations against a common enemy. He even managed, temporarily, to make the Jaʿaliyyīn and the Danāgla forget their rivalry, and the *jallāba* forget their maltreatment by the Baqqāra, who became the most important force in the Mahdist camp, and from whom was recruited the Mahdī's successor, the Khalīfa ʿAbdullāhi. The Mahdī appealed both to those who were outraged by what they perceived as Turkish corruption of Islam, to those who saw in the Mahdī a leader who could free them from heavy taxation and arbitrary injustices, to those whose slave trade business was seriously hampered by government interference, and to those who had personal grievances of various kinds against the Turks.

The government proved unable to deal with the situation, although it had a better equipped army. The lack of resolution must also be attributed to the British occupation of Egypt in 1882, which detracted attention away from what was building up in the Sudan. Al-Ubayyiḍ fell to the Mahdists after a long siege in January 1883. After this success the Mahdists were well prepared to meet the expedition of Hicks Pasha in the autumn, which they crushed at Shaykān. The road was now open to Khartoum. For the third time the Egyptian government called upon Gordon to assist them, and he arrived in the Sudan in the early part of 1884. His mission was apparently to evacuate Khartoum, but this was not made known in order not to discourage the still loyal people of the north. It seems also that Gordon himself hoped to turn the tide or at least keep the Mahdī from gaining more territory. Ḥusayn Pasha Khalīfa was reinstated as governor of the combined provinces of Berber and Dongola, substantial tax-reductions were announced, slavery was not to be abolished after all, and Gordon promised that the Sudan would henceforth be governed by the Sudanese themselves. Rather than pacifying the people of Berber Province, Gordon's unclear mission convinced many that the Sudan was to be evacuated and given over to the Mahdī. That Gordon later announced that he had actually been appointed governor-general of the Sudan, did not make much impression on the Sudanese.

Until the arrival of Gordon, Berber Province had been relatively quiet, the people there expected probably that the Turks would regain power. Gordon, however, who had crushed so many of their *jallāba* relatives, was not the right man to assure the Jaʿaliyyīn that the government was still in control and had only good intentions. After he had reached Khartoum, support among the Jaʿaliyyīn for the Mahdist cause became widespread, under the leadership of ʿAbd Allāh w. Saʿd and his brother, ʿAlī, and Aḥmad w. Ḥamza.[25] In March the Jaʿaliyyīn cut the telegraph line between Khartoum and Berber, and it was cut again north of Berber. By April the whole province was ripe for revolt; the Turkish garrison at Shendi demanded more money, ammunition and grain, and panic broke out in Berber.[26] Towards the end of April, the future Mahdist *amīr* of Berber and former teacher of the Mahdī, Muḥammad Khayr, was sent to join the rebellious Jaʿaliyyīn and lead them to take the town of Berber. As he advanced downstream, the villagers rose and joined him. The remaining troops at Shendi offered little effective resistance, and the same may be said about the followers of the Khatmiyya brotherhood there.[27] After a siege of seven days, Berber fell on 19 May. Ḥusayn Pasha submitted and was sent to Omdurman, from where he later managed to flee to Egypt. Gordon was now trapped in Khartoum, and was killed by the Mahdists when they stormed the town on 26 January 1885. A leading general in the assault was al-Zubayr's former general, ʿAbd al-Raḥmān w. al-Nujūmī, a Jaʿalī.

The Mahdist uprising occurred in a most decisive period in world history and this fact has coloured and distorted contemporary as well as later understanding of the phenomenon. 'Darkest Africa' was about to be divided between the European powers, and here they were already faced with the first genuine African resistance movement. Although some observers expressed understanding of the hatred felt against the Turks, the general attitude against the Mahdiyya was one of condemnation and outrage. It was thought to represent the victory of barbarism and fanaticism over the forces of civilisation, inspired by an imposter and 'false prophet'.

The events leading up to the fall of Khartoum and the killing of Gordon, the subsequent anti-Mahdist propaganda war and the re-occupation, made it difficult to search for the causes of the revolution beyond the slogans of 'Islamic fanaticism'. Seen in retrospect, however, it was only natural that the protest movement should adopt Islam as its unifying ideology. What alternatives were there? It was also natural to propagate the coming political and social changes in the language of religious reform, rather than to fight for a meaningless return to the happy old days of the Funj Sultanate. There is no reason to doubt the seriousness of the Mahdī when he expressed his disgust of being ruled by the immoral and irreligious Turks and their European 'infidel' partners. For him and many of his followers, fighting against the Turks and calling for religious, political and social reform were inseparable.

From this analysis of economic and social change as result of and response to a colonial regime, it follows that the causes of the Mahdist revolution can be found in the growing feeling of despair and hatred in the population against dislocation, arbitrary rule, physical oppression and disregard for Sudanese moral and religious sentiments. The early revolt of the Jaʿaliyyīn and subsequent 'disturbances' showed that both the peasantry and nomads were against the regime and that local, spontaneous revolts by the poorer classes against oppression were futile. This situation had changed dramatically around 1880. Now the government had managed to alienate large sections of the religious and trading middle class, who consequently allied themselves with the peasants and nomads and, armed with capital, military training and a strong religious conviction, gave the opposition groups the unity, ideological direction, courage and strength they needed. The cross-ethnic nationalist ideas about being 'Sudanese' were now formulated for the first time. The Mahdist uprising was not the revolt of the poorest and the most oppressed peoples and it did not start in the poorest areas of the Sudan, but on the contrary in Kordofan and along the Blue and White Niles. The Mahdī entered the historical stage in response to the historical situation and the expectations of the people.

The present study has described and analysed the political, economic and social changes that the northern Sudan underwent in the nineteenth century up to 1885. It has mainly followed the history of the Jaʿaliyyīn in this period and their two main towns, Shendi and al-Matamma, but it has tried always to situate them in a broader historical context. It was not meant to be a history of a tribe. In the analysis of peasants and traders, it was sought to break out of the somewhat artificial tribal framework and see their history also in terms of cross-ethnic social groups. By relating the various phenomena we are studying to a concrete population group, however, we are able all the time to tie our abstractions and generalisations to the concrete history of a people, a social group, a family or a town.

Ample evidence has shown how an alien economic policy with emphasis on cash crops and taxation in marketable crops and in cash, undermined the eco-system and the subsistence peasant economy and society. A collaborating class of merchants contributed to surplus extraction by providing the peasants with cash with which to pay their taxes, but which also tied them permanently to the merchant-creditors. Many peasants and traders emigrated in this period as a result of the diminishing economic possibilities in the north and discovered that the areas further south and west offered a variety of new options.

Although the decline had begun before, and despite all the efforts at 'economic development', the Turkiyya struck the final blow at the political and economic vitality of the Nile Valley north of Khartoum. Thenceforward, the north acted and continues to act as the birth-place of many prominent religious, political and intellectual figures, whose careers have unfolded outside their homeland. The regularity of emigration has made its heavy imprint on social organisation and world-view, and is frequently a theme in local folk-tales. A Jaʿalī saying expresses in a nut-shell how the people have come to regard emigration as a fact of life: 'The North gives birth and the South gives manhood.' The north has become a source of cheap labour, tenants on government schemes, civil servants, teachers and engineers for the rest of the Sudan, for Egypt, Libya and the Gulf States. And finally the north has continued to produce merchants, particularly in the Shendi area, who handle much of the commodity trade in the Sudan. The present study has shown how this lop-sided development started, and how the more central areas became the economic and political gravity point of the modern Sudan.

Appendix: Three contracts from the archive of ʿAbd Allāh Bey Ḥamza

1 Berg. NI 363. 15/91 (13 Shawwāl 1299/28 August 1882)

A paper for guarantee, conditions and agreements and similar documents without a stated sum, its price [stamp duty] being six piastres.

6[1]

Abū Ḥanīfa al-Nuʿmān, may God be pleased with him.

On the blessed day of Monday the 13th of the month of Shawwāl 1299 – one thousand two hundred and ninety nine – [28 August 1882] a blessed partnership contract [*ʿaqd sharika*] took place between the honourable Shaykh Sulaymān ʿAbd al-Ghanī, living in Egypt [or Cairo], and Shaykh ʿAbd Allāh Ḥamza of the merchants of al-Matamma, staying in Kordofan, concerning those profits realised on goods sold in Egypt by Shaykh Sulaymān ʿAbd al-Ghanī, and bought in the Sudan under the supervision of the aforementioned Shaykh ʿAbd Allāh Ḥamza. Its [the partnership's] capital is constituted by ten thousand *safariyya tōbs* from the capital of Shaykh Sulaymān ʿAbd al-Ghanī, consigned to Ilyās Pasha upon [his] receipt of them in Kordofan, free [of] all expenses. The retail price is one *riyāl* for two *tōbs* according to the instructions of the said Shaykh Sulaymān ʿAbd al-Ghanī. Shaykh ʿAbd Allāh Ḥamza has no share in the capital, rather he is to receive half of the profit of the sale of the goods in Egypt as has been mentioned, and he is not responsible for any losses. Shaykh ʿAbd Allāh Ḥamza has no right to dispose of what Shaykh Sulaymān ʿAbd al-Ghanī sends him from Egypt, except according to the price which he learns from him, and with his permission according to his instruction, either by telegraph or letter. Likewise he is not to buy anything from the Sudan except at the behest of and with the consent of Shaykh Sulaymān ʿAbd al-Ghanī. Likewise Shaykh ʿAbd Allāh Ḥamza is to inform Shaykh Sulaymān ʿAbd al-Ghanī immediately about the prices of goods in the Sudan in order that he may authorise him to buy what should be bought. Shaykh ʿAbd Allāh Ḥamza may not sell anything on credit but only for ready cash. As for what he buys of goods and sends to Shaykh Sulaymān ʿAbd al-Ghanī from the Sudan, whether by sea or land, and any of these goods are lost, God forbid, it will not be counted against Shaykh ʿAbd Allāh Ḥamza in any way, after a confirmation that they have been sent by him. In accordance with what has been mentioned here, let there be content and agreement between the two. Done in the presence of the witnesses mentioned below. Two copies were made, each having a copy in order that he may proceed in accordance with it. And God Most High is the best of witnesses.

The undersigned ʿAbd Allāh Ḥamza [seal]	Sulaymān ʿAbd al-Ghanī [2 seals]	By the testimony of ʿAbd Allāh al-Falālī. Seal	By the testimony of al-Sayyid Muḥammad al-Ghālī al-Ḥusaynī. Seal. [seal]
	By the testimony of . . .		

I witnessed it, with my signature, Muḥammad ʿAlī Miyās	I witnessed it, with my signature, ʿAlī Masʿūd	I witnessed it, *al-Ḥājj* ʿAbd al-Salām al-Nānī. Seal. [seal]

2 Berg. NI 383. 15/111 (15 Shawwāl 1299/30 August 1882)

A paper for guarantee, conditions and agreements and similar documents without a stated sum, its price [stamp duty] being six piastres.
6

On the blessed day of Wednesday the 15th Shawwāl 1299 [30 August 1882] the two men, sound of mind and of legal age, came together. The two referred to, being in a state of legal competence, and whose names and seals appear on it [the document] below, are the honourable Shaykh Sulaymān ʿAbd al-Ghanī, resident in Egypt, and *al-ḥājj* ʿAbd Allāh Ḥamza, resident in al-Matamma. They have agreed and consented to a partnership that, if God is willing, may be profitable. The said honourable Shaykh Sulaymān has contributed from his personal capital a sum of one hundred and fifteen Egyptian gold pounds, and likewise the said Shaykh ʿAbd Allāh has contributed from his personal capital the sum of one hundred and fifteen Egyptian gold pounds; the total sum contributed by the two parties, being thus two hundred and thirty Egyptian gold pounds, have been mixed one with the other and become one capital. We purchased with it goods from Egypt and all the goods were delivered to *al-ḥājj* ʿAbd Allāh Ḥamza, the partner, in order that he should take them to the Sudan to sell and buy with them with his [Sulaymān's] knowledge so that after the sale it would be possible to acquire, as a result of exchanging them, goods from the Sudan, with his [Sulaymān's] knowledge. These should then be sent to the said Sulaymān mentioned for him to dispose of in Egypt with his [ʿAbd Allāh's] knowledge. The partnership contract will last for a complete year starting from the date below [*sic!*], and after the completion of the said year, each of them will be free to continue or not. And the stipulations of the partnership, in so far as God provides some profit, from the proceeds of the Egyptian and Sudanese goods, after settling the capital and expenses, are that in so far that God provides some profit, half will go to the said Shaykh Sulaymān and the other half to *al-ḥājj* ʿAbd Allāh Ḥamza. If the opposite should happen, may God forbid, the losses will be divided equally. To this they have agreed without duress or compulsion, in the presence of the witnesses named below, and [the document which contains] these stipulations, will remain in the hand of the honourable Shaykh Sulaymān [to the benefit of?] the two parties. And God, may He be exalted, is the best of witnesses.

I witnessed it, Aḥmad ʿAbd Allāh al-Falālī. Seal. [seal]

The guarantor of its validity. Sulaymān ʿAbd al-Ghanī [seal]

The guarantor of its validity. ʿAbd Allāh Ḥamza Mūsā [seal]

I, the undersigned Ṭāhā Yūsuf, witnessed it.

I, the undersigned ʿAlī Masʿūd, witnessed it.

The testimony of al-Sharīf Muḥammad al-Ghālī al-Ḥusaynī. Seal. [seal]

I, the undersigned Muḥammad ʿAlī Mīyās, witnessed it.

3 Berg. NI 347. 15/75 (27 Shaʿbān 1307/18 April 1890)

A document for up to forty five thousand piastres to fifty thousand piastres, its price [stamp duty] being hundred piastres.

100

In the presence of the witnesses below, Muḥammad Maḥmūd ʿAbd al-Raḥīm of the people of Binabāna [?], sound of mind and of legal age, acknowledges and confirms and swore personally, without anyone else, that he took and received from His Excellency ʿAbd Allāh Bey Ḥamza of the merchants of the Sudan, now living in Rammādī a sum in the amount of 117 *afrankī* pounds – one hundred and seventeen *afrankī* pounds – each pound being equal to ninety seven and a half piastres of standard state currency, in the hope of successful trade. And as to what the Creator, He being praised and exalted, allows in terms of profit, Muḥammad Maḥmūd shall receive half of the profit and His Excellency ʿAbd Allāh Bey will receive the other half, in addition to his original capital, the sum whose amount was stated above, namely one hundred and seventeen *afrankī* pounds. This sum is separate from the earlier partnership [contract] preserved among the papers in [his] hands, namely ʿAbd Allāh Bey's. And the duration of the partnership will be as long as he wishes and until he chooses to terminate the accounts. And this took place before witnesses. And God is sufficient as a Witness.

The guarantor of its validity, Muḥammad Maḥmūd ʿAbd al-Raḥīm [seal]

27 Shaʿbān 1307 [18 April 1890]

I witnessed it, Ibrāhīm Ḥāmid Māshā ʿAbduh [seal]

I witnessed it,
the undersigned
Muḥammad [Ibrāhīm?]

I witnessed it,
Muḥmūd ʿAbd al-Raḥīm [seal]

I witnessed it,
Ḥasan Ḥamza,
the merchant
[seal]

Notes

INTRODUCTION

1 O'Fahey and Spaulding (1974), 15–25. Spaulding (1985).
2 Yūsuf Faḍl Ḥasan (1973); MacMichael (1922a); Al-Faḥl al-Fakī al-Ṭāhir (1976).
3 For an example, see Crowfoot (1911), 13.
4 Lorimer (1936b), Hill (1976), 265.
5 Spaulding (1985) argues strongly in favour of a feudal model in his analysis of Sinnār. A different view of the political economy of Sudanic states can be found in Watts' voluminous study of Hausaland (1983).

I THE JAʿALĪ KINGDOM OF SHENDI AND ITS DESTRUCTION

1 Yūsuf Faḍl Ḥasan (1973), 146–47. On the origin of the Jaʿaliyyīn Group, see pp. 145–54. P. M. Holt, 'Djaʿaliyyūn' in *EI*[2]
2 Hurreiz (1972), 404, and Holt (1981), 262–72.
3 Interview C2/A.
4 Interview C8, and Institute of Folklore (hereafter IF), IAAS 619; Yūsuf Faḍl Ḥasan (1973), 147–48; MacMichael (1922a), I, 200 II, 110; Hurreiz (1972), 57.
5 Biberfeld (1892), 12; Hillelson (1933), 61; Crawford (1951), 132–42.
6 Interview C10, and interview with Muḥammad Nimr Jamāl al-Dīn, not recorded on tape. See also Hurreiz (1972), 378–79.
7 Interview, C1, even *makk* Muḥammad Nimr and *makk* Nimr used the title *arbāb* in their land charters. See Berg. NI 163. 13/26 (10 Shaʿbān 1208/13 March 1794); Berg. NI 179. 13/41 (14 Jumādā (?) 1220/August or September (?) 1805), and Berg. NI 180. 13/42 (1168/1754–55).
8 A not yet identified battle of Abramād is said to have terminated the payment of tribute to the Funj. Interview C8.
9 O'Fahey and Spaulding (1974), 94; Spaulding (1985) discusses in great detail the period of decline and it is therefore not necessary here to elaborate on the very complicated political history leading up to 1821.
10 *Makhṭūṭa*, 27 and 32; Parkyns, MS, 26; Bruce (1790), iv, 531.
11 The Awlād Nimr are today believed to be a branch of the Saʿdāb. Robinson (1925), 105, however, maintains that the founder of the section, Nimr 'the elder' belonged to the Nifīʿāb and that he married into the Saʿdāb. See also Interview C5/B, and C9/A.
12 Nimr was young around 1800 and about forty years in 1821, Robinson (1925), 111; English (1822), 158 n., however, says that he was sixty-five in 1821, but that must be an exaggeration. See also Burckhardt (1822), 247.
13 Berg. NI 164. 13/26 (10 Shaʿbān 1208/13 March 1794).
14 Berg. 181. 13/64 (1216/1801–2). At the same time Nāṣir was placed on the ʿAbdallāb throne.
15 *Makhṭūṭa*, 43–44.

16 *Ibid.*, 44; Interviews C5/A, C9/A and C10, and Jackson (1912), 71.
17 Burckhardt (1822), 242 and 247. See also Bruce (1790), iv, 518.
18 Burckhardt (1822), 242; Bruce (1790), iv, 545, paints the same picture of them in 1772.
19 Cailliaud (1826), ii, 135.
20 Interview C5/A.
21 Burckhardt (1822), 248.
22 *Ibid.*, 244.
23 *Ibid.*, 249. There was a chief judge (*qāḍī*) attached to the court by the name of Wad Murtada, from the Shaqalwa family in Shendi (Interview C9A). They formed a section of the Jaʿaliyyīn, according to MacMichael (1922a), ii, 133. Saʿd, Nimr's uncle and guardian during the events in 1800, seems to have acted as vizier. Linant de Bellefonds (1958), 79–80 and 110–11, met him on several occasions in 1821–22. The same man was probably seen by Lepsius (1852), 159, in 1844. The vizier represented the king also in the market, Thibaut in Santi and Hill, eds. (1980), 75.
24 Burckhardt (1822), 254; Cailliaud (1826), iii, 107, says that if the country was threatened, the subjects mobilised *en masse*. English (1822), 136, reported that the country could muster 30,000 horsemen in conjunction with the ʿAbdallāb, which seems vastly exaggerated.
25 Robinson (1929), 243; and al-Ḥājj Ḥāmid Muḥammad Khayr and Spaulding (1980).
26 O'Fahey (1980), 39.
27 English (1822), ix–x. For historical treatment of these events and their background, see Robinson (1925–26), and Douin (1944), i. Muḥammad ʿAlī's motives are also formulated in his letter of 30 October 1821, to Muḥammad Bey the Daftardar, see Marsot (1984), 205.
28 English (1822), 109; Waddington and Hanbury (1822), 29; Cailliaud (1826), ii, 37–8; Nicholls (1913), 30–42; and Douin (1944), i, 96–135.
29 Marsot (1984), 86, quoting a letter in the Dār al-Wathā'iq al-Miṣriyya, *Sudan*, dated 9 Rabīʿ ii 1236/14 January 1821. See also Waddington and Hanbury (1822), 94–5; Cailliaud (1826), ii, 31–2; Cadalvène and Breuvery (1836), ii, 261.
30 Robinson (1925), 110; Hoskins (1835), 45; and al-Ḥājj Ḥāmid Muḥammad Khayr and Spaulding (1980).
31 English (1822), 117 and 131; and Cailliaud (1826), ii, 96–7.
32 Douin (1944), i, 142 (Abidin Archive Cairo, Maʿiyya, Reg. Turc. 7, piece 167).
33 Cailliaud (1826), ii, 121; and English (1822), 110–11.
34 English (1822), 117; see also Douin (1944), i, 142 (Abidin Archive Cairo, Maʿiyya, Reg. Turc. 7, piece 172). A son of Shawīsh accompanied them to ask for mercy for the Shāyqiyya encamped opposite Shendi, English (1822), 117–18.
35 Cailliaud (1826), ii, 121–2; Douin (1944), i, 147.
36 Douin (1944), i, 147–8, 150–1; English (1822), 133, 136–8, 140–1; Cailliaud (1826), ii, 181–2.
37 English (1822), 150n; Linant de Bellefonds (1958), 79; Cailliaud (1826), ii, 300, met *makk* Nimr in Sinnār.
38 Linant de Bellefords in Douin (1944), i, 296; Linant de Bellefonds (1958), 108.
39 There are numerous references to this event in the sources, see Rüppell (1929), 106–12; Hoskins (1835), 92; Cadalvène and Breuvery (1836), ii, 269–70; Shuqayr (1903), iii, 14–15; Robinson (1925), 112; Hill (1959a), 16; *Makhṭūṭa*, 90; and *Ta'rīkh*, 23–4. Interview C6 and C7.
40 A short eyewitness report by shaykh al-Faḍlī, subsequently living as a refugee in the Banī Shanqūl, is given in Toniolo and Hill (1974), 241.
41 Rüppel (1829), 110; Shuqayr (1903), ii, 15; The bloody revenge of the Daftardar is described in the *Makhṭūṭa*, 94; Parkyns, MS, 108; and by an anonymous chronicler in Hill (1970), 5. Pükler-Muskau (1844), ii, 161, thought that the Daftardar had killed half the population of Shendi area. Hartmann (1872), 501, n.2, estimated the number of dead as 30,000, which seems exaggerated; if correct, it must also include numerous non-Jaʿalī victims.

42 Rüppell (1829), 104–8; and Rüppell (1836), 139–40; Thibaut in Santi and Hill (1980), 81; Shuqayr (1903), ii, 15.

2 SHENDI'S ECONOMY ON THE EVE OF THE TURKIYYA

1 Bruce (1790), iv; Burckhardt (1822); English (1822); Cailliaud (1826); Finati (1830); Linant de Bellefonds (1958).
2 Poncet (1709), 17; Biberfeld (1892), 12; Hillelson (1933).
3 Krump (1710); Le Mascrier (1740); Crawford (1951), 288–96.
4 Le Mascrier (1740), ii, 362–3; Giamberardini (1963), 381–6, 392–3, 412–14, 417, 421–3.
5 Giamberardini (1963), 386.
6 Bruce (1790), iv, 509, 525, 527.
7 O'Fahey and Spaulding (1974), 109.
8 Bruce (1790), iv, 514–15, 517.
9 English (1822), 144; Linant de Bellefonds (1958), 85.
10 O'Fahey (1980), 26, 139–44.
11 Bruce (1790), iv, 529–30, 536. On the trade of Sinnār, see also p. 485.
12 Burckhardt (1822), 283.
13 Rüppell (1829), 104–5; Hall (1907), 560; Linant de Bellefonds (1958), 169–70.
14 Churi (1853), 90, says that Berber was so named because of its good autumn pastures.
15 Burckhardt (1822), 193, 223. For a similar practice in Kobbei, see O'Fahey (1980), 141.
16 Burckhardt (1822), 247.
17 Cailliaud (1826), iii, 104–5; English (1822), 134–7; Finati (1830), 387. Much of the information given by Cailliaud follows Burckhardt's narrative in structure and details and one may question whether his statements about Shendi are in fact independent.
18 English (1822), 134–5; interview C8.
19 Thibaut in Santi and Hill (1980), 75. Al-Matamma was also called 'Shendi of the West', English (1822), 133–4; a short outline of al-Matamma's history may be found in Bjørkelo (forthcoming), 'Al-Matamma' in EI 2nd edn.
20 Finati (1830), ii, 385. Finati travelled together with Linant de Bellefonds and arrived in Shendi on 9 November. His narrative is not always reliable. He says, for instance, that they were received by *makk* Nimr there (p. 384), but he was still in Sinnār at that time, only returning to Shendi in December.
21 Thibaut in Santi and Hill (1980), 75. See also Burckhardt (1822), 247, 250, 253; English (1822), 137; Cailliaud (1826), iii, 109.
22 Burckhardt (1822), 248. The Jaʿaliyyīn considered it an insult to be called a Dongolāwī.
23 *Ibid.*, 265.
24 *Ibid.*, 264–5.
25 *Ibid.*, 235, 264–5, 329. The main markets of an area held their big markets on different weekdays so as to enable people to attend more than one big market during the same week. Hoskins (1835), 123–4.
26 Burckhardt (1822), 254; Cailliaud (1826), iii, 109–10.
27 Burckhardt (1822), 261, 245–6, 276. Salt was a vital export product from Shendi, being exported also to Ethiopia. The salt works of the Buwayḍa hamlets, near Wādī Dushayn on Linant de Bellefonds' map, belonged to the king. See also IF, IAAS 597 and 619.
28 Thibaut in Santi and Hill (1980), 75.
29 Al-Shahi and Moore (1978), 104–6.
30 Cailliaud (1826), iii, 115 and 121.
31 *Ibid.*, iii, 121; Burckhardt (1822), 282; Thibaut in Santi and Hill (1980), 75; Paul (1954), 17–31.
32 Bruce (1790), iv, 546–7.

33 Burckhardt (1822), 267–8. A *zāmila* could be part of a woman's bridewealth, see Berg. NI 177. 13/39 (20 Rajab 1259/16 August 1843).
34 Burckhardt (1822), 268–70. Arkell (1937), 300–5.
35 Burckhardt (1822), 274–5.
36 *Ibid.*, 214, 273–4, 277.
37 *Ibid.*, 282.
38 *Ibid.*, 290; see also Cailliaud (1826), iii, 115–16.
39 Walz (1979), 216.
40 Le Mascrier (1740), ii, 339–40, 363. The author seems to contradict himself in regard to whether the Ethiopian caravans go as far as Cairo or not.
41 Browne (1806), 324; O'Fahey (1980), 139–40.
42 Burckhardt (1822), 273.
43 Browne (1806), 251 and 266.
44 Burckhardt (1822), 291; O'Fahey (1973b), 31–6.
45 Burckhardt (1822), 214, 273.
46 *Ibid.*, 274. Unlawful expropriation like this was not common. See Thibaut, in Santi and Hill (1980), 75.
47 Burckhardt (1822), 282.
48 Interview C2.
49 Linant de Bellefonds in Douin (1944), i, 47.
50 This subject is examined by Spaulding (1984).
51 Weber (1969), 202–3.
52 Burckhardt (1822), 217 and 285; O'Fahey (1980), 134.
53 Burckhardt (1822), 257–8, 216–17; Cailliaud (1826), ii, 117, 296–7, iii, 121. For other sources on this subject, see Krump (1710), 267–88; Bruce (1790), iv, 486–7.
54 English (1822), 135; Burckhardt (1822), 257; O'Fahey (1980), 97.
55 Cailliaud (1826), ii, 117.
56 Finati (1830), ii, 410.
57 Burckhardt (1822), 216.
58 *Ibid.*, 216.
59 *Ibid.*, 263. For an illuminating theoretical discussion of barter and currency transactions, see Webb (1982).
60 Spaudling (1982a).
61 'There is not a single family which is not connected, more or less, with some branch of traffic, either wholesale or retail, and the people of Berber and Shendy appear to be a nation of traders in the strictest sense of the word', says Burckhardt (1822), 289–90. This statement would undoubtedly have been endorsed by H. A. Nicholson, a Condominium Official, who wrote about Shendi area 120 years later, 'It is the home of the "Gallaba", all except the very poor have relations in trade and it is the ambition of most people to be a merchant & 90% of the people [are] considering that if they had a chance they would be successful.' NRO, Northern Province, 1/27/273, Trade 1939.
62 See the Mīrafābī folktale of 'The Cheat' in al-Shahi and Moore (1978), 192–4. Another relevant story from the Ṭabaqāt is discussed by Spaudling in his unpublished doctoral thesis (1971), 243–5.
63 Burckhardt (1822), 219–20.

3 THE JAʿALIYYĪN UNDER TURKISH ADMINISTRATION

1 One of the first to use the term 'Turco-Egyptian' was Brehm, travelling in the Sudan 1847–52, see Brehm (1975), 149 and 173; see also Werne (1849), ii, 2, and Hartmann (1863), 283.
2 A contemporary document from Shendi states clearly the provinces belonged to 'the

Ottoman Kingdom', *al-mamlakat al-ʿuthmāniyya* (NRO, Misc. 1/13/119 (25 Dhu'l-hijja 1282/11 May 1866).

3 According to English (1822), 108–9, Ismāʿīl Pasha told the Shāyqiyya who had fled to Shendi and asked for *amān* (peace), that there would be no peace for them unless they gave up their horses and arms, and stopped robbing their neighbours. The Shāyqiyya replied that they 'had no other means to live', to which the pasha answered, 'cultivate your land, and live honestly'. The Shāyqiyya had been bred to that kind of life, they said, and were not willing to work and change their way of life. 'I will make you change it', replied the pasha.

4 Hill (1970), xvi.

5 Brehm (1975), 146.

6 Hill (1959a), 13; Linant de Bellefonds (1958), 41–3; Finati (1830), ii, 368; Rüppell (1829), 26.

7 Douin (1944), i, 177 and 187.

8 Linant de Bellefonds (1958), 36, 106–9, 112; Cailliaud (1826), iii, 73–4.

9 Douin (1944), i, 187.

10 Linant de Bellefonds (1958), 106; Hartmann (1863), 236; Pückler-Muskau (1844), iii, 226–8; Hill (1970), 165.

11 Hill (1959a), 19.

12 *Ibid.*, 80–1; Hill (1958), 83–87; Lepsius (1852), 139–42. When Lepsius came to al-Dāmir in January 1844, he said he was now in the province of Amīn Pasha (of Khartoum Province). At the same time a top-level meeting took place in al-Dāmir between Hasan Pasha, *mudīr* of Dongola, and the *mudīr* of Berber (about to retire or be degraded?), the *mudīr* of Khartoum, and Aḥmad Pasha Maniklī.

13 Hill (1959a), 94; NRO, Dakhlia I, 112/4/20; *L'Isthme de Suez*, Wednesday 25 March 1857, 89–95.

14 Beatty (1956), 148–9.

15 Stewart (1883), 9.

16 *Ibid.*, 89.

17 Hoskins (1835), 48.

18 *Ibid.*, 49.

19 Douin (1944), i, 369–79; Hill (1959a), 5–6.

20 Pückler-Muskau (1844), iii, 296. Some higher officials were former Mamluks, as for instance Mūsā Pasha Ḥamdī, one time governor of Berber Province and later, 1862–5, Governor-General; for his biography, see Petherick (1869), ii, 48–52.

21 Hoskins (1835), 92–3; see also Brocchi (1843), iv, 123–4.

22 Pückler-Muskau (1844), iii, 144–5.

23 Hill (1970), 166–7.

24 Petherick (1861), 127; Brehm (1975), 168, 267; Thibaut in Santi and Hill, eds. (1980), 48; Prudhoe (1835), 39, 53; Hill (1970), 96, 139, 146, 164–5, 180, 197; Hill (1959a), 68; Selim Bimbachi (1842).

25 English (1822), 196; Linant de Bellefonds (1958), 76; Hoskins (1835), 87; Russegger (1841–8), ii/1, 493. Shendi *khuṭṭ* is referred to in NRO, Misc. 1/13/119.

26 Hill (1970), 146, 164–5.

27 Hill (1959a), 23; Douin (1944), i, 84; Brehm (1975), 91; Hill (1970), 43, 167; Werne (1849), ii, 325; Holroyd (1839), 170; Lejean (1865a), 41; Hill (1967), xiv.

28 Based on a Report by N. Shuqayr in NRO, Cairint. 3/8/147.

29 Hill (1970), 109. About eight or nine years before, a *muʿallim* was hanged in Shendi apparently for similar reasons, Cadalvène and Breuvery (1836), ii, 279.

30 Hill (1970), 107; Lepsius (1852), 204; Brehm (1975), 348; Taylor (1862), 260–1.

31 Brehm (1975), 292, 343–4, 348; Petherick (1861), 117. Travelling in the early 1860s, Heuglin took a present from Ḥusayn Aghā to Brehm.

32 Stewart (1883), 11 and Sāmī Amīn (1916–35), iii, 646.

33 Hill (1959a), 23.
34 Warburg (1974), 236.
35 Twenty years would be nearer the truth, as he was appointed by Nāṣir (the ʿAbdallāb *mānjil*), whose letter concerning the appointment, written about 1800 to the people of Berber, has been published by al-Ḥājj Ḥāmid Muḥammad Khayr and J. L. Spaulding in 1980.
36 Hoskins (1835), 45–6.
37 Hill (1959a), 96–7, 108; Hill (1967), 30, 269.
38 Aḥmad Pasha hired local people to dig wells and erect waterwheels at al-Matamma, but some of the strongest were sent to Khartoum to be enlisted into the army. When the order came to conscript 4,000 free men, the males left their homes and farms and fled. At Shendi some men had been taken while at Friday prayer, but they were later released. Thibaut in Santi and Hill (1980), 86–7; Werne (1852), 106. In the 1830s the settled population of Berber Province was perhaps as low as 25,000 to 30,000. As many as 400,000 tax-paying nomads have been suggested as belonging to Berber. Hoskins (1835), 57; Pallme (1844), 463; Russegger (1841–8), ii/1, 464, and Hill (1970), 137.
39 Hoskins (1835), 205–12; Rüppell (1829), 28, and Cadalvène and Breuvery (1836), ii, 329–31.
40 Hill (1970), 69–70; Thibaut in Santi and Hill (1980), 76–9.
41 Hoskins (1835), 57–8; Rüppell (1829), 28; Vayssière in Santi and Hill (1980), 108.
42 Hill (1970), 202–5.
43 Interview C1 and C10.
44 Interview C7; Cailliaud (1826), ii, 130–1, iii, 357; see also Russegger (1841–8), ii/1, 472 and 484–5, where the border is located at Jabal Egedah (ʿAqīda), that is approximately Cailliaud's area, and also near the Turkish border between *qism* Zaydāb and *qism* al-Matamma.
45 Hoskins (1835), 124–5.
46 Interviews C7 and C10; see also Shuqayr (1903), iii, 15, and NRO, Intel. 5/1/6, Chapter 10.
47 Rüppell (1829), 117; see also *Ta'rīkh*, 23, n.1; Shuqayr (1903), 15.
48 *Funj Chronicle* in MacMichael (1922a), ii, 390.
49 Interview C7.
50 *Makhṭūṭa*, 106; *Funj Chronicle* in MacMichael (1922a), ii, 393, and *Ta'rīkh*, 28.
51 *Ta'rīkh*, 23 and n.1, quoting a report in Abidin archive in Cairo, *Daftar* 26, *raqm* 125, date 28 Shaʿbān 1242/27 March 1827.
52 *Funj Chronicle* in MacMichael (1922a), ii, 395.
53 Pückler-Muskau (1844), iii, 162, 172; Hoskins (1835), 124–5.
54 Pückler-Muskau (1844), iii, 163, 165, 169, 171 and 173–5.
55 Interview C7, and Cuny (1862–3), iii, 313.
56 Spaulding (1977).
57 Holt (1968), 408. For more references, see also, Ḥusayn Sīd Aḥmad al-Muftī (1378/1959), i, 73–126; Hill (1959a), 42–6; Stewart (1883), 11–13.
58 The signature of a *qāḍī khuṭṭ* Shendi appears in the following documents, NRO, Misc. 1/13/119 (25 Dhu'l-hjja 1282/11 May 1866); NRO, Misc. 1/13/120 (14 Ṣafar 1298/17 January 1881); Berg. NI 464. 15/187 a+b (undated), and NRO, Misc. 1/14/125, piece 1 (13 Rabīʿ I 1286/23 June 1869).
59 For instance in NRO, Misc. 1/13/120 (14 Safar 1298/17 January 1881); Berg. NI 477. 15/200 (15 Ṣafar 1266/31 December 1849), and NRO, Misc. 1/14/125, piece 25 (27 Rajab 1261/1 August 1845). We have also a document issued by the *qāḍī* of Berber Province, Berg. NI 340. 15/68 (14 Muḥarram 1281/20 June 1864).
60 Hill (1970), 146.
61 *Ibid.*, 137.
62 *Ibid.*, 163; when ʿAbbās Aghā was about to be removed from the office of governor, this

qāḍī went to Berber to assist in the investigations against him, following accusations of administrative and financial misconduct. His title of *muftī* appears in NRO, Misc. 1/14/125, piece 1 (13 Rabīʿ I 1286/23 June 1869), and NRO, Misc. 1/13/119 (25 Dhu'l-hjja 1282/11 May 1866).

63 Churi (1853), 221.

64 *Ibid.*, 166; see also Brocchi (1843), iv, 112, and 118–19.

65 Pückler-Muskau (1844), iii, 162.

66 Hill (1970), 195.

67 Hoskins (1835), 37–9.

68 Hill (1970), 46–7.

69 Hartmann (1863), 307–8; *L'Isthme de Suez*, no. 10, 25 March 1857, 91–5; Merruau (1858), 318–34.

70 Churi (1853), 252.

71 In Santi and Hill (1980), 84.

4 THE TRANSFORMATION OF AGRICULTURE

1 SAD 542/6/1–48, Report on Berber Land Commission, 1904, 30–1; NRO, Misc. 1/13/118; NRO, Northern Province, 2/72/735–45, Petitions.

2 Al-Shahi and Moore (1979), 1–60; Cailliaud (1826), ii, 116–17; Burckhardt (1822), 250; Interview C6; NRO, Northern Province, 1/13/74, Educational Policy.

3 Al-Shahi and Moore (1978), 50–1.

4 For a historical and sociological study of house styles among the Jaʿaliyyīn, see Lee (1967).

5 Brocchi (1843), v, 95–6.

6 Rüppell (1829), 39.

7 Lee (1967), 295–319.

8 Some historical and present-day references to village morphology may be found in Krump (1710), 235 (tr. Spaulding); Burckhardt (1822), 196; Cailliaud (1826), ii, 132–3 and 221; Rüppell (1829), 110; Russegger (1841–8), ii/1, 448, 451, 460–1, 484 and 492–3; Nelson (1973), 127–30; Randell (1974), 1–4.

9 Rüppell (1829), 107.

10 For a study of the changes in the *sadāq* among the Jaʿaliyyīn, see Kjerland (1982).

11 Descriptions of the Nubian Nile Valley may be found in Chélu (1891), 30–65; Gleichen (1905), i, 83ff.; Adams (1977), 20–43.

12 Crowfoot (1911), 10–11; he added in a footnote that in 1907 the amount of durra in Berber Province alone from this cultivation was about 150,000 ardabbs. See also Hewinson in Tothill (1948), 743; NRO, Siv. Sec. 38/3/9, Land Settlement Question, and Interview C6. Lepsius (1852), 150, for instance, noted that the people of Shendi and al-Matamma used to cultivate in the Wādī al-ʿAwātīb during the rains.

13 Chélu (1891), 107; NRO, Siv. Sec. 38/3/17, Land tenure in Fung area, Singa (by Matthew); al-Shāṭir Buṣaylī (1966), 263–6; SAD 542/6/1–48 (1904), 7; Chélu was of the opinion that the making of ridges (*turus*) and cultivating in the *karrū* were tasks fit only for slaves as they were allegedly more resistant to the kind of fever one could get from the work.

14 Notes and reports by MacMichael in SAD 542/3/36–44, 48–66, 70–5, 80–2.

15 Spaulding (1982b).

16 Chélu (1891), 106.

17 Spaulding (1982a), 7.

18 SAD 542/6/1–48, 12; SAD 542/7/49–75, Reports on the Karu Lands in Shendi, Tippets (1906), 66.

19 Burckhardt (1822), 126–7.

20 For an analysis of the changing *sāqiya* system in Dongola in the present century, see El Haj Bilal Omer (1985).

21 See for instance Saeed M. A. El Mahdi (1976) and (1971).
22 Paul (1936), 348, 350.
23 SAD 542/6/1-48 (1904), 8–9; NRO, Siv. Sec. 38/1/1, Land Registration; Tothill (1948), 191; Spaulding (1982a), 4–5.
24 The *dhirāʿ* was usually equal to the length of the forearm from elbow to finger-tips, plus the breadth of the hand and a finger. The *ʿūd* varied from one village to the next, but according to Ryder, MS, 68, the Jaʿaliyyīn usually employed the *ʿūd* of three *dhirāʿ*. For measuring land in this way a durra stalk (*qaṣab*, hence *qaṣaba*) of the length of an *ʿūd* (the village yard-stick) or a rope (*ḥabl*) was used.
25 See the sketch map by Settlement Officer Ryder, included in his MS in the possession of his widow, Mrs Elizabeth Ryder, to whom I am most grateful for a copy. For another copy which lacks the sketch map, see SAD 400/8/1–25.
26 NRO, Intel. 8/1/2, Land tenure among Arab tribes in rain cultivations.
27 Hill (1970), 54; NRO, Siv. Sec. 38/3/17, Land tenure in Fung Area. For more on measures and measurements, see Cailliaud (1826), ii, 297, 290–1; Brocchi (1843), v, 420, 449, 463–4; Douin (1933–41), iii/3B, 1180.
28 Ryder, MS, 66–7; SAD 400/8/14–16; NRO, Siv. Sec. 38/4/22, Seluka Land in Berber; and Saeed M. A. El Mahdi (1976), 83–7.
29 Spaulding (1982a), 3.
30 Tothill in Tothill (1948), 210–21.
31 See for instance Holroyd in Bowring (1840), 88; Hill (1970), 29–30.
32 Churi (1853), 152.
33 For a study of the Sudanese *sāqiya*, see Abū Salīm (1980). For the Egyptian *sāqiya*, see Ménassa and Laferrière (1974).
34 For more details, see Burnett in Tothill (1948), 289; El Haj Bilal Omer (1985), 37–8.
35 The stages of the growth of the durra and the calamities that might occur, are described in Jackson (1919a), 1–16. See also Burckhardt (1822), 129.
36 Bjørkelo (1982).
37 See Bond (1925), 97–103; Nicholson (1935), 314–22; Paul (1936), 346–49; Burnett in Tothill (1948), 300–1.
38 Wituki (1967), 24.
39 Paul (1936).
40 Rüppell (1929), 38, calculated that those dependent on a *sāqiya* had a net income of 1,000 piastres at their disposal for a full year (in Dongola 1823–5). With the introduction of indigo cultivation, the income of a *sāqiya* was reduced to 637 piastres a year, according to Hoskins (1835), 232, in the early 1830s. Rüppell estimated the harvest of a *sāqiya* to be between 17 and 20 Cairo *ardabb* (exclusive of the seed required for the next sowing), bringing the annual harvest up to between 34 and 40 *ardabb* of grain with the market value of between 1,000 and 1,500 piastres (2½ to 3 dollars or 32½ to 39 piastres per *ardabb* of 198 litres which contained 151.2 kg of durra). If the average yield of a *faddān* of *sāqiya* land was about five *ardabbs*, the average *sāqiya* would then irrigate three to four *faddāns*, which agrees with other information; see Wituki (1967), 32.
41 Chayanov (1966); Grønhaug (1976).
42 Poncet in Nicholls (1913), 59.
43 Bruce (1790), iv, 526, 538.
44 Burckhardt (1822), 240.
45 Rivlin (1961), 102–4.
46 Rüppell (1829), 109.
47 *Ibid.*, 112; Prudhoe (1835), 52; Brocchi (1843), v, 115, 193, 666 and Table 8; Pallme (1844), 218; Brun-Rollet (1855), 302–3; Baker (1874), 13; Hill (1959a), 53; (1970), 52–3.
48 Rüppell (1829), 112 (my translation). Military supervision and control of agricultural

production became therefore a necessity under this system, see Cadalvène and Breuvery (1836), ii, 265.

49 Brocchi (1843), v, 115, 192–3.

50 Hoskins (1835), 53, gives the figures of 500 *sāqiyas* in the whole of Berber Province in 1833 and estimated the number to 800 in 1821, which must be far too low, if he is really talking about the whole province and not Berber District. Unfortunately these figures were reproduced by Russegger (1841–8), ii/1, 465, in 1837, without any reference to his source.

51 Hoskins (1835), 53. For comparative purposes, see also Cadalvène and Breuvery (1836), ii, 339–49.

52 Russegger (1841–8), ii/1, 465, 484.

53 Pückler-Muskau (1845), ii, 164.

54 Russegger (1841–8), ii/3, 9, 13, 28–9, 64; ii/1, 465; Pückler-Muskau (1845), iii, 146.

55 Hill (1970), 196.

56 Brun-Rollet (1855), 302; Hill (1970), 66–7, 188, 200; Southworth (1875), 172–3; Dufton (1867), 10; Werne (1849), i, 63 and (1852), 102; Hartmann (1863), 381; Lejean (1865a), 114; Heuglin (1869), 258; Hill (1970), 69–70.

57 Thibaut in Santi and Hill (1980), 86.

58 Holroyd (1839), 184. See also Hamilton (1857), 369; Hill (1970), 133–4; similarly the cultivation of opium, rice, coffee, silk and vines failed.

59 Hill (1970), 66–7. At the same time huge numbers of cattle were exported to Egypt. Burckhardt had noted that durra used to be thinly planted (1822), 244, which is confirmed by Rüppell (1829), 37. During the Turkiyya, large tracts of exhausted agricultural land went permanently out of use; see Cuny (1862–3), 199–200; and Hoskins (1835), 179.

60 Petherick (1861), 117–18; (1869), ii, 54; Hoskins (1835), 52–3; Santoni in Santi and Hill (1980), 219; Brocchi (1843), v, 193.

61 Du Bisson (1868), 22; Heuglin (1869), 248–9, 260–1; Baker (1874), 386; and Douin (1933–41), iii/1, 161–2.

62 Southworth (1875), 235.

63 Abidin Archives, Reg. 1938. *Ordres superieures*, piece 4, 18, to the *mudīr* of Berber, 9 January 1871. Ref. to in Douin (1933–41), iii/2, 477–8.

64 Douin (1933–41), iii/2, 446–7, 449–50 and n.1, 488–9. The number of 3,000 *sāqiyas* in Berber province in 1871 is confirmed by Abū Salīm (1980).

65 Chélu (1891), 131; Douin (1933–41), iii/2, 485–6; iii/3B, 1168ff. A critical summary of why cotton production failed, can be found in C. Ch. Giegler Pasha (1984) (ed. by R. Hill), 54.

66 Hill (1970), 53.

67 Thibaut in Santi and Hill (1980), 84.

68 Cadalvène and Breuvery (1836), ii, 279, n.1; Russegger (1841–8), ii/3, 11; Werne (1852), 78, 99; Hamilton (1857), 369, 371; Lepsius (1852), 150.

69 Taylor (1862), 221–2, 259, 261–2, 265, 403, 438; Churi (1853), 90.

70 Hamilton (1857), 381. See also Werne (1852), 77–8, 106; Taylor (1862), 443, 468.

71 *L'Isthme de Suez* (1857), 91–5, 109. See also Beatty (1956), 148–9; Hamilton (1857), 382; Merruau (1958), 318–34.

72 *L'Isthme du Suez* (1857), 92 (my translation).

73 Petherick, letter to Stanton, 26 December 1863, PRO, FO, 78/2253; ref. in Santi and Hill (1980), 190.

74 Schweinfurth (1918), 19; Heuglin (1869), 18–19, 38, 248–9, 253, 259–61; Baker (1874), 13; (1875), 11; Frobenius (1893), 98. For an example of emigration from this area during this period, see the family of Babikr Bedri in his memoirs (1969), i, 1.

75 Lafargue in Douin (1933–41), iii/1, 440–1 (my translation).

76 *Ibid.*, 431–2, 436.

77 *Ibid.*, 488–9.

78 Hill (1959a), 41.

79 Estimates based on Stewart (1883), 17. Stewart reports that there were 1,442 abandoned *sāqiyas* in Berber province at that time, but it is uncertain whether they should be counted among the 3,000 or not. The worst interpretation of these data is that nearly half of the counted *sāqiyas* were actually out of work. The next chapter will explain why broken *sāqiyas* were still kept in the ledgers of the taxation officials.
80 Rüppell (1829), 25–9.
81 Hasan A. A. Ahmed (1980), 112.
82 Dawkins in Alford and Sword (1898), 160.
83 Pückler-Muskau (1844), iii, 149–2. See also Sāmī Amīn (1916–35), iii, 646.
84 Hamont (1843), i, 150; Russegger (1841–8), ii/2, 53 and ii/3, 40–3, 48–9.
85 Russegger (1841–8), ii/3, 66–7.
86 Hamont founded and was in charge of the Egyptian veterinary service in the 1830s and 1840s and wrote a very critical report about the project to Muḥammad ʿAlī, (1843), i, 140–51.
87 O'Fahey and Spaulding (1974), 103.
88 Santoni in Santi and Hill (1980), 217. For references to small-scale trading in slaves along the Nile, see SAD 465/2, H. C. Jackson, Safaria Notes (December 1924); and Spaulding (1982a), 11.
89 Holroyd (1839), 185.
90 Holroyd in Bowring (1840), 88–9; Hill (1970), 29–30.
91 Chélu (1891), 131; Douin (1933–41), iii/3B, 1145–6, 1262, 1271.
92 Burckhardt (1822), 290; Russegger (1841–8), ii, 1, 493; see also ii/2, 20.
93 Buchta (1888), 28, 89.
94 Southworth (1875), 212.
95 Williams (1884), 152; Thibaut in Santi and Hill (1980), 86, 91; Santoni in Santi and Hill (1980), 217.

5 TAXATION

1 Interviews C1, C2 and others. See also Ohrwalder (1892), 284.
2 Kremer (1863), ii, 18.
3 Spaulding (1985), 79–91.
4 Interview C1.
5 Rivlin (1961), 121; on taxation and finances, see 119–36.
6 Hill (1970), 43.
7 Linant de Bellefonds (1958), 79; *Makhṭūṭa*, 88; Douin (1944), i, 272, 291; Cailliaud (1826), iii, 90; Hill (1959a), 41.
8 Douin (1944), i, 273; Cailliaud (1826), 75ff.; *Makhṭūṭa*, 88, 90.
9 *Funj Chronicle* in MacMichael (1922a), ii, 287, and *Makhṭūṭa*, 89–90. Shuqayr (1903), iii, 11, gives somewhat lower rates, namely five dollars for a slave, half a dollar for a cow, a sheep or a donkey.
10 Douin (1944), i, 276–8; Cailliaud (1826), iii, 88, 91.
11 Douin (1944), i, 279.
12 *Ibid.*, 283–4; *Ta'rīkh*, 23; Shuqayr (1903), iii, 12; Linant de Bellefonds (1958), 142.
13 Douin (1944), i, 277, 296, 281, 284; *Makhṭūṭa*, 88; Shuqayr (1903), iii, 12.
14 Actually the fiscal year followed the Coptic calendar until 1876, when the Christian calendar was introduced. Kremer (1863), ii, 31, says it commenced on 10 September. In the first Coptic month of the year, Thōt (29–30 September to 27–8 October), the provincial accounts were closed as the new tax estimates were worked out and the revenues of the last year were entered into the books as far as they had been collected. SAD 404/10 [AR].
15 Letter of 27 August 1822 from Muḥammad ʿAlī to the governor of Berber. Abidin Archive, Maʿiyya saniyya, Reg. Turc. 19, piece 360; quoted in Douin (1944), i, 298 (my translation).

16 Cailliaud (1862), iii, 94; Douin (1944), i, 275; Dehérain (1898), 176; English (1822), 137–8.
17 In 1840, 'The concession for the sale of liquor in the canton [district?] of al-Matamma is fixed at 10 purses a year,' Hill (1970), 196. The French diarist says furthermore that the customs revenues of Berber District had been assessed at 416 purses a year, *ibid.*, 195. The year before we learn from Thibaut that the customs contract was increased to 300 purses, farmed out to a merchant from Aswan, who was made to make up for a deficit of 70 purses; Thibaut in Santoni and Hill (1980), 84. 1 purse (*kīs*) = 500 piastres.
18 Pückler-Muskau (1844), iii, 40–1; Hill (1970), 166–60.
19 Quoted in Brun-Rollet (1855), 367.
20 Quoted in Dehérain (1898), 168, note 2. (My translation and emphasis).
21 *Ibid.*, 168; Melly (1851), travelling downstream from Khartoum in 1851, noted depopulation along the Nile as a result of 'heavy taxation' and that the nomads had started to invade agricultural land with their flocks. In Berber (Province), 6,000 purses were collected annually, and as there were only 5,000 persons (families or taxation units?), who could pay, that meant £6 (c.600 piastres or 30 dollars) from each on average; see also Santi and Hill (1980), 89–90.
22 Brocchi (1843), v, 78–9, 314–15. See also Cailliaud (1826), i, 355.
23 Hill (1970), 43–4, 53–5; Brocchi (1843), v 306–7, 479–80, 666–7. In 1825–6, a good milking cow cost 8 dollars (c.12 piastres), a bull 5, a donkey 3 to 4, a sheep half a dollar, a transport camel 12 dollars and slaves from 20 to 30 dollars; see Russegger (1841–8), ii/1, 493; ii/2, 20 and 536.
24 Brocchi (1843), v. 479; Cadalvène and Breuvery (1836), ii, 164–5, say that the capitation or *furdat al-ru'ūs* was unknown in Nubia; see also Petherick (1861), 130. This tax was originally meant for non Muslims and was apparently an innovation for the Muslims in Egypt as well; see Rivlin (1961), 133.
25 Brocchi (1843), v, 487, n.b.
26 Rüppell (1829), 26–7.
27 *Ibid.*, 24–9. See also Cadalvène and Breuvery (1836), ii, 167. If carried out, this would have seriously affected indigo cultivation as it was known from Egypt that a *sāqiya* devoted to indigo required nine men working continuously for eight months a year; Richards (1981), 48.
28 Thus the increase in the number of *sāqiyas* in Dongola given by Cadalvène and Breuvery, (ii, p. 167), refers to the ideal rather than to the reality. More reliable figures are given by Abū Salīm (1980), 230, in which we learn that in 1834/5 the number of *sāqiyas* in Dongola was 5,416. The most dramatic decrease occurred in al-Maḥas District, namely from 775 to 292 *sāqiyas*; see, for instance, Reboul in Santi and Hill (1980), 51. As for Arqū Island, see Rüppell (1829), 40; Cadalvène and Breuvery (1836), ii, 339; Hamilton (1857), 381–3; Hartmann (1863), 156–7.
29 Rüppell (1829), 27–8, 37–8, 43; Melly (1851), 183, says that about a quarter was paid in cash and the rest in kind, estimated according to government prices. Hoskins (1835), 128, says that 75 per cent or 300 piastres were paid in cash. See also Cadalvène and Breuvery (1836), ii, 166–7.
30 Rüppell (1829), 37–8; Hoskins (1835), 232.
31 Rüppell (1829), 26, 43; Brocchi (1843), v, 315, 478, 480, 666–7.
32 Pückler-Muskau (1845), ii, 174; Russegger (1841–8), ii/3, 49, 66.
33 Brocchi (1843), v, 667; see also Hill (1970), 7.
34 NRO, Misc. 1/27/386.
35 Bredin (1961), 39.
36 Hill (1970), 45.
37 *Ibid.*, 46; see also Lefèvre in Santi and Hill (1980), 59. We are also informed that the Kabābīsh camel nomads, who nominally paid 6 piastres a head of camel, had offered to pay 1 dollar a head and be rid of the extra contributions, an offer which the Turks flatly rejected; Hamilton (1857), 382.

38 Hill (1970), 55–6.
39 *Ibid.*, 108–9; Thibaut in Santi and Hill (1980), 84. In order to break the monopoly of the Copts, officers knowledgeable in book-keeping were instructed to audit the books.
40 Hoskins (1835), 38, 178; Pückler-Muskau (1844), iii, 39 or (1845), ii, 173; Russegger (1841–8), iii/1, 443–7; Petherick (1861), 105; Hartmann (1863), 220; Hill (1970), 202, 205.
41 Baker (1875), 53; Pückler-Muskau (1845), ii, 173.
42 Taylor (1862), 443, 468; Hamilton (1857), 381–3.
43 Taylor (1862), 443, 468.
44 Beatty (1956), 148–9; *L'Isthme de Suez* (1857), 109.
45 *L'Isthme de Suez* (1857), 91–5.
46 Petherick (1861), 130ff.; Cuny (1862–3), 199–200; Munzinger (1864), 570; Lejean (1865a), 110; Baker (1874), 52; Douin (1933–41), iii/1, 133–4.
47 Heuglin (1941), 151–2.
48 Grant (1885), 24, 33; Petherick (1869), ii, 21; Hill (1959a), 112–13; Du Bisson (1868), 53–5, 258; Douin (1933–41), iii/1, 139; Lejean (1865a), 48, 60, 137–8; Southworth (1875), 172.
49 Petherick to Stanton, 26 December 1863, PRO, FO, 78/2253. Reference in Santi and Hill (1980), 190. Heuglin (1869), 18–19, 248–9, 260–1. According to Brownell (1862), 318, the prices of meat and eggs were relatively low.
50 Douin (1933–41), iii/1, 139–40; 175–6, 229; Hill (1959a), 107.
51 Douin (1933–41), iii/1, 213, 215, 217–18; Hill (1959a), 112.
52 Douin (1933–4), iii/1, 218, 221–3, 226.
53 *Ibid.*, 140, 228–9, 433–5; iii/2, 455.
54 *Ibid.*, iii/1, 436.
55 *Ibid.*, 439–41.
56 Baker (1874), 11; Schweinfurth (1918), 19.
57 Baker (1874), 11; Southworth (1875), 234–5; Douin (1933–41), iii/2, 473, 476, 488, 543. It is said that he managed to persuade as many as 5,000 to return; Abū Salīm (1980), 217.
58 Giegler (1984), 12–13; Douin (1933–41), iii/2, 458, 480–1.
59 *Ibid.*, 477–8, 485; Letters from Ḥusayn Bey, 15 November 1870, Abidin Archive, Reg. 1849, Maʿiyya saniyya, piece 4, 13; 2 December 1870, Reg. 1849, piece 7, 15; 2 December 1870, piece 8, 15. Before the reductions in 1881, the tribute from the nomads reached 800,000 piastres; Stewart (1883), 22.
60 Compared with the revenue for the previous year, Douin (1933–41), iii/2, 477, n.7, gives 2,346 purses as the deficit, while a deficit of about 2,200 purses may be deduced from the list provided by Stewart (1883), 45.
61 Douin (1933–41), iii/2,477, note 7; Ismāʿīl Ayyūb's letter of 20 April 1874; Abidin Archive, reg. 1875, Maʿiyya saniyya, piece 22, 88.
62 *Ibid.*, 489.
63 *Ibid.*, 482–5, 491.
64 Sāmī Amīn (1916–35), iii, 646.
65 Douin (1933–41), iii/2, 528, 584, 601–2; iii/3B, 1095ff.
66 *Ibid.*, iii/2, 594.
67 Giegler (1984), 13–14.
68 Douin (1933–41), iii/3B, 1099.
69 Letter from Ḥusayn Bey of 11 June 1774, in Abidin Archive, Reg. 24 *Arr. Abd.*, ref. to in *Ibid.*, iii/3B, 1101–3. Ḥusayn spent his exile in Upper Egypt, but was reinstated as *mudīr* of Berber 1884 by Gordon, only to surrender Berber to the Mahdists in May the same year. From Omdurman he shortly afterwards made a narrow escape to Egypt, where he was accused of cooperation with the enemy.
70 *Ibid.*, iii/3B, 1112, note 1; 1118, note 1.
71 Slatin (1896), 4.
72 Hill (1959a), 154–5; Abū Salīm (1980), 220–1. Mumtaz' efforts to promote cotton

production in the east had the Khedive's enthusiastic support but, as in Berber, they did not meet expectations. However, thereafter for a long time 'the name of Mumtaz was used as a synonym for cotton', Holt and Daly (1979), 81. A still optimistic Khedive transferred him to Khartoum (1871) after the deposition of his rival and 'anti-cottonist' Jaʿfar Pasha Maẓhar and the abolition of the *ḥikimdāriyya*, but within a year Mumtāz was deprived of his position because of grave irregularities; Hill (1967), 37–8.

73 Abū Salīm (1980), 221–2; Stewart (1883), 14–15.

74 Stewart (1883), 14. Stewart was sent by the British, rulers of Egypt since 1882, to report on the alarming situation in the Sudan.

75 *Ibid.*, 14–15.

76 *Ibid.*, 13–14.

77 *Ibid.*, 21, 17–18, 36.

78 Giegler (1984), Map 2.

79 Holt (1977), 33; Holt and Daly (1979), 89; Shuqayr (1903), iii, 109–12.

80 Boserup (1965), 32–42; Rivlin (1961), *passim*; Abū Salīm (1980), 213–14; Richards (1981), 46–52.

6 THE TRANSFORMATION OF COMMERCE

1 Lejean (1862), 205–21; an important manuscript by Thibaut, a French merchant and traveller in the Sudan, entitled, *Aperçue du Commerce du Soudan*, in Bibliothèque de la Société de Géographie de Paris, n.d., contains much information on commerce during the first decades of the Turkiyya. A copy of the MS has most kindly been provided by Dr Alfred Fierro.

2 Bjørkelo (1984).

3 Rüppell (1829), 27; (1836), 169–70; Russegger (1841–8), ii/2, 768; Hamont (1843), i, 42; ii, 591; Thibaut, MS, Bibliothèque de la Société de Géographie, Paris, 9–10, 16; Cailliaud (1826), ii, 57; Linant de Bellefonds (1858), 152.

4 Churi (1853), 142–3; Santoni in Santi and Hill (1980), 225.

5 Hamilton (1935), 61; Shukry (1935), 130; Gray (1961), 21.

6 Holt (1977), 39; Wilson and Felkin (1882), ii, 285; Ohrwalder (1892), 12, 35; Slatin (1896), 133, 142, 144–5.

7 The tax paid by the merchants was called *wīrkū*. The *humāyūnī* merchant law is referred to in Du Bisson (1868), 50–1; Stewart (1883), 12; SAD 404/10 [AR].

8 English (1822), 204; Cailliaud (1826), i, 365, ii, 116–17; Finati (1830), ii, 360, 385, 410; Pückler-Muskau (1845), ii, 152.

9 Cailliaud (1826), ii, 116–17.

10 Waddington and Hanbury (1822), 53, 81, 83.

11 Cadalvène and Brauvery (1836), ii, 168; Russegger (1841–8), ii/1, 494; ii/2, 36; Hill (1979), 150–2; Rivlin (1961), 329.

12 Both the piastre and the para contained an increasingly higher percentage of copper, see Rivlin (1961), 121; *taʿarīfa*, 'understood', origin of our word *tariff*, referred to the official exchange rate as opposed to the commercial or current rate. *Taʿarīfa* was also the name of the ½ piastre coin.

13 Russegger (1841–8), ii/1, 494. Berg. NI 477. 15/200 (15 Ṣafar 1266/31 Dec. 1849).

14 Hill (1970), 163, 167.

15 Russegger (1841–8), ii/2, 36, ii/1, 494. For an analysis of the weights, contents and current values of the Egyptian coins, see Lambert (1842), MS; the Turkish coins are discussed in Belin (1864), 417–65.

16 Hill (1959a), 38; Junker (1889–92), i, 159–60; Job (1920), 163–96.

17 Giegler (1984), 63; see also Hartmann (1863), 144.

18 Russegger (1841–8), ii/2, 36, noted a loss of up to 30 to 50 per cent.

19 Hill (1970), 52; see also Werne (1849), i, 35.
20 Giegler (1984), 63; Marno (1874), 135, 262–3; Gray (1961), 51.
21 Petherick (1861), 283–4; on the profitability of collecting gum, see Lauture (1853), 171.
22 Giegler (1984), 63; Lauture (1853), 573; Taylor (1862), 386; Antognoli in Santi and Hill (1980), 193–4. The Banque du Soudan in Cairo failed to finance trade and development in the Sudan and was closed in 1873.
23 Letter of 1 April 1863, Abidin Archive, MS Carton 30, piece 54, referred to in Douin (1933–41), iii/1, 170–2.
24 Marno (1874), 441.
25 NRO, Misc. 1/13/119 (25 Dhu'l-hijja 1282/11 May 1866).
26 SAD 281/3, Notes on the History of Kordofan, 24; Rüppell (1829), 139; Pallme (1844), 303; Lauture (414/15); O'Fahey (1980), 134.
27 Brocchi (1843), v, 667.
28 Russegger (1841–8), ii/2, 240; Bjørkelo (1983), 136, Table 1.
29 Junker (1889–92), i, 158, 176.
30 Berg. NI. 347. 15/75. (27 Shaʿbān 1307/17 April 1890). See also Pfund (1876–7), 285.
31 Hoskins (1835), 87–8; Brocchi (1843), v, 480, 666–7; Junker (1889–92), i, 158; Pallme (1844), 270; Hill (1970), 157.
32 Born (1968), 88.
33 Abbate (1858), 20; Wingate (1891), 162.
34 Russegger (1841–8), ii/1, 494.
35 Hoskins (1835), 87–8.
36 Taylor (1862), 493–4, 258–61.
37 Gleichen (1905), i, 105; ii, 107; Budge (1911), 824; Sudan Intell. Report, no. 56 (1897), 7.
38 Didier (1858), 20–60; Brownell (1862), Private Papers, 320; Poncet (1863), 6; Lejean (1865a), 27, 35; Lesseps (1857), MS., 3. On the history of Khartoum, see Edwards (1922); Walkley (1935–6); Stevenson (1966).
39 Slatin (1896), 107–8.
40 See for example Junker (1889–92), i, 123.
41 Lejean (1865b), 294–300; Chélu (1891), 105, 144.
42 As is evident from a partnership contract, Berg. NI 363. 15/91 (13 Shawwāl 1299/28 August 1882); See also Lejean (1865b), 277.
43 Southworth (1875), 367–80; Cox (1952), 199.
44 Walz (1979), 71–2.
45 Petti Suma (1964).
46 Le Mascrier (1740), i, 50–4, 261; ii, 338ff.
47 Abbas A. Mohamed (1980), 116; Sarkassian (1913), 40; L. O. Manger (personal communication).
48 Garnier in Douin (1933–41), iii/1, 161.
49 Ḥamza Mūsā, the merchant in al-Matamma who entered into partnership with Ahmad Pasha in the famous indigo factory, is referred to as '*khawāja*' in a land sale contract from 1849 (Berg. NI 477. 15/200). Today the title has the mixed meaning of 'foreigner', 'Christian', and 'merchant' in the Sudan.
50 In a letter from the sultan of Dār Fūr, Ibrāhīm Qarad (1873–4) to al-Zubayr Pasha, the former refers contemptuously to the merchant prince as *al-jallābī*. Al-Zubayr in his reply fiercely asserts his ʿAbbāsī descent. Shuqayr (1903), iii, 73.
51 Taylor (1862), 385.
52 Cadalvène and Breuvery (1836), ii, 149; Marno (1874), 236.
53 Schweinfurth (1917), 502.
54 Pallme (1844), 267–70, 287. On the commodities brought by the *jallāba* from Egypt, see Taylor (1862), 386, and Cuny (1862–3), 283.
55 Pallme (1844), 301.

56 Poncet (1863), 10; Petherick (1861), 189–90.
57 Marno (1874), 192–4, 232.
58 NRO, Northern province, 1/27/273, Trade 1939.
59 Werne (1849), ii, 214.
60 Cuny (1862–3), 43.
61 Marno (1874), 236.
62 Interview C2/B.
63 Thibaut, MS; Lauture (1853), 460.
64 Poncet (1863), 8.
65 Marno (1874), 192–4, 232. See also Hartmann (1872), 499.
66 Taylor (1862), 385.
67 Spaulding (1985), 238–72.
68 Lejean (1865a), 4; (1865b), 275–6.
69 Cuny (1862–3), 214, 216; Munzinger (1864), 563, 581.
70 Lejean (1862), 208–11, 216; (1865b), 297.
71 Munzinger (1864), 566, 569–70: Hartmann (1872), 499.
72 Munzinger (1864), 553; Beurmann (1973), 59–60; Yūsuf Mikha'īl (1962), 41, 48.
73 Hill (1970), 56; SAD 404/10/20 [AR], 3.
74 I am now working on a more detailed biography of this merchant.
75 Inalcik (1969), 99–100.
76 Karrār (1985), 65, 74.
77 O'Fahey, personal communication.
78 Cadalvène and Breuvery (1836), ii, 314; Cuny (1862–3), 302, 308–9.
79 Berg. NI 477. 15/200 (15 Ṣafar 1266/31 December 1849).
80 Berg. NI 300. 15/28 (1273/1856–7).
81 Berg. NI 340. 15/68 (14 Muḥarram 1280/1 July 1863); NI 399. 15/67 (27 Rajab 1281/26 December 1864).
82 Berg. NI 404/15. 127 (20 Rabīʿ I 1289/28 May 1872); NI 396. 15/119 (Muḥarram 1290/March–April 1873); NI 343. 15/71 (19 Jumādā I 1288/6 August 1871); NI 345. 15/73 (6 Rabīʿ II 1299/25 February 1882); NI 303. 15/31 (8 Rabīʿ II 1301/4 February 1884).
83 Letter no. 752 (22 Shaʿbān 1302/7 June 1885), Abū Salīm (1969), 363.
84 Berg. NI 393. 15/116 (1291/1874–5) and NI 360. 15/88 (22 Dhu'l-Qaʿda 1295/17 November 1878).
85 Cuny (1862–3), 329; Hartmann (1863), 118.
86 Douin (1933–41), iii/3B, 166–7. *Al-ḥājj* ʿAbd al-Ghanī was the agent for Morocco in Cairo and associated with the Moroccan al-Sharīf al-Sayyid Aghalī alʿUmarānī, chief of a commercial house in the Sudan. He was given permission to extend his operations to Dār Fūr by a Superior Order of 17 February 1875 to the Governor of the Sudan. A copy of this document, dated 11 Muḥarram 1292, and catalogued under *Awāmir ʿarabī, daftar* 1, no. 3, p. 3, in the Dār al-Wathā'iq al-Miṣriyya was most kindly provided to me by Dr Alī Sālih Karrār.
87 Berg. NI 353. 15/81 (letter); Berg. NI 349. 15/77; NI 354. 15/82; NI 351. 15/79; NI 352. 15/80.
88 Berg. NI 424. 15/147 (20 December 1890).
89 See for instance: Berg. NI 277. 15/5 (Rabīʿ II 1299/February–March 1882); NI 363. 15/91 (13 Shawwāl 1299/28 August 1882); NI 383. 15/111 (15 Shawwāl 1299/30 August 1882); NI 350. 15/78 (end of Rabīʿ I 1303/January 1885).
90 Berg. NI 275. 15/3, letter of appointment; NI 276. 15/4 (1296/1878–79), seal of the Khedive.
91 Bedri (1969), i, 101, 104–9, 123.
92 Interview C11
93 Relevant documents: Berg. NI 287. 15/15 (27 Rajab 1330/12 July 1912), ʿAbd Allāh repays loan extended to him by al-Zubayr; NI 462. 15/185 (11 July 1913), letter from the Midland

Engineering Company; NI 461. 15/184 (1 May 1913), Receipt from the Midland Engineering Company.

94 Udovitch (1970), 86–7.
95 Du Bisson (1868), 226.
96 Spaulding (1982b), 4.
97 Travellers going to the Sudan might obtain letters of credit in Egypt on persons in the Sudan, to avoid the risk of transporting cash. Thus Taylor obtained from an Armenian merchant a letter of credit on his brother in Khartoum for 2,000 piastres, on which he was to pay a discount of 20 per cent when cashing the letter in Khartoum, Taylor (1862), 49. The personal character of such transactions made them vulnerable to external events. Cadalvène and Breuvery had a letter of credit on a *muʿallim* in Shendi, but found him hanged before they could reach him and exchange the letter for cash (1863), ii, 279.
98 Udovitch (1970). For comparative purposes, see also Postan (1973).
99 Goitein (1967–83), i; Walz (1979); Postan (1973).
100 Udovitch (1970), 171.
101 Udovitch (1970), 174–5; Goitein (1967–83), i, 171.
102 Berg. NI 340. 15/68 (14 Muḥarram 1280/1 July 1863) and Berg. NI 222. 13/83 (20 Shaʿbān 1277/3 March 1861).
103 Udovitch (1970), 183–4.
104 *Ibid.*, 143, 145–6, 147, 150.
105 Bjørkelo (1982).
106 Walz (1979).

7 CONCLUSION: DISPERSION AND RETURN

1 Hill (1970), 183.
2 Müller (1851), 131.
3 O'Fahey (1980), 115–30.
4 The kingdom of Taqalī may be a case in point, see Ewald (1985).
5 Hartmann (1872), 499–501.
6 Munzinger (1864), 519.
7 Browne (1806), 271–2; Cailliaud (1826), ii, 23, 183; Cadalvène and Breuvery (1836), ii, 191; Nicholls (1913), 18ff.
8 The rebel state of the Jaʿaliyyīn remains to be studied. A MS in Durham, SAD 110/2/3, gives valuable first hand information. Parkyns was probably the last traveller who saw *makk* Nimr alive in 1844; Parkyns (1868), 445. For a later (1851) anonymous visitor to the Jaʿaliyyīn on the Setit River, see Santi (ed.) (1965), 135–8.
9 These terms are also used by Geiser (1975), 172.
10 NRO, Misc. 1/81/1292: This document belongs to Shaykh al-Rayyaḥ al-ʿAydarūs. Members of this family spread from al-Matamma to Shendi, Atbara, Khartoum North, al-Fāshir, al-Rūṣayris, al-Duwayn, Omdurman, Berber, al-Raḥad and al-Tabā. I am grateful to Dr J. Spaulding for drawing my attention to this document.
11 Combes (1946), ii, 206.
12 Cailliaud (1826), iii, 108; ii, 116–17; English (1822), 115; Cadalvène and Breuvery (1836), ii, 242; Chélu (1891), 48; Combes (1846), ii, 206; Marno (1878), 155.
13 NRO, Misc. 1/14/125, piece 1 (13 Rabīʿ I 1286/26 June 1869).
14 Al-Shahi and Moore (1978), 104–6.
15 Abdulla El Tayib (1956–64), part ii, 1956, 66–8.
16 Cuny (1862–63), 329; Junker (1889–92), i, 169; Petherick (1869), i, 108.
17 Babikr Bedri (1969), i, 1–2.
18 Nachtigal (1879–89), iii, 320–21.

19 Shuqayr (1903), iii, 60–87; Jackson (1913). I am grateful to R. S. O'Fahey for the information on al-Zubayr's early career.
20 Slatin (1896), 122ff.; Holt (1977), 45 ff.
21 For firsthand information on the political situation in Kordofan just prior to the Mahdiyya, see Yūsuf Mikha'īl (1962), 31–106. For a summary, see Holt (1977), 49. The deputy and associate of Ilyās Pahsa, ʿAbd al-Raḥmān Bey Bān al-Naqā, appears probably in document Berg. NI 422. 15/145.
22 Holt (1977), 38.
23 Hallam (1977); Bjørkelo (1976), 16.
24 Holt (1977), 39.
25 Slatin (1896), 280; Broadbent (1940), 125–6. Aḥmad w. Ḥamza gained control of Shendi and became *amīr* of Salawa area. ʿAlī w. *al-ḥājj* Saʿd became the first *amīr* of the Jaʿaliyyīn under the Mahdiyya and was succeeded by ʿAbd Allāh. The latter came to oppose the successor of the Mahdī, the Khalīfa ʿAbdullāhi, refusing to evacuate al-Matamma when British troops advanced south through Dongola in 1896–97. The Khalīfa sent therefore an army against the Jaʿaliyyīn of al-Matamma and a large part of the population was killed. Holt, Box 1 1/2 120 (1315) (undated), is a copy of a letter from the Khalīfa ordering the evacuation of al-Matamma. I am grateful to Dr Lidwien Kapteijns for a copy of this letter. A posthumous daughter of ʿAbd Allāh, Surra, and a grandson, al-Zayn, were interviewed in Shendi in 1980. C 5/B. See also NRO, Cairint. 1/50/291, Report on the fate of the Jaalin at Metemma 1897.
26 Cuzzi (1968), 59–60.
27 Wingate (1891), 162; NRO, Dakhlia I, 112/3/12.

APPENDIX: THREE CONTRACTS FROM THE ARCHIVE OF ʿABD ALLĀH BEY ḤAMZA

1 This 'heading' is stamped on the paper and indicates that such paper could be bought for the purpose of setting up contracts. The following contract has a heading with exactly the same wording, whereas the third contract also indicates the limits of the partnership's capital and has cost the partners 100 piastres in stamp duty, as opposed to the 6 piastres of the two first. It may also be noted that the same circular seal with some unreadable text has been impressed without ink into the paper on top of all the three contracts, which also indicates that we are dealing with officially issued paper for the writing of contracts.

Sources and bibliography

The primary source material utilised in this study can be divided into four main categories: travel literature, government archives, private collections, and interviews. These are familiar categories to any historian working on Africa and the Middle East, and their historical value will be discussed here only in so far as the nineteenth century in the Sudan is concerned. Each category poses specific methodological problems, particularly with regard to origin, nearness to the events reported, human biases or hidden motives. There is also the problem of completeness in the sources, which means that an area is not covered continuously over a long period of time. This is most commonly the case with the travel literature which has left both geographically and diachronically scattered information. The authors of travel books naturally followed the caravan routes across the deserts or along the Nile, they were more or less compelled to visit the administrative and economic centres without seeing much of the remoter villages and nomadic camps. These considerations were, of course, important when the present author chose to study an area of the Nile Valley which is relatively well covered in the historical sources, compared to most other areas in the Sudan. The source situation may also account for the concentration on Shendi rather than on al-Matamma and al-Dāmir, and the concentration on the riverain communities to the near exclusion of the neighbouring pastoral nomads. However, to be guided to an area and a historical period by the available sources *is not* the same as adopting the perspectives, values and themes prevalent in them.

A fundamental rule in dealing with travel literature, and indeed with most written sources and interviews, is to separate the normative from the cognitive elements. The first may be of high value in a study of the author's background, ethos and worldview, when his writings are studied as a remnant of the past. Our concern has been to extract data based on the author's own observations or on what he has learned from others. Data from different sources have been compared as far as possible in order to enhance the reliability by discarding or at least qualifying unconfirmed information.

The author has consulted six archives: (1) the National Records Office in Khartoum; (2) the Sudan Archive in Durham; (3) the Public Record Office in Kew, London; (4) the Bergen Archive at the Department of History, University of Bergen; (5) the Folklore Institute, University of Khartoum; (6) the Maḥkama Archive in Shendi. Some material was sent to me from the Bibliothèque Nationale de Paris, the Bibliothèque de la Société de Géographie, and the Bibliothèque de l'Arsenal, all in Paris. The archive in Shendi contains registers of land sales, some of which date from the nineteenth century. The NRO has much more land-sales contracts, chronicles and other manuscripts originating in the period under study. The Mahdiyya papers and the Condominium Archives are also housed there. The latter have been used extensively in order to become acquainted with socio-economic features on the local level. They also contain numerous reports by British officials on local customs, politics, and history, particularly with regard to the Turkiyya. This information was collected from interviews and from material left from the Turkiyya, and must, of course, be subjected to the same precautions as the travel literature.

Several officials wrote books about Sudanese history and their personal experiences there. They kept private archives and wrote diaries and drafts for articles and books; much of this material is now deposited in Durham University.

The Egyptian archives in Cairo have not been consulted partly because much of the relevant material would be in Ottoman Turkish, with which I am unfamiliar. However, some information has been obtained from the body of sources translated into Arabic and published by Sāmī Amīn.

Under the heading of private collections comes Arabic documentation in private hands in the Sudan. These are letters, contracts and religious and historical manuscripts, which are continually being located, photographed and transferred to the NRO. Much material has been found during fieldwork by R. S. O'Fahey and J. L. Spaulding, who have deposited copies both at the NRO and at the Department of History, University of Bergen. Of particular importance to the present study is the collection of papers discovered by the author in al-Matamma in the possession of the decendants of a rich merchant, ʿAbd Allāh Bey Ḥamza, who started his career in the latter half of the Turkiyya. Only a fraction of the more than 230 documents photographed in 1980 and 1984 have been used in the present study. They will form the basis of a separate work. The most original documents are commercial contracts on the classical Islamic pattern. The other interesting category are land sale contracts which testify to the extent of the commercialisation of the agricultural sector.

As part of the fieldwork in 1980 a series of interviews were conducted in order to obtain historical and socio-economic data. The informants were chosen among people reputed to be knowledgeable in history. However, I soon discovered that the transmitted information on the nineteenth century was on many points inconsistent and unreliable. Some information could also be checked against written evidence, which worked as an important yardstick of the value of the interviews. On the other hand, in the fields of agriculture, trade and crafts, society, religion and culture, the interviews as well as the continuous informal discussions were crucial sources of information which cannot be found in any archive or book.

The voice of the Sudanese themselves has also survived in a few edited and published manuscripts written by local authors, such as Wad Ḍayf Allāh's *Tabaqāt* and the *Funj Chronicle* (also known as *Makhṭūṭa Kātib al-Shūna*). The first collection of tribal genealogies, religious and historical manuscripts to appear in English was MacMichael's two-volume work *A History of the Arabs in the Sudan* from 1922. The voluminous work from 1903 by Shuqayr, *Ta'rīkh al-Sūdān*, draws also heavily upon Sudanese sources (written and oral) as well as on Turkiyya material and ought to be rated among the primary sources.

ABBREVIATIONS

AAS	*Asian and African Studies*
BSG	*Bulletin de la Société de Géographie de Paris*
BSOAS	*Bulletin of the School of Oriental and African Studies*
EI 2nd edn	*Encyclopaedia of Islam*
IJAHS	*International Journal of African Historical Studies*
JAH	*Journal of African History*
JAL	*Journal of African Law*

JAS	*Journal of the African Society*
JESHO	*Journal of the Economic and Social History of the Orient*
JRGS	*Journal of the Royal Geographical Society*
MEJ	*Middle East Journal*
MES	*Middle Eastern Studies*
NAV	*Nouvelles Annales des Voyages*
PM	*Petermann's Mitteilungen*
SNR	*Sudan Notes and Records*
Berg.	The collection of Sudanese Arabic documents at the Department of History, University of Bergen
C	Tape cassette recording
IF	Institute of Folklore, Khartoum
NRO	National Records Office, Khartoum (formerly Central Records Office, CRO)
PRO	Public Record Office, Kew
SAD	Sudan Archive, Durham

ORAL SOURCES

Muḥammad Nimr Jamāl al-Dīn, age 85 (in 1980), village shaykh in Ḥōsh Bān Naqā village. Interviews: (1) C1, 19 February 1980 in Ḥōsh Bān Naqā; (2) C9/A, 6 March 1980 in Shendi; (3) Notes, 20 April in Ḥōsh Bān Naqā.

Al-fakī al-Amīn Yūsuf, age 70, teacher at the Quran school (*khalwa*) of Old Shendi. Interviews: (1) C2/A, 21 February 1980 in Shendi; (2) C4, 26 February in Shendi.

Sharīf Ḥāmid Maḥmūd, age 89. Interview, C2/B and C3, 24 February 1980 in Shendi.

Muḥammad ʿUthmān Nūr, age 70, retired railway officer, now merchant. Interview C5/A, 27 February 1980 in Shendi.

Surra bt. ʿAbd Allāh w. Saʿd, age 85, and Al-Zayn w. Saʿd w. ʿAbd Allāh w. Saʿd, teacher, interviewed together, C5/B, 27 February 1980 in Shendi.

Abbashir Majdhūb, age 60, teacher. Interview, C6, 28 February 1980 in Shendi.

Muḥammad Khayr (Al-ʿUmda) age 50, post office employee. Interview, C7, 1 March 1980 in Shendi.

Muḥammad w. al-Bashīr Muḥammad ʿUthmān, age 44, merchant. Interview, C8, 3 March 1980 in Shendi.

Al-Shūl bt. al-Shaykh Sirrūr, age late 80s. Interview C9/B, 10 April 1980 in Shendi.

Sulaymān ʿAbd Allāh Bey Ḥamza, age 81, farmer and builder. Interviews (1) C10, 9 March 1980 in al-Matamma; (2) C11, 18 March in al-Matamma.

Muḥammad Ḥāmid al-Jamrī, retired army officer. Interview, C12/A, 14 April 1980 in Shendi.

Al-Shaykh al-Muzammil, age c.70, religious shaykh in Misiktāb village. Notes.

Muḥammad al-Ṭūm Ziyād, village shaykh of Basabīr village, and head of the Basabīr Shāyqiyya. Notes, 4 March 1980 in Shendi.

Al-fakī Aḥmad Jabbūr, age 100. Notes, 28 April 1980 in Shendi.

Muḥammad Bābikr ʿAbd al-Kāfī, age 59, former farmer from ʿĀlīāb, now ferry captain. Notes, 1 May 1980 in Shendi.

Tijānī al-Mardī, age 80, merchant. Notes, 24 October 1978 in Omdurman.

IF Oral material collected by and deposited at the Institute of Folklore in Khartoum.

PRIVATE PAPERS

A typed MS by Col. Ryder, in the possession of the family, pp. 57–82 (Great Britain).

Brownell's Diary (1862). A typed MS in the possession of the family (United States).

Sources and bibliography

ARCHIVAL MATERIAL – IN EUROPEAN LANGUAGES

La Bibliothèque de la Société de Géographie, Paris

G. Thibaut, uncatalogued MS, 'Aperçu du commerce du Soudan'.

G. Lejean (1862), 'Rapport adressé à son Excellence M. le Ministre des affaires Étrangères, par M. G. Lejean, chargé d'une mission dans la région du Haut Nil'.

La Bibliothèque Nationale de Paris

F. de Lesseps (1857), MS, 'Rapport.'

La Bibliothèque de l'Arsenal, Paris

C. Lambert (1842), *Tarif des monnais en Egypte*, MS, Fonds Enfantine No. 7740.

University of Nottingham

Mansfield Parkyns, MS. a copy of the *Funj Chronicle*, PA. X3, copied 1847, 143 folios/pages.

SAD (Sudan Archive, Durham) (Condominium sources)

SAD 110/2/3: Abyssinia-Sudan Frontier. An account of Mc [*sic*] Nimr and his sons on the Abyssinian Frontier.

SAD 110/2/4: A full account of the military revolt of the 14th Sudanese Battalion (1865), as related by Mahmud El Mahallawi and corroborated by several other eyewitnesses.

SAD 178/5–6: El-Obeid. Siege 1883. Fr P. Rossignoli's account.

SAD 195/7: Sudan Correspondence 1915. Na'ūm Shuqayr, History of the Majdhūbiyya Tarīqa.

SAD 245/7: Chronology for Wingate's Draft, 1883, 1918.

SAD 281/3: Notes on the History of Kordofan (MacMichael).

SAD 292/18: Report on the Sudan by Lieutenant-Colonel J. D. H. Stewart, presented to Parliament in 1883; published as Command Paper 3670, London, 1885.

SAD 294/18/4: H. A. MacMichael, Reminiscences of Kordofan, 1906.

SAD 303/12: Letter from Johann Hedenborg, 10 October 1835.

SAD 400/8/1–25: Part of Col. Ryder's typed memoirs, pp. 48–75 (see above, private papers).

SAD 404/10 [AR]: Anonymous History of al-Ubayyiḍ from about 1863 to 1883. Arabic text and English translation.

SAD 406/2: Sd. Yūsuf b. al-Sayyid Ahmad, born 1200/1785–86. History of the Awlād Hindī.

SAD 444/8/4: Chronological Table of Events, 1849–94.

SAD 465/2; H. C. Jackson's Safaria Notes. December 1924.

SAD 542/3: Notes and reports by MacMichael.

SAD 542/6/1–48; Report on Berber land commission (1904), by J. F. Kershaw.

SAD 542/7/49–75: Report on certain lands on the Atbara. Reports on the Karru Lands in Shendi (1906), by S. A. Tippetts.

NRO (National Records Office, Khartoum, formerly Central Records Office, CRO)

Condominium sources

The following groups have been consulted: Northern Province, Kordofan Province, Dakhlia I (Interior), Intelligence, Cairint., Civil Secretary, Miscellaneous (see section under Arabic documentation below). A detailed list of these files can be found in my thesis, 1983, 395–400.

ARCHIVAL MATERIAL: SUDANESE ARABIC DOCUMENTATION

1 NRO, Miscellaneous, which includes private Arabic documents from the nineteenth century.

2 *Dār al-Wathā'iq al-Miṣriyya*. (The Egyptian National Archives). *Awāmir ʿarabī, daftar* 1, no. 3, p. 3. A document concerning ʿAbd al-Ghanī al-Ṭayyib al-Ṭāzī.

3 Berg., which includes photographic copies of Arabic documents deposited at the Department of History, University of Bergen, Norway. The majority of the documents have been found and photographed by R. S. O'Fahey, J. L. Spaulding and the present author. Some are copies of documents in the NRO, Misc. collection. The documents are catalogued according to owner of the respective archives and province of origin. NI stands for Nile Province (the old Berber province), and NO stands for Northern Province (the old Dongola province); the two collections are the most relevant to the present study.

4 SOAS, Holt's Papers. Holt Box 1 1/2 120 1315. A letter from the Khalīfa (1897).

THESES, MIMEOGRAPHS, PAPERS AND FORTHCOMING ARTICLES

Abū Salīm, M. I., '*Al-Murshid ilā wathā'iq al-Mahdī*', mimeograph, Khartoum, 1969.

Bjørkelo, A., 'State and society in three Central Sudanic kingdoms, Kanem Bornu, Bagirmi and Wadai', MA thesis, University of Bergen, 1976.

'From King to Kāshif: Shendi in the Nineteenth Century', PhD thesis, University of Bergen, 1983.

'al-Matamma', forthcoming in EI².

'The buying and selling of land in the Northern Sudan, c.1770–1910', unpublished article, 77pp.

Ewald, J. J., 'Leadership and social change on an Islamic Frontier: The Kingdom of Taqali, 1780–1900'. PhD thesis, University of Wisconsin-Madison, 1982.

Farah Hassan Adam, 'Contribition of land tenure structures to agricultural development in the Sudan through incentives, knowledge and capital', PhD thesis, Iowa State University, 1965.

Hargey, T., 'The suppression of slavery in the Sudan, 1898–1939', PhD thesis, University of Oxford, 1981.

Hurreiz, S. H., 'Jaʿaliyyīn folktales. An interplay to African and Islamic elements', PhD thesis, University of India, 1972.

Kapteijns, L., 'Mahdist faith and Sudanic tradition. History of Dār Masālīt, 1870–1930', PhD thesis, University of Amsterdam, 1982.

Karrār, A. S., 'The Sufi Brotherhoods in the Sudan until 1900. With special reference to the Shāyqiyya region'. PhD, University of Bergen, 1985.

Kjerland, K., 'The fetters of memory. The changing pattern of marriage among the Jaʿaliyyīn, 1915 to 1981', MA thesis, University of Bergen, 1982.

Kuhn, M. W., 'Markets and trade in Omdurman, Sudan', dissertation, Los Angeles, 1970.

Lee, D. R., 'The geography of rural house types in the Nile Valley of Northern Sudan', PhD thesis, 1967.

Salih Mohammad Nur, 'A critical edition of the Memoirs of Yūsīf Mikha'īl', PhD thesis, University of London, 1962.

Shukry, M. F., 'The Khedive Ismail and slavery in the Sudan', PhD thesis, University of Liverpool, 1935.

Spaulding, J. L., 'Kings of Sun and Shadow: A history of the ʿAbdullab Provinces of the Northern Sinnar Sultanate, 1500–1800 AD', PhD thesis, Columbia, 1971.

Wituki, L. A., 'The transformation of agriculture in the Merowe area of Northern Sudan', PhD thesis, University of Wisconsin, Madison, 1967.

Yūsuf Mikha'īl, see above, Salih Mohammad Nur.

TRAVEL LITERATURE AND OTHER PRIMARY SOURCES

Abbate, O. (1858), *De l'Afrique Central ou voyage de S. A. Mohammad Saïd Pacha dans ses Provinces du Soudan*, Paris.

Alford, H. S. L. and Sword, W. D. (1898), *The Egyptian Sudan, Its Loss and Recovery*, New York, repr. 1969.

Baker, S. W. (1874), *The Nile and Its Tributaries of Abyssinia and the Sword Hunters of the Hamran Arabs*, London.

(1875), *Ismailia. Berättelse om den af Ismail, Khediv af Egypten, för undertryckande af slafhandeln i Centralafrika utsände expedition*, Stockholm.

Bedri, Babikr (1969), *The Memoirs of Babikr Bedri*, London, 2 vols., vol. i.

Bellefonds, L. M. A. L. de (1958), *Journal d'un voyage à Méroé dans les années 1821 et 1822*, Khartoum, ed. by M. Shinnie.

Beurmann, K. M. von (1973), *Voyages et explorations 1860–1863: Nubie, Soudan, Libye, Fezzan, Lac Tchad, Bornu*, Paris.

Biberfeld, E. (1892), *Der Reisebericht des David Rëubēni. Ein Beitrag zur Geschichte des xvi. Jahrhunderts.* (Doctoral thesis at Leipzig). Berlin.

Bowring, J. (1840), *Report on Egypt and Candia addressed to the Right Hon. Lord Viscount Palmerstone, Her Majesty's Principal Secretary of State for Foreign Affairs*, London.

Bredin, G. R. F. (1961), 'The Life-Story of Yuzbashi 'Abdullah Adlan', *SNR*, xlii, 37–52.

Brehm, A. E. (1972), *Reisen im Sudan, 1847 bis 1852*, Tübingen and Basel.

Broadbent, P. B. (1940), 'Reminiscences of a Berber Merchant', *SNR*, xxiii/1, 123–30.

Brocchi, G. B. (1843), *Giornale delle osservazioni fatte ne' viaggi in Egitto nella Siria e nella Nubia*, Bassano, 5 vols.

Browne, W. G. (1806), *Travels in Egypt, Syria and Africa*, London, 2nd edn.

Bruce, J. (1790), *Travels to Discover the Source of the Nile in the Years 1768–1773*, Edinburgh, 5 vols., repr. 1972.

Brun-Rullet, M. (1855), *Le Nil Blanc et le Soudan: moeurs et coutumes des sauvages*, Paris.

Buchta, R. (1888), *Der Sudan unter Aegyptischer Herrschaft, Rückblicke auf die letzen sechzig Jahre*, Leipzig.

Budge, E. A. W. (1907), *The Egyptian Sudan*, London, 2 vols.

(1911), *Cook's Handbook for Egypt and the Egyptian Sudan*, London, 3rd edn.

Burckhardt, J. L. (1822), *Travels in Nubia*, London, 2nd edn repr. 1978.

Cadalvène, E. de and Breuvery, J. de (1836), *L'Egypte et la Turquie de 1829 à 1836*, Paris, 2 vols., vol. 1, *L'Egypte et la Nubie.*

Cailliaud, F. (1826), *Voyage à Méroé, au Fleuve Blanc, au-delà de Fāzogl dans le Midi du Royaume de Sennār, à Syouah et dans cinq autres oasis: fait dans les années 1819, 1821 et 1822*, Paris, 4 vols.

Chélu, A. (1891), *Le nil, le Soudan, l'Egypte*, Paris.

Churi, J. H. (1853), *Sea Nile, The Desert, and Nigritia: Travels in the Company of Captain Peel, RN. 1851–1852*, London.

Colston, R. E. (1876), 'Le Cordofan. Itinéraire de Débé à l'Obeyad', *L'Explorateur*, 250.

(1878), *Report on the Northern and Central Kordofan*, Cairo.

Combes, E. (1846), *Voyages en Egypte, en Nubie dans le Deserts de Beyouda, des Bisharys, et sur les côtes de la Mer Rouge*, Paris, 2 vols.

Cox, F. J. (1952), 'Munzinger's Observations on the Sudan, 1871: "The Little America of Africa" ', *SNR*, xxxiii/2, 189–200.

Cuny, Ch. (1858), 'Observations générales sur le Mémoire sur le Soudan par M. le Comte d'Escayrac de Lauture', *NAV*, 3–28.

(1862–3), 'Journal de voyage de Siout à El-Obeid du 22 novembre 1857 à avril 1858', *NAV*, iii (1862), 254–391 and iv (1863), 22–85 and 175–225.

Cuzzi, G. (1968), *Fifteen Years Prisoner of the False Prophet*, Khartoum.

Ḍayf Allāh (1971), *Kitāb al-ṭabaqāt*, ed. Yūsuf Faḍl Ḥasan, Khartoum.

Desplaces, E. (1857), 'Progrès nouveaux de l'Administration Egyptienne. Organisation du Soudan', *L'Isthme de Suez*, no. 10, Wednesday 25 March, 89–91.

Didier, Ch. (1858), *500 Lieus sur le Nil*, Paris.

Du Bisson, R. (1868), *Les Femmes, les eunuques et les guerriers du Soudan*, Paris.
Dufton, H. (1867), *Narrative of a Journey through Abyssinia in 1862–3*, London.
English, G. B. (1822), *A Narrative of the Expedition to Dongola and Sennaar under the Command of his Excellence Ismaïl Pasha, Undertaken by Order of His Highness Mehemmed Ali Pasha, Vice Roy of Egypt, by an American in the Service of the Vice Roy*, London.
Ensor, F. S. C. E. (1881), *Incidents on a Journey through Nubia to Darfoor*, London.
Finati, G. (1830), *Narrative of the Life and Adventures of Giovanni Finati*, ed. W. J. Bankes, London, 2 vols.
Fraccaroli, A. (1880), 'Gita commerciale nel Cordofan e Darfur', *L'Exploratore*, iv, 161–6 and 205–7.
Frobenius, H. (1893), *Die Heiden-Neger des ägyptischen Sudan*, Berlin.
Gessi, R. (1892), *Seven Years in the Sudan: Being a Record of Explorations, Adventures and Campaigns against the Arab Slave Hunters*, London, repr. Farnborough 1968.
Giamberardini, G. (1963), 'I viaggiatori francescani attraverso la Nubia dal 1698 al 1710', *Collectanea no. 8, Studia Orientalia Christiana*, 361–438.
Giegler, C. Ch. (1984), *The Sudan Memoirs of Carl Christian Giegler Pasha 1873–1883*, ed. R. Hill, London.
Gleichen, A. W. E. (1905), *The Anglo-Egyptian Sudan: a Compendium Prepared by Officers of the Sudan Government*, London, 2 vols.
Grant, J. A. (1885), *Khartoom, as I saw it in 1863*, London.
Hall, H. E. (ed.) (1907), *Murray's Handbook for Egypt and the Sudan*, London, 11th edn.
Hamilton, J. (1857), *Sinai, the Hedjaz and Soudan, Wanderings Around the Birth-Place of the Prophet and Across the Aethiopian Desert, from Sawakin to Khartoum*, London.
Hamont, P. N. (1843), *L'Egypte sous Méhémet-Ali*, Paris, 2 vols.
Hartmann, R. (1863), *Reise des Freiherrn Adalbert von Barnim durch Nord-Ost-Afrika in den Jahren 1859 und 1860. Beschrieben von seinem Belgeiter Dr. Robert Hartmann*, Berlin.
(1872), 'Einiges über Ursachen und Wirkungen der im älteren und neueren Afrika stattgehabten und noch gegenwärtig stattfindenden Völkerbewegungen', *Zeitschrift des Gesellschaft für Erdkunde zu Berlin*, vii, 497–537.
(1884), *Die Nilländer*, Prague.
Head, Major Sir F. B. (1842), *The Life and Adventures of Bruce, the African Traveller*, New York.
Henniker, F. (1823), *Notes During a Visit to Egypt, Nubia, the Oasis, Mount Sinai and Jerusalem*, London.
Heuglin, Th. von (1869), *Reise in das Gebiet des Weissen Nil*, Leipzig.
(1941), 'Travels in the Sudan in the Sixties. Translations from Petermanns Mitteilungen. Letters from Th. v. Heuglin to Dr Petermann, July, 1862 to January 1863', *SNR*, xxiv/1, 145–66.
Hill, R. (1948), 'An unpublished itinerary to Kordofan', *SNR*, xix/1, 58–70.
(1956–7), 'An unpublished chronicle of the Sudan 1822–41', *SNR*, xxxvii (1956), 2–19, and xxxviii (1957), 130–46.
(1970), *On the Frontiers of Islam: Two Manuscripts Concerning the Sudan under Turco-Egyptian Rule, 1822–1845*, Oxford.
Hillelson, S. (1923), 'Tabaqāt wad Dayf Allāh: studies in the lives of scholars and saints', *SNR*, vi/2, 191–230.
(1933), 'David Reubini, an early visitor to Sennar', *SNR*, dvi/1, 54–66.
Holroyd, A. T. (1838–9), 'Iron money in Kordofān', *Numismatic Chronicle*, i, 210–13.
(1839), 'Notes on a journey to Kordofan in 1836–37', *JRGS*, ix, 163–91.
Hoskins, G. A. (1835), *Travels in Ethiopia above the Second Cataract of the Nile*, London.
L'Isthme de Suez, no. 10, Wednesday 25 March 1857, 'Ordres de son altesse le Vice-roi', 91–5.

Italian Missionaries (1960), 'Three impressions of Khartoum during the Turkiyya', *SNR*, xli, 101–6.

Jomard, E. F. (1839), *Études geógraphiques et historiques sur l'Arabie, suivies de la relation du voyage de Mohammed-Aly dans le Fazogl*, Paris.

Junker, W. J. (1889–92), *Reisen in Afrika, 1875–1886*, Vienna, 3 vols.

(1890–2), *Travels in Africa during the Years 1875–1886*, London, 3 vols.

Kremer, A. von (1863), *Aegypten. Forschungen über Land und Volk während eines zehnjährigen Aufenthalts*, Berlin, 2 vols.

Krump, T. (1710), *Hoher und fruchtbarer Palm-Baum des Heiligen Evangelj*, Augsburg, unpubl. English transl. by J. L. Spaulding.

Laponouse, J. (1802), *Mémoire sur les Caravannes du Darfour et du Sennaar*, Paris.

(1802), 'Mémoire sur les caravannes qui arrivent du royaume de Darfour en Egypte, avec des détails sur les lieux où elles passent et sur les commerce qui se fait des esclaves et des autres marchandises précieuses qui viennent de ce pays', *Mémoires sur l'Egypte*, xi/4, 77–89.

Lauture, E. de (1850), 'Extrait d'un mémoire sur le commerce du Soudan oriental', *BSG*, 3e série, xii, 391–410.

(1851), 'Notice sur le Kordofan', *BSG*, 4e série, i, 357–73.

(1853), *Le Désert et le Soudan*, Paris.

(1855–6), 'Mémoire sur le Soudan', *BSG*, 4e série, x (1855), 89–184 and 209; xi (1856), 24–69.

(1856), *Mémoire sur le Soudan*, Paris.

Legh, T. (1817), *Narrative of a Journey in Egypt and the Country beyond the Cataracts*, London, 2nd edn.

Lejean, G. (1862), 'Rapport adresse' à son Excellence M. le Ministre des Affaires Etrangères, par M. G. Lejean, Chargé d'une mission dans le région du haut Nile', *BSG*, 5e série, iii, 205–21.

(1865a), *Voyage aux Deux Nils (Nubie, Kordofan, Soudan Oriental) executé de 1860 à 1864*, Paris.

(1865b), *Théodore II. Le Nouvel Empire d'Abyssine et les interets français dans le sud de la Mer Rouge*, Paris.

Le Mascrier, J. B. (1740), *Déscription de l'Égypte contenant plusieurs remarques curieuses sur la géographie ancienne et moderne de ce Païs. Composée sur les Mémoires de Monsieur De Maillet, ancien Consul de France au Caire*, Paris, 2 vols.

Lepsius, R. (1852), *Briefe aus Aegypten, Aethiopien und er Halbinsel des Sinai geschrieben in den Jahren 1842–1845*, Berlin, repr. 1958.

Lesseps, R. de (1884), 'Souvenirs d'un voyage au Soudan', *La Nouvelle Revue*, 491–516.

Light, H. K. C. B. (1818), *Travels in Egypt, Nubia, Holy Land, Mount Libanon and Cyprus, in the Year 1814*, London.

Lobo, J. (1789), *A Voyage to Abyssinia*, London, repr. New York, 1978.

Makhṭūṭa (1961), *Makhṭūṭa kātib al-shūna, fi-ta'rīkh al-sulṭāna al-sinnāriyya wa'l-idāra al-miṣriyya*, ed. al-Shāṭir Buṣaylī ʿAbd al-Jalīl, Cairo.

Marno, E. (1874), *Reisen im Gebiete des blauen und weissen Nil, im egyptischen Sudan und an den angrenzednen Negerländern, in den Jahren 1869 bis 1873*, Vienna.

(1878), *Riese in der Egyptischen Aequatorial-Provinz und in Kordofan in den Jahren 1874–1876*, Vienna.

Melly, G. (1851), *Khartoum and the Blue and White Nile*, London, 2 vols.

Mengin, F. (1823), *Histoire de l'Egypte sous le gouvernement de Mohammed-Aly*, Paris, 2 vols.

Merruau, P. (1858), *L'Egypte contemporaine de Méhémet-Ali à Said Pacha*, Paris, 2nd edn.

Mohammad b. ʿAlī b. Zayn al-ʿAbidīn (1981), *Le Livre du Soudan*, Paris, transl. M. Grisard and J. C. Bacqué-Grammont.

Müller, J. v. (1851), *Fliegende Blätter aus meinem Tagebuche, geführt auf einer Reise in Nord-Ost-Afrika in den Jahren 1847, 1848, und 1849*, Stuttgart.

Munzinger, W. (1864), *Ostafrikanische Studien*, Schaffhausen.
Murray, A. D. D. (1808), *Account of the Life and Writings of James Bruce*, Edinburgh.
Nachtigal, G. (1876–7), 'Handel im Sudan', *Mitteilungen der Geographischen Gesellschaft*, 205–26.
(1879–89), *Sahara und Sudan*, Berlin and Leipzig, 3 vols., repr. Graz, 1967.
Neufeld, C. (1899), *A Prisoner of the Khaleefa. Twelve Years' Captivity at Omdurman*, London.
Ohrwalder, J. (1892), *Aufstand und Reich des Mahdi im Sudan und meine zehnjährige Gefangenschaft dortselbst*, Innsbruck.
Pallme, I. (1844), *Travels in Kordofan*, London.
Parkyns, M. (1854), 'The Kababish Arabs between Dongola and Kordofan', *JRGS*, xx, 254–75.
(1868), *Life in Abyssinia. Being Notes Collected during Three Years' Residence and Travels in that Country*, London, 2nd edn., repr. London, 1966.
Peney, A. (1882–4), 'Mémoires sur l'ethnographie du Soudan égyptien', *Revue d'Ethnographie*, i (1882), 397–409; ii (1883), 487–99, and iii (1884), 45–50.
Petherick, J. (1861), *Egypt, the Soudan and Central Africa, with Explorations from Khartoum on the White Nile to the Regions of the Equator, Being Sketches from Sixteen Years' Travel*, Edinburgh.
Mr and Mrs (1869), *Travel in Central Africa, and Explorations of the Western Nile Tributaries*, London, 2 vols., repr. Farnborough, 1969.
Petti Suma, M. T. (1964), 'Il viaggio in Sudan di Evliyā Celebī (1671–1672)', *Annali dell'Instituto Universitario Orientale di Napoli*, nuova serie, xiv/2, 433–52.
Pfund, J. (1876–7), 'Reisebriefe aus Kordofan und Darfur', *Mitteilungen der Geographischen Gesellschaft*, i, 121–305.
Poncet, J. (1863), 'Notice géographique et ethnologique sur la région du Fleuve Blanc et sur ses habitants', *NAV*, iv, 5–62.
Poncet, M. D. (1709), *A Voyage to Æthiopia, Made in the years 1698, 1699, 1700*, London.
Prout, G. H. (1877), *General Report on the Province of Kordofan submitted to General C. P. Stone, Chief of the Egyptian General Staff*, Publications of the Egyptian General Staff, Cairo, 232 pp., 6 maps.
Prudhoe, Lord (1835), 'Private Memoranda Kept by Lord Prudhoe on a Journey From Cairo to Sennar, in 1829', *JRGS* (*Geographical Journal*), 38–58.
Pückler-Muskau, H. L. H. von (1844), *Aus Mehmet Ali's Reich*, Stuttgart, 3 vols.
(1845), *Egypt under Mehmet Ali*, London, 2 vols.
Rüppell, E. (1829), *Reisen in Nubien, Kordofan und dem Peträischen Arabien. Vorzüglich in geographisch-statisticher Hinsicht*, Frankfurt am Main.
(1836), 'Voyages en Nubie, en Kordofan, et dans l'Arabie-Pétrée', *NAV*, 137–211 and 265–315.
Russegger, J. R. von (1839), 'Lettres de J. R. von Russegger sur la Nubie, le Sennaar, le Kordofan, le Fazokhl', *NAV*, 3rd series, 283–321.
(1841–8), *Reisen in Europa, Asien und Afrika*, Stuttgart, 4 vols.
Sāmī Amīn (1916–35), *Taqwīm al-Nil*, Cairo, 6 vols.
Sammarco, A. (1929), *Il viaggio di Muhammed Ali al Sudan (15 Ottobre 1838–15 Marzo 1839)*, Cairo.
Santi, P. (1965), *Mémoire d'un voyage en Haute-Nubie en 1851. D'après un manuscrit anonyme annoté et transcrit par Paul Santi*, Beyrouth.
Santi, P. and Hill, R., eds. (1980), *The Europeans in the Sudan, 1834–1878*, Oxford.
Schweinfurth, G. (1869), 'Skizze eines neuen Weges von Suakin nach Berber, zurückgelegt im September 1868 von Dr. G. Schweinfurth', *PM*, xv, 281–91.
The Heart of Africa. Three Years' Travels and Adventures in the Unexplored Regions of Central Africa from 1868 to 1871, London, 2 vols.

(1884), 'The future of the Soudan', *The Pall Mall Gazette*, xxxix, no. 5962, Thursday, April 17.
(1918), *Im Herzen von Afrika. Reisen und Entdeckungen im Centralen Aequatorial Afrika während der Jahre 1868 bis 1871*, Leipzig, 3rd edn.
Selim Bimbachi (1842), 'Premier voyage à la recherche des sources du Nil-Blanc, ordonné par Mohammed-Aly, vice-roi d'Egypte. Journal du voyage fait par Selim Bimbachi, capitaine de frégate, chargé de l'expedition envoyée par S.A. la vice-roi d'Egypte, pour découvrir la source de fleuve Blanc', *BSG*, xvii, 5–30, 81–106 and 161–85.
Shaw, F. (1887), 'The story of Zubehr Pasha, as told by himself', *The Contemporary Review*, lii, 333–49, 564–85 and 658–83.
Shendy, Map of (1885), 'Intended Route of Lord Wolseley from Korty to Shendy', *Illustrated News*, 86, 13.
Shuqayr, N. (1903), *Ta'rīkh al-Sūdān al-qadīm wa'l-ḥadīth wa-jughrāfīyatuhu*, Cairo, 3 vols. in one.
Slatin, R. K. von (1896), *Fire and Sword in the Sudan: a Personal Narrative of Fighting and Serving the Dervishes, 1879–1895*, London, 4th edn.
Sonini, C. G. (1799), *Voyage dans la Haute et Basse Egypte, fait par ordre de l'ancien gouvernement*, Paris, 3 vols.
Southworth, A. S. (1875), *Four Thousand Miles of African Travel: Being a Personal Record of a Journey up the Nile and through the Sudan to the confines of Central Africa*, London.
Speedy, Mrs (1884), *My Wanderings in the Sudan*, London, 2 vols.
Statistique (1879), *Essais de statistique générale de l'Egypte, années 1873, 1874, 1875, 1876, 1877*, Ministère de l'Interieur, Bureau de la Statistique, Cairo.
Stewart, L.-C. (J. D. H.) (1883), *Report on the Sudan.* In *Egypt*, no. 11, presented to both Houses of Parliament in 1883. Published as Command Paper 3670, London 1885. Copy in SAD, Box 292/18.
Ta'rīkh (1948), *Ta'rīkh mulūk al-sūdān*, ed. Shibayka, Khartoum.
Taylor, B. (1862), *A Journey to Central Africa; or Life and Landscapes from Egypt to the Negro Kingdoms of the White Nile*, New York, 11th edn.
Thilo, M. (1921), *Ez-Zibēr Rahmet Paschas Autobiographie. Ein Beitrag zur Geschichte des Sudan*, Leipzig.
Toniolo, E. and Hill, R. (eds.) (1974), *The Opening of the Nile Basin. Writings by members of the Catholic Mission to Central Africa on the geography and ethnography of the Sudan 1842–1881*, London.
Trémaux, P. (1856), 'Episode d'un voyage au Soudan Oriental et remarques sur l'esclavage', *BSG*, 4th series, xi, 153–64.
(1862), *Voyage en Ethiopia au Soudan Oriental et dans la Nigritie*, Paris, 2 vols.
Waddington, G. and Hanbury, B. (1822), *Journal of a Visit to Some Parts of Ethiopia*, London.
Werne, F. (1848), *Expedition zur Entdeckung der Quellen des Weissen Nil*, Berlin.
(1849), *Expedition to Discover the Sources of the White Nile, in the Years 1840, 1841*, London, 2 vols.
(1851), *Feldzug von Sennaar nach Taka, Basa und Beni-amer, mit besonderen Hinblick auf die Völker von Bellad Sudan*, Stuttgart.
(1852), *African Wanderings or an Expedition from Sennaar to Taka, Basa and Beni-amer with a Particular Glance at the Races of Belled Sudan*, London.
Whitehead, G. O. (1934), 'Italian Travellers in the Berta Country', *SNR*, xvii/1, 217–27.
(1938), 'André Melly's visit to Khartoum 1850', *SNR*, xxi/2, 291–305.
Williams, J. (1884), *Life in the Sudan*, London.
Wilson, R. W. and Felkin, C. T. (1882), *Uganda and the Egyptian Sudan: an account of travel and a description of the slave districts of Bahr-el-Ghazal and Darfour*, London, 2 vols.
Wingate, F. R. (1893), *Ten Years' Captivity in the Mahdi's Camp 1882–1892*, London.

SECONDARY SOURCES

Abbas Ahmed Mohamed (1980), *White Nile Arabs. Political Leadership and Economic Change*, New Jersey.

Abbas Ibrahim Muhammad Ali (1972), *The British, the Slave Trade and Slavery in the Sudan 1820–1881*, Khartoum.

(1974), 'A history of European geographical exploration of the Sudan 1820–1865', *SNR*, lv, 1–15.

Abdulla el Tayib (1955–64), 'The changing customs of the riverain Sudan', part 1, *SNR*, vol. xxxvi, 1955, 146–57; part 2, vol. xxxvii, 1956, 56–69; part 3, vol. xlv 1964, 12–28.

Abū Salīm, M. I. (1967), *al-Funj wa'l-arḍ. Some Land Certificates from the Fung*, Occasional papers, no. 2, Sudan Research Unit Khartoum.

(1970), *al-arḍ fi'l-Mahdiyya*, Khartoum.

(1975), *al-Fūr wa'l-arḍ: wathā'iq tamlīk*, Khartoum.

(1980), *al-sāqiya*, Khartoum.

Adams, W. Y. (1977), *Nubia, Corridor to Africa*, London.

Ahmed Abdel Rahman Mustafa (1968), 'The breakdown of the monopoly system in Egypt after 1840', in P. M. Holt (ed.), *Political and Social Change in Modern Egypt*, London, 294–8.

Arkell, A. J. (1937), 'Hebron beads in Darfur', *SNR*, xx, 300–5.

(1945), 'Beads made in Darfur and Wadai', *SNR*, xxvi/2, 305–11.

Asad, T. (1970), *The Kababish Arabs: Power Authority and Consent in a Nomadic Tribe*, London.

ʿAwaḍ ʿAbd al-Hādī al-ʿAṭā (1972), *Ta'rīkh Kurdufān al-siyāsī fi'l-Mahdiyya, 1881–1899*, Khartoum.

Awad, M. H. (1971), 'The evolution of landownership in the Sudan', *MEJ*, xxv/2, 212–28.

Barbour, K. M. (1961), *The Republic of the Sudan: A Regional Geography*, London.

Beatty, Ch. (1956), *Ferdinand de Lesseps, a Biographical Study*, London.

Beckman, P. (1982a), 'Investing in farmers', *Sudanow*, vii/9, 16–17.

(1982b), 'Still viable?', *Sudanow*, vii/10, 41–2.

Belin, M. (1864), 'Essais sur l'histoirc économiques de la Turquie', *Journal Asiatique*, 6th series, iii, 416–89.

Bjørkelo, A. (1982), 'Partnerskap i jordbruk og handel i Sudan', *Historisk Tidsskrift*, 3, 228–46.

(1984), 'Turco-*jallāba* relations, 1821–1885', in L. O. Manger, ed., *Trade and Traders in the Sudan*, Bergen Occasional Papers in Social Anthropology, no. 32, 81–107.

(1987), 'Bønder, kontantavlingar og skattar i Nord-Sudan under den første koloniperioden (Turkiyya-perioden), 1821–1885', in *Bønder og stat i den tredje verden*, Centre for Development Studies, Seminar Proceedings, no. 1, Bergen, 11–28.

and Wickens, G. E. (1981), *A bibliography of the Dār Fūr/Wadai Region*, Occasional Paper, no. 5, Department of History, University of Bergen.

Bond, W. R. G. (1925), 'Some curious methods of cultivation in Dongola Province', *SNR*, viii, 97–103.

Born, M. (1965), *Zentralkordofan. Bauern und Nomaden in Savannen-gebieten des Sudan*, Marburger Geographische Schriften, Heft 25, Marburg.

(1968), 'El Obeid, Bemerkungen zur Stadtentwicklung im östlichen Sudan', *Geographische Rundschau*, xx, 87–97.

Boserup, E. (1965), *The Conditions of Agricultural Growth. The Economics of Agrarian Change under Population Pressure*, London.

Census (1962), *First Population Census of the Sudan 1955–1956, Final Report*, Department of Statistics, Khartoum.

Chayanov, A. V. (1966), *The Theory of Peasant Economy*, ed. D. Thorner *et al.*, Homewood, Illinois.

Cohen, A. (1969), *Custom and Politics in Urban Africa. A Study of Hausa Migrants in Yoruba Towns*, London.
(1971), 'Cultural strategies in the organization of trading diasporas', in C. Meillassoux, *The Development of Indigenous Trade and Markets in West Africa*, London, 266–81.
Cordell, D. D. (1979), 'Blood partnership in theory and practice', *JH*, xx/3, 379–94.
Corkill, N. L. (1948), 'Weight equivalent of Sudan Foods sold by measures of capacity', *SNR*, xxix, 126–7.
Crabites, P. (1969), *Gordon, the Sudan and Slavery*, New York, 2nd edn.
Crawford, O. G. S. (1951), *The Fung Kingdom of Sennar, With a Geographical Account of the Middle Nile Region*, Gloucester.
Crowfoot, G. M. (1921), 'Spinning and weaving in the Sudan', *SNR*, iv/1, 20–39.
Crowfoot, J. w. (1911), *The Island of Meroë*, vol. xix, in F. L. L. Griffith (ed.), *Memories of the Archaeological Survey of the Egypt Exploration Fund*, London.
(1918), 'Customs of the Rubātāb', *SNR*, i/2, 119–34.
(1919), 'Angels of the Nile', *SNR*, ii/3, 183–94.
(1922), 'Wedding customs in the Northern Sudan', *SNR*, v, 1–28.
Cumming, D. C. (1937–40), 'The history of Kassala and the Province of Taka', *SNR*, xx/1 (1937), 1–46 and xxiii/2 (1940), 1–54.
Cunnison, I. (1966), *Baggara Arabs: Power and Lineage in a Sudanese Nomadic Tribe*, London.
Darling, H. S. (1951), 'Insects and grain storage in the Sudan', *SNR*, xxxii/1, 131–49.
Davies, R. (1957), *The Camel's Back: Service in the Rural Sudan*, London.
Dehérain, H. (1898), 'Le Soudan Egyptien de Mohamed Aly à Ismaïl Pacha', in G. Hanotaux (ed.), *Histoire de la Nation Égyptienne*, Paris, vi, *L'Egypte de 1801 à 1882.*
Douin, G. (1933–41), *Histoire de Règne du Khedive Ismaïl*, Cairo, 3 vols., iii/1, 2, 3A, 3B, *L'Empire Africain.*
(1944), *Histoire de Soudan Egyptien*, Cairo, i, *La pénétration 1820–1822.*
Dugmore, A. R. (1924), *The Vast Sudan*, London.
(1938), *Through the Sudan*, London
Edwards, F. A. (1922), 'The Foundation of Khartoum', *SNR*, v/3–4, 157–62.
Elles, R. J. (1935), 'The Kingdom of Tegali', *SNR*, xviii, 1–35.
El Haj Bilal Omer (1985), *The Danagla Traders of the Northern Sudan. Rural Capitalism and Agricultural Development.* London.
El-Sayed El Bushra (1971), 'Towns in the Sudan in the eighteenth and early nineteenth centuries', *SNR*, lii, 63–70.
Al-Faḥl al-Fakī al-Ṭāhir (1976), *Ta'rīkh wa-uṣūl al-'arab bi'l-sūdān*, Khartoum.
Fleming, G. J. (1922), 'Kassala', *SNR*, v/2, 65–77.
Geiser, P. (1967), 'Some differential factors affecting population movements: the Nubian case', *Human Organization*, xxvi/3, 164–77.
Gerber, H. (1982), 'The monetary system of the Ottoman Empire', *JESHO*, xxv/3, 308–24.
Goitein, M. (1967–83), *A Mediterranean Society. The Jewish Communities of the Arab World as Portrayed in the Documents of the Cairo Geniza*, Berkeley, 4 vols.
Gray, R. (1961), *A History of the Southern Sudan, 1839–1889*, London.
Grönhaug, R. (1976),, 'Chayanov's regel', *Lov og struktur*, 1–17.
Al-Ḥājj Ḥāmid Muḥammad Khayr and Spaulding, J. L. (1980), 'The deposition of a Makk of Berber', *Sudan Text Bulletin*, no. 2, 47–58.
Hallam, W. K. R. (1977), *The Life and Times of Rabih Fadl Allah*, Devon.
Hamilton, A. A. de C. (ed.) (1935), *The Anglo-Egyptian Sudan from within*, London.
Hasan A/Aziz Ahmed (1974), 'Aspect of Sudan's foreign trade during the 19th century', *SNR*, lv, 16–32.
(1975), 'The Zeidab Estate, 1903–1924', *Adab*, 2–3, 83–97.

(1977), 'Some economic factors hampering the development of Sudanese trade during the 19th century', *Sudan Journal of Economic and Social Studies*, ii/1, 31–9.

(1980), 'The Turkish taxation system and its impact on agriculture in the Sudan', *MES*, xxvi/1, 105–14.

Hassan Dafalla (1969), 'Land Economy of old Halfa', *SNR*, l, 63–74.

Hassanuzzaman, S. M. (1971), 'The liability of partners in an Islamic s̲h̲irkah', *Islamic Studies*, x, 319–41.

Hayyim Nahum Effendi (1935), *Recueil des firmans imperiaux Ottomans*, Cairo.

Hewins, H. P. (1921), 'Weights and measures', *SNR*, iv/4, 225–6.

Hill, R. (1939), *A Bibliography of the Anglo-Egyptian Sudan from the earliest times to 1937*, London.

(1951), 'Rulers of the Sudan 1820–1885', *SNR*, xxxii/1, 85–95.

(1958), 'Death of a Governor-General', *SNR*, xxxiv, 83–87.

(1959a), *Egypt in the Sudan, 1820–1881*, London.

(1959b), 'The period of Egyptian occupation', *SNR*, xl, 101–16.

(1965), *Slatin Pasha*, London.

(1967), *A Biographical Dictionary of the Sudan*, London, 2nd edn.

Hillelson, S. (1925), *Sudan Arabic English-Arabic Vocabulary*, London.

(1935), *Sudan Arabic texts*, Cambridge.

Holt, P. M., 'Dja'aliyyūn', in *EI* 2nd edn, ii, 351–2.

(1968), 'Modernization and reaction in the nineteenth-century Sudan', in Polk and Chambers (eds.), *Beginnings of Modernization in the Middle East. The Nineteenth Century*, London, 401–15.

(1969), 'Four Funj land-charters', *SNR*, l, 2–14.

(1977), *The Mahdist State in the Sudan 1881–1898. A Study of its Origins, Development and Overthrow*, Nairobi, repr. of 2nd edn, 1972, London.

(1981), 'The Geneology of a Sudanese Holy Family', *BSOAS*, xliv/2, 262–72.

and Daly, M. (1979), *The History of the Sudan. From the Coming of Islam to the Present Day*, 3rd edn, London.

Hopkins, A. G. (1975), *An Economic History of West Africa*, London.

Hurst, H. E. (1952), *The Nile, a General Account of the River and the Utilization of Its Waters*, London.

Ḥusayn Sīd Aḥmad al-Muftī (1959), *Taṭawwur niẓām al-qaḍā' fi'l-Sūdān*, Khartoum.

Inalcik, H. (1969), 'Capital formation in the Ottoman Empire,' *Journal of Economic History*, xxix, 1, March 1969, 97–140.

Innes, N. M. (1931), 'The Monasir country, 1930', *SNR*, xiv/2, 185–91.

Ismā'il 'Abd al-Qādir al-Kurdufānī (1972), *Sa'ādat al-Mustahdī bi-sīrat al-Imām al-Mahdī*, Khartoum.

Jackson, H. C. (1912), *Tooth of Fire: Being Some Account of the Ancient Kingdom of Sennār*, Oxford.

(1913), *Black Ivory, or the Story of el-Zubeir Pasha, Slaver and Sultan*, Khartoum, repr. New York, 1970.

(1919a), 'Seed-time and harvest', *SNR*, ii/1, 1–16.

(1919b), 'Two Gezira families', *SNR*, ii/2, 94–106.

(1919c), 'The Mahas of 'Eilafūn', *SNR*, ii/4, 276–90.

(1919d), 'Desiccation?', *SNR*, ii/4, 341–2.

(1926), 'A trek in Abu Hamed District', *SNR*, ix/2, 1–35.

(1954), *Sudan Days and Ways*, London.

Job, H. S. (1920), 'The coinage of the Mahdi and the Khalifa', *SNR*, iii/3, 163–96 and 5 plates.

Kenrick, J. W. (1948), 'The kingdom of Tegali, 1921–1946', *SNR*, xxi/2, 143–50.

Klein, M. A. (ed.) (1980), *Peasants in Africa: Historical and Contemporary Perspectives*, London.

Leach, T. A. (1919), 'Date-trees in Halfa Province', *SNR*, ii, 98–104.
(1926), 'The Selima oasis', *SNR*, ix/2, 37–49.
Leake, H. (1933), 'Studies in tropical land tenure', *Tropical Agriculture*, x/5, 126–31.
Lebon, J. H. G. (1965), *Land Use in the Sudan*, Monograph no. 4 in *World Land Use Survey*, Cornwall.
Lorimer, F. C. S. (1936a), 'The Rubatab', *SNR*, xix/1, 162–7.
(1936b), 'The Megadhib of el Damer', *SNR*, xix/2, 335–43.
Lyall, C. E. (1921), 'Rights, dues and customs prevailing among Arab tribes in the White Nile Province', *SNR*, iv/4, 199–203.
MacMichael, H. A. (1912), *The Tribes of Northern and Central Kordofan*, Cambridge, repr. London, 1967.
(1920), 'The Kheiran', *SNR*, iii/4, 231–44.
(1922a), *A History of the Arabs in the Sudan: and some account of the people who preceded them and the tribes inhabiting Darfur*, Cambridge, 2 vols., repr. 1967.
(1922b), 'Pottery making of the Blue Nile', *SNR*, v/1, 33–8.
(1927), 'Notes on the Gebel Haraza', *SNR*, x/1, 61–7.
Majer, H. G. (1982), 'Ein osmanisches Budget aus der Zeit Mehmeds des Eroberers', *Der Islam*, 59/1, 40–63.
Manger, L. O. (1981), *The Sand Swallows our Land*, Bergen Occasional Papers in Social Anthropology, no. 24.
(1984), *Trade and Traders in the Sudan*, Bergen Occasional Papers in Social Anthropology, no. 32.
Marsot, A. L. al-S. (1984), *Egypt in the Reign of Muhammad Ali*, Cambridge.
Martin, P. F. (1921), *The Sudan in Evolution. A Study of the Economic, Financial and Administrative Conditions of the Anglo-Egyptian Sudan*, London.
Matthew, J. G. (1921), 'Land customs and tenure in Singa District', *SNR*, iv/1, 1–19.
McLoughlin, P. F. M. (1962), 'Economic development and the heritage of slavery in the Sudan Republic', *Africa*, xxxii, 355, 89.
Ménassa, L. and Laferrière, P. (1974), *La Sāgia. Technique et vocabulaire de la roue à eau égyptienne*, Cairo.
Miskin, A. B. (1949), 'Land registration', *SNR*, xxx/2, 274–86.
Muhammad Ahmad Abdel Ghaffar and Mustafa Abdel Rahman (1979), *Urbanization and Exploitation: The Role of Small Centres*, SRC Monograph Series, no. 11, Development Studies and Research Centre, University of Khartoum, Khartoum.
Mutwakil A. Amin (1970), 'Ancient trade routes between Egypt and Sudan', *SNR*, li, 23–30.
Nadel, S. F. (1945), 'Notes on Beni Amer Society', *SNR*, xxvi, 51–93.
Nelson, H. D. (1973), *Area Handbook for the Democratic Republic of Sudan*, Washington.
Newbold, D. (1924), 'The history of Gallabat', *SNR*, vii, 103–7.
Nicholls, W. (1913), *The Shaikiya. An Account of the Shaikiya Tribes and of the History of Dongola Province from the XIVth to the XIXth Century*, Dublin.
(1918), 'The Sakia in Dongola Province', *SNR*, i, 21–4.
Nicholson, H. A. (1935), 'Saqia terminology in Dongola', *SNR*, xviii/2, 314–22.
O'Fahey, R. S. (1973a), 'Kordofan in the eighteenth century', *SNR*, liv, 32–42.
(1973b), 'Slavery and the slave trade in Dār Fūr', *JAH*, xiv/1, 29–43.
(1977), 'The office of *qāḍī* in Dār Fūr: a preliminary enquiry', *BSOAS*, xl/1, 110–24.
(1980), *State and Society in Dār Fūr*, London.
'Kordofan', in *EI*, 2nd edn, 266–8.
and Spaulding, J. L. (1972), 'Hāshim and the Musabbaʿat', *BSOAS*, xxxv/2, 316–33.
and Spaulding, J. L. (1974), *Kingdoms of the Sudan*, Studies in African History, 9, London.
and Abū Salīm, M. I. (1983), *Land in Dār Fūr*, Fontes Historiae Africanae: Series Arabica, iii, Cambridge.
Paul, A. (1936), 'Sagia custom in Shendi District', *SNR*, xix/2, 346–50.

(1954), 'Some aspects of the Fung Sultanate', *SNR*, xxxv/1, 17–31.
Penn, A. E. D. (1934), 'Traditional stories of the 'Abullab Tribe', *SNR*, xvii/1, 59–82.
Pensa, H. (1895), *L'Egypte et le Soudan Egyptien*, Paris.
Postan, M. M. (1973), *Medieval Trade and Finance*, London.
Purves, W. D. C. L. (1935), 'Some aspects of the Northern Province', in J. A. de C. Hamilton (ed.), *The Anglo-Egyptian Sudan from Within*, London, 165–80.
Randell, J. R. (1974), 'Landsbybebyggelse i Nordöst Sudan', *Kulturgeografi*, ix/121.
Raymond, A. (1973–4), *Artisans et commerçants au Caire au XVIIIe siècle*, Damascus, 2 vols.
Rehfisch, F. (1962), 'A study of some Southern migrants in Omdurman', *SNR*, xliii, 50–104.
(1964), 'A sketch of the early history of Omdurman', *SNR* xlv, 35–47.
(1965), 'An unrecorded population count of Omdurman', *SNR*, xlvi, 33–9.
(1967), 'Omdurman during the Mahdiyya', *SNR*, xlviii, 33–61.
Richards, A. (1981), 'Growth and technical change: "internal" and "external" sources of Egyptian underdevelopment, 1800–1914', *AAS*, xv, 45–67.
Rivlin, H. A. B. (1961), *The Agricultural Policy of Muḥammad 'Alī*, Cambridge, Mass.
Robinson, A. E. (1922), 'The Mamelukes in the Sudan', *SNR*, iii/2, 88–94.
(1925), 'Nimr, the last king of Shendi', *SNR*, viii, 105–18.
(1924–6), 'The conquest of the Sudan by the wali of Egypt, Muhammad Ali Pasha, 1820–1824', *JAS*, October 1925, 47–58, and January 1926, 164–82.
(1929), 'Abu el Kaylik, the kingmaker of the Fung of Sennar', *American Anthropologist*, n.s., xxxi, 231–64.
Sadik Nur (1956), 'Land tenure in the time of the Fung', *Kush*, iv, 48–53.
Saeed Mohammed Ahmed El Mahdi (1976), 'Some general principles of acquisition of ownership of and rights over land by customary prescription in the Sudan', *JAL*, xx/2, 79–99.
(1971), *A Guide to Land Settlement and Registration*, Khartoum.
Sagar, J. W. (1922), 'Notes on the history, religion and customs of the Nuba', *SNR*, v/3–4, 137–56.
Sandars, G. E. R. (1933), 'The Bisharin', *SNR*, xvi/2, 119–49.
Sanderson, G. N. (1963), 'The modern Sudan 1820–1956: the present position of historical studies', *JAH*, iv/3, 435–61.
Sarkassian, G. (1913), *Le Soudan egyptien, Etude de Droit Internationale Publique*, Paris.
Schacht, J. (1975), *An Introduction to Islamic Law*, London.
Al-Shahi, A. and Moore, E. F. T. (1978), *Wisdom from the Nile. A Collection of Folk-Stories from the Northern and Central Sudan*, London.
Shanin, T. (ed.) (1971), *Peasants and Peasant Societies*, London.
Al-Shāṭir Buṣaylī 'Abd al-Jalīl (1966), *Ma'ālim ta'rīkh Sūdān wādī al-Nīl*, Cairo.
Shaw, W. B. K. (1929), 'Darb el arba'in', *SNR*, xii, 63–71.
Shukry, M. F. (1938), *The Khedive Ismail and Slavery in the Sudan*, Cairo.
Simpson, S. R. (1955), 'Land law and registration in the Sudan', *Journal of African Administration*, vii/1, 11–17.
Spaulding, J. L. (1973), 'The government of Sinnar', *IJAHS*, vi/1, 19–35.
(1977), 'The evolution of the Islamic judiciary in Sinnār', *IJAHS*, x/3, 408–26.
(1979), 'Farmers, herdsmen and the state in rainland Sinnār', *JAH*, xx/3, 329–47.
(1982a), 'Slavery, land tenure and social class in the Northern Turkish Sudan', *IJAHS*, xv/1, 1–20.
(1982b), 'The misfortunes of some – the advantage of others: land sales by women in Sinnar', in M. J. Hay and M. Wright (eds.) (1982), *African Women and the Law. Historical Perspectives*, Boston University Papers on Africa, vii.
(1984), 'The management of exchange in Sinnār, c. 1700', in L. O. Manger (ed.) (1984), 25–48.

(1985), *The Heroic Age in Sinnār*, Ethiopian Series Monograph, no. 15, African Studies Centre, Madison State University, East Lansing.
Stevenson, R. C. (1966), 'Old Khartoum, 1821–1885', *SNR*, xlvii, 1–38.
Sudan (1892–8), *Sudan Intelligence Reports*, 1–60, 3 vols., repr. NRO, Khartoum, n.d.
Theobald, A. B. (1949), 'The Khalifa ʿAbdullahi', *SNR*, xxx/2, 254–73.
Thompson, C. F. (1965), *The Land of the Sudan: Cases and Materials*, Khartoum, 3 vols.
Thornton, D. S. (1964), 'The organisation of production in irrigated areas of the Sudan', *Journal of Agricultural Economics*, xvi, 286–95.
Tothill, J. D. (ed.) (1948), *Agriculture in the Sudan: Being a Handbook of Agriculture as Practised in the Anglo-Egyptian Sudan*, London.
Trimingham, J. S. (1949), *Islam in the Sudan*, London.
Triulzi, A. (1975), 'Trade, Islam, and the Mahdia in Northwestern Wallagā, Ethiopia', *JAH*, xvi/1, 55–71.
Udovitch, A. L. (1970), *Partnership and Profit in Medieval Islam*, New Jersey.
Walkley, C. E. J. (1935–6), 'The story of Khartoum', *SNR*, xviii/2 (1935), 221–41, and xix/1 (1936), 71–92.
Walz, T. (1979), 'Trading into the Sudan in the sixteenth century', *Annales Islamologiques*, xv, 211–33.
(1982), 'Family archives in Egypt: new light on nineteenth-century provincial trade', in *L'Egypte au XIXe siècle*, Paris, 15–33.
(1983), 'Gold and silver exchange between Egypt and Sudan, 16th–18th centuries', in J. F. Richards, ed. (1983), *Precious Metals in the Later Medieval and Early Modern Worlds*, Durham, N. Carolina, 305–28.
Warburg, G. (1971), *The Sudan under Wingate. Administration in the Anglo-Egyptian Sudan 1899–1916*, London.
(1974), 'Popular Islam and tribal leadership in socio-political structure of North-Sudan', in N. Milson (ed.), *Society and Political Structure in the Arab World*, New York, 231–80.
Watts, M. (1983), *Silent Violence. Food, Famine and Peasantry in Northern Nigeria*, Los Angeles.
Webb, J. L. A. (1982), 'Toward the comparative study of money: a reconsideration of West African currencies and neoclassical monetary concepts', *IJAHS*, xv/3, 455.
Weber, M. (1969), *The Theory of Social and Economic Organization*, London.
West, L. C. (1918), 'Dongola Province of the Anglo-Egyptian Sudan', *Geographical Review*, v, 22–37.
Whitehead, G. O. (1940), 'Mansfield Parkyns and his projected history of the Sudan', *SNR*, xxiii/1, 131–8.
Wilmington, M. W. (1955), 'Aspects of moneylending in Northern Sudan', *MEJ*, ix, 139–46.
Wingate, F. R. (1891), *Mahdiism and the Egyptian Sudan*, London, 2nd edn, repr. 1968.
(1930), 'The siege and fall of Khartoum', *SNR*, xiii/1, 1–82.
Wolf, E. R. (1966), *Peasants*, New Jersey.
Yūsuf Faḍl Ḥasan (1965), 'The Umayyad geneology of the Funj', *SNR*, xlvi, 27–32.
(ed.) (1971), *Sudan in Africa*, Khartoum.
(1973), *The Arabs and the Sudan. From the Seventh to the Early Sixteenth Century*, Khartoum, 3rd reprint.

Index

Kararī, 41, 71, 116, 125, 143
Karkōj, 116, 123, 142
Kassala, 75, 80, 93, 114, 116, 123
Kawaḥla, 8
kāshif in Shendi, 40
kāshif of al-Matamma, 40, 47
kāshiflik, 36, 40ff
Khalīfa ʿAbdullāhi, 144
Khalīfa family, 105
khalwa, 4, 142
Khandaq, 70, 71, 124ff
Khartoum, 6, 35ff, 71, 74, 75, 78, 79, 88, 91, 93, 97, 102, 103, 106ff, 119ff, 142ff
Khartoum North, 16
Khartoum Province, 36, 96
khashm, 63
Khatmiyya brotherhood, 125, 128, 145
Khayr Ḥamza, 126
khayrān, 140
Khedive Ismāʿīl, 73, 93–4, 95–7, 109, 127
Khedive Muḥammad Tawfīq, 128
khurj (land-tax), 83
khuṭṭ of Rās al-Wādī, 48
kifāyat yad principle, 58
kirkhāna, indigo factory, 71
Kitiāb, 43
Kobbei, in Dār Fūr, 16, 18, 25, 26, 27, 116, 123, 125, 126, 127
Kordofan, 3ff and *passim*
Kremer, 82
Krump, 15
Kurd, 34, 36ff
Kurgos Island, 43, 67
kursī, 4
Kurtī, 7, 15, 17
Kuruskū – Abū Ḥamad – Berber route, 35
Kuruskū, 95
Küchük ʿAlī, 106

labour, 5, 65ff, 73
Lafargue, 75–6, 93
Lake Chad, 25, 117, 123, 144
landownership, 32, 53ff, 58ff
land, 4–5, 47
legal instruments, 130–31
Lejean, 104, 122
lending of money, 110
Levantine, 138
Libya, 147
Linant de Bellefonds, 12, 29
long distance trade, 3, 22, 127, 134–6
Lower Nubian, 3

ma'mūr, 36–7
ma'mūriyya, 37
Maghārba (North African) cavalry, 36
Maḥas, 91
the Mahdi, 103, 106, 126, 128, 134, 142
Mahdist camp, 144; cause, 145; revolt, 88; revolution, 103, 146; uprising, 145–6
Mahdists, 51, 128, 134, 139
Mahdiyya, 103, 111, 114, 115, 146
'Mahomet' (the Prophet), 44
Maḥū Bey Urfalī, 13, 36–7, 72, 84–6, 88
Main Nile, 5, 58
Majādhīb, 4, 9, 48
makk Saʿd, 8
makk Musāʿd, 9
makk Naṣr al-Dīn, 11, 44
makk (of Shendi), (*see also* Nimr); 8ff and *passim*
Makniyya, 9
Makuria, 1
malik Shāwīsh of the Shāyqiyya, 45
Mamluk military show, 40
Mamluk panache, 39
Mamluks, 11, 17, 34, 40
Mamluks in Dongola, 125
Manaṣīr, 7, 56
Manfalūṭ, 15
manufacture, 20–1
Marawī, 70
market due to the king, 22
Marno, 110, 120, 122
Masallamāb, 9, 46, 47
Masallamiyya, Blue Nile, 78, 122–3
mashaykha, 4
Massawa, Red Sea, 102, 123
al-Matamma, 3ff and *passim*
Mālikī law, 58, 141, 142
Mālikī school, 132
Mecca, 44
means of production, 5
mechanical pump schemes, 56
media of exchange, 23
mercenaries and slave hunters on the White Nile, 97
merchant capital, 6, 32, 135–6
merchant class, 55, 59
merchant princes, 106
merchants and money lenders, 82
merchants of al-Matamma, 74
merchants, 4, 17–18
Meroe, 1
Middle Ages, 131
Middle Nile region, 35
migrant Jaʿaliyyīn, 96
migration, 3–4, 26
military expenses, 93
Mīrafāb, 7
Mīrafābī, 11
mīrī land, i.e. government land, 58
modernisation, 83
monetary policy, 85–6
monetisation, 88, 109–11, 135–6
money exchange, 23

moneylending, 6
monopoly policy, 28
monopoly system, 69, 82, 105, 118, 135
mudīr of Berber, 28–9
mudīriyya, 37
Mufti, 48
Muḥammad Abū Likaylik, 8
Muḥammad Aḥmad b. ʿAbd Allāh (*see also* the Mahdī), 143ff
Muḥammad Aḥmad Jalāl al-Dīn, *qāḍī*, 141
Muḥammad Aḥmad Ḥamza, 126
Muḥammad ʿAlī Ḥamad al-Sīd, 142
Muḥammad ʿAlī Pasha, 10ff, 28, 35, 36, 37, 39, 40, 46, 52, 68–70, 83ff, 103, 107, 125, 138
Muḥammad Bey Rāsikh, 45
Muḥammad Bey, the Daftardar, 13–14
Muḥammad ʿUthmān al-Mīrghanī, 125
Muḥammad Darwīsh, 94
Muḥammad Efendī Ḥijil, 95
Muḥammad Khayr al-Arqāwī, 106
Muḥammad Khayr, 145
Muḥammad Ra'ūf Pasha, 101
Muḥammad Saʿīd Efendi; 84
Muḥammad Saʿīd Pasha (Viceroy of Egypt 1854–63), 37ff, 43, 49, 51–2, 74–5, 91
Muḥammad Saʿīd Pasha, (gov. of Kordofan); 143
Muḥammad Ṣāliḥ, 125
Muḥammad w. Nimr al-Kabīr, 8–9
Mukābrāb section of the Jaʿaliyyīn, 9, 75
Mukhayrif, 17
Mumtāz Pasha, 99
Munzinger Pasha, 95, 97, 99, 123, 139
Musāʿd, *makk*, 9, 11ff, 46
Muslim pilgrims, 3
Muslim teachers, 3
Muslims, 52
Muṣṭafā, brother of Bashīr, 47
Mūsā Pasha Ḥamdī (1862–65), 75, 92ff, 97, 106, 110
Mūsā, son of Abbakr, 125
Mūshū, 15, 26
Müller, 137

Nachtigal, 142
nafīr (work party), 20
Naṣr al-Dīn, *makk*, 11, 46
Naṣūb, 13
natural flood (*fayyaḍān*); 64
Nāfaʿāb, 9
nās al-baḥr, 26
Negro countries, 19
networks, 27, (*jallāba*) 117ff, 122, 136, 139–40
Nifīʿāb, 8–9
Nigeria, 144
Nile; Nile Valley, 1ff and *passim*
Nile Confluence, 36, 137
Nimr, *makk*, 8ff
Nimrāb, 8–9, 46, 93
Nimro, 16
Ninth Regiment, 43
Nobatia, 1
North Africans, 26
Northern Sudan, 3, 54, 112, 129, 136
Northern Sudanese (Nubians), 122; culture, 4; slave hunters and traders, 103, 104; merchant capital, 138
al-Nūba, village, 43
Nuba Mountains, 78
Nubia, 1, 26, 55, 78
Nubian caravan, 26; desert, 17, 22, 35; families, 3; kingdoms, 7;language, 3; Nile valley, 60; Nubian or Sudanese origin of *jallāba*, 117
Nubians, 1, 3, 7, 26, 133, 137
al-Nūr w. Abbakr, 125

Omdurman, 105, 128, 143, 145
Ottoman, 34, 35, 52; commercial law (the *humāyūnī*), 106; dominion, 141; Emprie, 34, 58, 104; practices in Egypt, 83; Turks, 10, 111, 132
over-exploitation, 67

Pallme, 119
partners, 123; partnership or *commenda*, 117; partnership, 28, 105; in production, 133
'Pasha in Cairo', 34
pastoralism, 19
peasant economy, 26
peasants, peasantry, 3, 4, 5, 13, 19, 31, 47ff, 53ff
Petherick, John, 92
Pharaonic, 32
pilgrim routes, 25
plantations, 69
plants, 67–8
Poncet, M. D., 15
Poncet, J., 119
population, 18, 115
Postan, 132
prices, 27, 112ff
primary producers, 19, 82
professionalisation, 20
promissory notes, 109
Province (*ma'mūriyya*) of Dongola, 36
Province of Sinnār, 36
Pückler-Muskau, 40, 47, 70, 77

Qaḍārif, *sūq* Shaykh Abū Sinn, 75, 88, 114, 116
Qallabāt, 75, 116, 123
Qarrī, 8, 9, 15ff, 26

Sulaymān (informant), 124, 126, 128–9
Sulaymān Abū Da'ūd Aghā, 41
Sulaymān, son of al-Zubayr, 106, 144
Sulaymān 'Abd al-Ghani, 127, 134–5
sultan of Sinnār, 5
sultan's caravans, 17
Surat, 23
surplus, 5, 34, 82, 102
surplus extractions, 82ff
Syrians, 26

Ṭāhir Ḥamza, 127–8
Tākā (Kassala), 94, 102
takkiyya (pl. *takākī*), strips of cotton cloth, 23
Tanqāsī, 17
ṭāqiyya, 4, 12
tax, 12–13, 58–9, 64, 73, 75, 85, 91, 140; arrears, 59, 95; collecting, 51–2; collectors, 5, 13, 84, 92; on slaves, 86; on the *sāqiya*, 90ff; reductions, 103, 145; reforms of Muḥammad Sa'īd, 91–2; immunities, 58; system, 67, 82ff; in cash, 87
Taylor, 91, 115
technology, 64–6
teddān contract, 4, 59, 66
Thamaniyyāt, 70
Thibaut, 52, 74, 94
Ṭīniyyāt, 142
tōb dammūr, 30–1
topography, 57
trade by way of sectors, 27
trade routes, 139
trade, 3–4, 54, 115
traders, 3, 4, 104ff, 117ff
trading networks of the Danāgla and the Ḥaḍāriba, 122–3
tribute, 5, 46, 82
Tripolitanians, 26
trust (*amāna*) holders, 47
Tu Bedawie, 13
ṭulba (tax), 82
Tumsāḥ ('Alī w.), 11
Tunisians, 26
Turk, Turkish, Turkiyya, *passim*
types of land, 57ff

al-Ubayyiḍ, 17, 25, 27, 78, 103, 105, 114, 116, 123, 126, 134, 142, 145
'Umar Bey, 93
Umayyads, 3
Umm al-Ṭuyyūr, 46
uncultivated land, 47
unequal exchange, 27–8
Upper Blue Nile, 3, 119
Upper Egypt, 17, 35, 50, 95, 117, 119, 142
Upper Egyptian *jallāba*, 26
Upper Nile, 75
Upper Nubia (Northern Sudan), 50
Upper White Nile, 106
urbanisation, 15–16, 106, 114ff
al-'Urḍī (lit. 'the camp'), 36
'Ushayr Island, 7
usufruct right, 58
usury capital, 82
'Uthmān Jarkas al-Birinjī, 37

Vaissière, 70
Venetian, 107
Venice, 23
viability, 77, 87
Viceroy, 11, 12, 52, 82; in Cairo, 34

Wad Bān al-Naqā, 8, 15, 54
Wad Bishāra, 36, 43
Wad Madanī, 13, 88, 114, 116
Wadai, 4, 16, 23, 26, 123, 142
Waddington and Hanbury, 107
Wādī Abū Dōm, 17
Wādī al-Milk, 17
Wādī Ḥalfā, 87
Wādī Qamar, 36
wage labour, 80, 101
al-Wāḥ, 15
Walz, 117, 132–3
Warburg, G., 44
water wheels (*sāqiyas*), 3, 4, 48, 53, 56–7, 74–5, 76–7, 87, 91
West, 68
Western market, 138
White Nile, 41, 79, 105, 106, 116, 117, 122, 129, 142–3, 146
White Nile trade, 92–3
work-parties, 20, 65–6
world market, 60

Yanbu' in Arabia, 26
Yemen, 28

Zaydāb, 57, 69
al-Zubayr (Pasha) Raḥma Manṣūr, 106, 118, 124, 129, 142–3

OTHER BOOKS IN THE SERIES

6 *Labour in the South African Gold Mines, 1911–1969* Francis Wilson
11 *Islam and Tribal Art in West Africa* Rene A. Bravmann
14 *Culture, Tradition and Society in the West African Novel* Emmanuel Obiechina
18 *Muslim Brotherhoods in Nineteenth-century Africa* B. G. Martin
23 *West African States: Failure and Promise: A Study in Comparative Politics* edited by John Dunn
25 *A Modern History of Tanganyika* John Iliffe
26 *A History of African Christianity 1950–1975* Adrian Hastings
28 *The Hidden Hippopotamus: Reappraisal in African History: The Early Colonial Experience in Western Zambia* Gwyn Prins
29 *Families Divided: The Impact of Migrant Labour in Lesotho* Colin Murray
30 *Slavery, Colonialism and Economic Growth in Dahomey, 1640–1960* Patrick Manning
31 *Kings, Commoners and Concessionaires: The Evolution and Dissolution of the Nineteenth-century Swazi State* Philip Bonner
32 *Oral Poetry and Somali Nationalism: The Case of Sayyid Mahammad Abdille Hasan* Said S. Samatar
33 *The Political Economy of Pondoland 1850–1930: Production, Labour, Migrancy and Chiefs in Rural South Africa* William Beinart
34 *Volkskapitalisme: Class, Capital and Ideology in the Development of Afrikaner Nationalism 1934–1948* Dan O'Meara
35 *The Settler Economies: Studies in the Economic History of Kenya and Rhodesia 1900–1963* Paul Mosley
36 *Transformations in Slavery: A History of Slavery in Africa* Paul E. Lovejoy
37 *Amilcar Cabral: Revolutionary Leadership and People's War* Patrick Chabal
38 *Essays on the Political Economy of Rural Africa* Robert H. Bates
39 *Ijeshas and Nigerians: The Incorporation of a Yoruba Kingdom, 1890s–1970s* J. D. Y. Peel
40 *Black People and the South African War 1899–1902* Peter Warwick
41 *A History of Niger 1850–1960* Finn Fuglestad
42 *Industrialisation and Trade Union Organisation in South Africa 1924–55* Stephen Ellis
44 *Slavery in Dutch South Africa* Nigel Worden
45 *Law, Custom and Social Order: The Colonial Experience in Malawi and Zambia* Martin Chanock
46 *Salt of the Desert Sun: A History of Salt Production and Trade in the Central Sudan* Paul E. Lovejoy
47 *Marrying Well: Marriage, Status and Social Change among the Educated Elite in Colonial Lagos* Kristin Mann
48 *Language and Colonial Power: The Appropriation of Swahili in the Former Belgian Congo, 1880–1938* Johannes Fabian
49 *The Shell Money of the Slave Trade* Jan Hogendorn and Marion Johnson
50 *Political Domination in Africa: Reflections on the Limits of Power* edited by Patrick Chabal
51 *The Southern Marches of Imperial Ethiopia: Essays in History and Social Anthropology* edited by Donald Donham and Wendy James
52 *Islam and Urban Labor in Northern Nigeria: The Making of a Muslim Working Class* Paul M. Lubeck
53 *Horn and Crescent: Cultural Change and Traditional Islam on the East African Coast, 500–1900* Randall L. Pouwels
54 *Capital and Labour on the Kimberley Diamond Fields 1871–1890* Robert Vicat Turrell
55 *National and Class Conflict in the Horn of Africa* John Markakis

African Studies Series

56 *Democracy and Prebendal Politics in Nigeria: The Rise and Fall of the Second Republic* Richard A. Joseph
57 *Entrepreneurs and Parasites: The Struggle for Indigenous Capitalism in Zaire* Janet MacGaffey
58 *The African Poor: A History* John Iliffe
59 *Palm Oil and Protest: An Economic History of the Ngwa Region, South-eastern Nigeria, 1800–1980* Susan M. Martin
60 *France and Islam in West Africa, 1860–1960* Christopher Harrison
61 *Transformation and Continuity in Revolutionary Ethiopia* Christopher Clapham